FORMAN'S GAMES

FORMAN'S GAMES

THE DARK UNDERSIDE OF THE LONDON OLYMPICS

LANCE FORMAN

First published in Great Britain in 2016 by
Biteback Publishing Ltd
Westminster Tower
3 Albert Embankment
London SE1 7SP

ISBN 978-1-78590-115-7

10 9 8 7 6 5 4 3 2 1

A CIP catalogue record for this book is available from the British Library.

Set in Caslon by Adrian McLaughlin

Printed and bound in Great Britain by
CPI Group (UK) Ltd, Croydon CR0 4YY

To my parents, Irene and Marcel

CONTENTS

FOREWORD

If you're looking for a nice, warm hagiography that lavishes praises on the wonders of the London Olympics, I'll have to 'fess up' and admit this isn't the book for you. It hasn't been officially approved by the International Olympic Committee, or the London Organising Committee for the Olympic Games, or the British government. It wasn't commissioned by Tony Blair, or Tessa Jowell, or Ken Livingstone, or Sebastian Coe, to brush up their tarnished reputations through association with the world's number one sporting event. It isn't packed to the rafters with vivid colour photographs of the Opening Ceremony, or the Men's 100m final, or triumphant Paralympians. If that's what you seek, I can point you in the direction of the *Official Commemorative Book* published by John Wiley & Sons.

What this book does instead is reveal an alternative narrative of the London Olympics from the perspective of one of the 350 businesses evicted from their premises, with just eighteen months' notice, to make way for the Olympic Park. It exposes the dark underside of the so-called festival of sport as it affected real people with real jobs. It shines a light on the frightening attitude and behaviour of the authorities as they set aside due process and fair treatment to get a job done. It shows how close many firms, including Forman's smoked salmon business, came to collapse as the onslaught and pressure intensified. It's a tale I've told in part to a number of audiences, including MBA students at the London Business School, and one I've often been encouraged to relay in full and for the record. Many of the details disclosed in the book are ones never previously divulged; all are supported by contemporaneous records and witness statements.

I haven't disguised the names of individuals in the book, but I should stress this – I'm not focused on settling old scores. Whilst many of those who played a significant role in the compulsory purchase of our factory do not, I think, emerge from these pages covered in glory, my aim has not been character assassination (in fact, many of those with whom I crossed swords have since done a medal-winning job of besmirching their reputations all by themselves). Instead, it has been to recount events honestly and objectively, whilst hopefully communicating a sense of what it was like for me, personally, to be caught at the vortex of such carnage.

I have spent a number of chapters describing challenges faced by me, and by Forman's, in the years before that fateful Wednesday in 2005 – for ever seared on my mind – when Jacques Rogge announced that London would be hosting the Games. I felt this was important because many of the solutions we devised to deal with previous crises had a bearing on our response to the land grab programme. Plus, I think, those earlier experiences are fascinating in their own right; one or two could arguably have merited a book all to themselves.

I'd like to acknowledge the support of my family – my wife René, my children Matthew, Oliver and Annabel – without whose forbearance I'd never have been able to run Forman's, let alone find time to reflect on recent history. Of course, I must thank the three former generations of Formans without whom I would not be endowed with this privileged position in the first place. I'd also like to give thanks to my publisher, Biteback, especially Iain Dale, Jeremy Robson, Olivia Beattie and Victoria Godden, who immediately agreed this story should be told, and have been unflinching in their backing ever since. To Laurence Smith, who has superbly assisted me in filleting, curing, carving and packaging this extraordinary tale. To Louise Jacobs, for her insightful recommendation to make contact with Jeremy Robson. To Spencer Debson, Lloyd Hardwick, Claire Bishop and René (again), who read through the manuscript as it was being drafted and gave invaluable feedback. And to many of those who were present during the events I've described, and kindly gave of their time to share their memories. The book wouldn't have been possible without all these contributions, and I'm for ever grateful.

I'll close by quoting a subtitle we once considered for *Forman's Games*, which provides simple advice for anyone facing the entire might of their government dumping an Olympic Stadium on their land: *Forewarned is Forearmed!*

CHAPTER 1

FORETASTE

October: the month we turn back the clocks and allow darkness to encroach; the month of Halloween, when children tremble in terror of the supernatural; and the month that's borne witness to every one of the greatest catastrophes suffered by H. Forman & Son during the past twenty-five years.

Comically, my birthday also happens to fall in October. There is a Yiddish proverb, '*Mann tracht und Got lacht*', meaning 'Man plans and God laughs'. There must have been an outbreak of heavenly chuckles when He arranged for me to enter this world bang in the middle of the month I've learnt to dread. When your mind's in turmoil from the latest disaster, it's not easy to blow out candles and unwrap presents with a cheery and carefree mien.

But, back in 2007, I was hopeful the curse had at last been broken. It was an unsettling time, but also one for fresh beginnings. The Forman's Marshgate Lane factory was standing alone, in the middle of vast wasteland, as if it was the sole remaining structure in a post-apocalyptic dystopia. Around the building, 500 cold and desolate acres, strewn with debris from the recent demolitions. A single makeshift track connected the factory to the outside world. It stretched through the mud to the remote cobalt-blue-fenced perimeter, where two bored and overweight guards stood on duty at the main entrance to the site. Beyond the gate, I could make out the distant outlines of bulldozers, excavators and loaders. These were the vehicles that had despatched havoc with such efficient brutality. Like medieval marauders, they had devastated a community. There was nothing left in their wake but twisted pipes, broken masonry and smashed glass.

A few months beforehand, the district had been abuzz with commerce, the largest concentration of manufacturing businesses in the entire Greater London area, including printers, dressmakers, galvanisers, stonemasons, tanners, concrete crushers and dozens more. Family-owned firms passed down through the generations, as well as the local operations of national and international companies. Over 350 employers, with a combined workforce of 12,000 skilled artisans and traders – every single one was being erased from the landscape to make room for just over two weeks of sport.

'Time to put the past behind us,' said René. 'We must stay positive.'

Even my factory, the newly built Forman's smokehouse, would not long defy the power of the wrecking ball. Since our produce cannot be kept in storage, we had negotiated a special dispensation from the authorities. Whilst every other business had been evicted from the future Olympic Park site during the summer, we'd been allowed to continue operating from Marshgate Lane until October. According to the authorities, this provided 'ample time' for our new Stour Road site to come on stream. And so it was that, on a bleak Saturday morning, the final boxes of Marshgate Lane smoked salmon were loaded onto our fleet of vans and despatched to over 100 top hotels and restaurants around the capital.

With the deliveries under way, my workforce of curers, smokers and packers set down their tools and transformed into the most dedicated crew of removal workers anywhere on the planet. We had precious few hours to transfer everything that wasn't nailed down from Marshgate Lane to our new facility. Steel tables, salmon blades, vacuum packers, office furniture, files, memorabilia – the mantra was simple: nothing of value could be left behind to fall victim to the blades and rippers of the returning bulldozers.

We'd quickly figured out there was no sense in preserving the structural integrity of a factory on the verge of demolition. So we used forklifts to smash out doors and windows, creating the largest possible apertures through which to pass our bounty. The last item I'd removed was an oil painting of Odessa, the town where my maternal grandfather had been born. René had banished it from our home on the grounds of its artistic failings. But I'd been loath to store or sell it. So it had found its way to the one section of my office wall that wasn't already crammed with smokehouse photography or the various awards we'd collected over the years. With Odessa always visible from the corner of my eye, it sometimes felt as if my forefathers were watching down, checking that my actions as Managing Director were staying true to their proud legacy.

'The Odessa painting made it out,' I confessed to René.

'Lance, that's just not news,' she replied. 'Some things aren't worth being sentimental over. Why not let the LDA have it as your parting gift?'

'They might be destroying my building,' I muttered. 'They're not taking my heritage as well. They can…'

For seven years, the London Development Agency had been the personal plaything of Mayor Ken Livingstone. Throughout his long career, Livingstone had cultivated an image of being an anti-establishment, lovable rogue. Shortly after the turn of the millennium, this had secured him a landslide victory as the UK's first directly elected Mayor. Yet his casual, jocular manner belied an inner ruthlessness, which had recently turned its artillery in my direction. As Mayor, Livingstone lacked the ability to raise conventional taxes, so he relied upon a complex web of quangos to secure his power base. At the core of this network was the LDA, with a budget approaching half a billion pounds and an ability to dispense Compulsory Purchase Orders like confetti. It was the LDA that had been charged with 'assembling' the land for the Olympics.

Overweening and opaque, the LDA was ruthlessly exploited by Livingstone. It was the lever of choice through which he brushed aside any nascent opposition and imposed his favoured projects upon the city's landscape. I'd learnt to my cost that, whilst the Mayor and his cronies paid lip service to 'vital small businesses' during hustings and public debates, their calculating actions were far removed from their soaring rhetoric. At heart, Livingstone was another scheming politician. His instinctive sympathy lay with the institutions of the state, rather than with independent traders who lacked the time and/or expertise to present a collective voice. Forman's had been a high-profile victim of the so-called regeneration of London's East End, but it was far from being the most unfortunate.

'I can't believe I was so close to giving up,' I said. 'It would've been so easy.'

'You would never have given up,' said René. 'I know you too well. But I feel sorry for the others who did. Not everyone has your drive and determination, Mr Long Game.'

'Well, some buried their heads in the sand, never thinking it was going to happen, but to be honest, it was difficult for them,' I replied. 'You can't compete when the LDA has the most expensive lawyers and can keep things dragging on and on. And they were always going to steamroller this through, come what may. It was never going to be fair. When the CPOs started to land, it's hardly surprising many businesses shut down their operations and laid off their staff. Rather that than start over. You can't blame them.'

We were speaking on the Monday after the factory move, about an hour before sunrise. The fish industry has always observed an unconventional working day. Trading gets under way at the Billingsgate Fish Market at 4 a.m., and is already winding down when most London commuters are checking their Oyster cards ready for the trip into work. There aren't many lifestyle advantages of such a manic schedule, but one is the almost-deserted state of London's road system for my early-morning drive between East Finchley and Stratford. At one time, I'd been able to drive the nine miles across London in about as many minutes. That was before the speed cameras started to proliferate. Unable to pump the throttle on the empty Holloway Road, I now maintained an absurdly serene twenty-nine miles an hour.

By 2007, I'd been making the journey for thirteen years, unaccompanied but for the easy-listening muzak wafting from the Land Rover's stereo system, if Radio 4's *Today* programme had nothing to keep me interested. Yet I wasn't travelling alone on that Monday. The past nine years had been burdened with so many negative emotions – anger, anxiety, frustration – that René had been keen to share in the wholehearted, unalloyed joy of our new start. And I was thrilled to have her alongside. We had just celebrated our twentieth wedding anniversary and I still felt the excitement of sharing a new experience with her. Even this morning, rising at 4.30 a.m., out of the house by 5 a.m., I'd spent a few more moments than usual brushing my jacket and combing my hair. Running a business can be lonely at times and René has always been a great sounding board, even if just to reflect on my own verbalised thoughts before putting them into action. Having her by my side at these special milestones made us both proud.

'I hope everyone managed to get a bit of rest over the weekend,' said René.

'I know a few of them crashed overnight on the office floor,' I replied. 'It was like Christmas two months early. I think Lloyd shot home for a couple of hours and then straight back to the ranch, and Darren lives close by, so he managed to get away for a few hours' kip. What a weekend, but we made it.'

'Maybe we should have invited Ken Livingstone, Gareth Blacker and Tony Winterbottom to show them what you achieved without their help. They ought to hire you and Lloyd to run the Olympics if they want to get it done in time.'

'And Coe,' I said. 'What a disappointment he's been. I never expected better from Livingstone. But Coe. Arrrgh. All of this could have been avoided if…'

'Yes?' prompted René, as my words petered out.

'He knew me. I'd met him when he came to race against Steve Cram round the college quad. I'd briefed him when I was working with Peter. All he had to do was have a conversation with me. What was he scared of? When he had the power to save a 100-year-old family business, he wouldn't even take my phone call. Pathetic.'

'I know, some people can't face up to problems.'

'No special treatment – I get that. But not even taking a call? He should have helped, not run away.'

Around Hackney, there was a little more roadside activity, the first fleeting signs of the approaching work day. On one corner, the proprietors of a deli café were rearranging half a dozen aluminium tables in anticipation of al fresco diners. Street-sweeper vans were pressure-washing the cycle lanes and scooping up litter that had clustered in the gutters. And lights were being switched on in Tube station ticket offices. London can never truly spring into life until its underground system, carrying up to 4 million passengers daily, has been primed.

Our new Stour Road factory was no more than 100 metres from the previous site. Designed to resemble a darne of a salmon, and (of course) painted a distinctive shade of pink, it had been built on the banks of the River Lea immediately opposite the Olympic Park site. The LDA's threat that we must relinquish Marshgate Lane within an absurdly concertinaed timetable meant there had been no chance to run production in parallel across the two properties. On Friday, our new factory had still been an industrial building site, swarming with construction and refrigeration engineers, plasterers, plumbers, locksmiths, electricians, communications and computer technicians, conditions which were certainly not suited for the meticulous and hygienic preparation of a luxury food product. Three days of frantic upheaval later, and it was time for operations to commence. In the catering trade, even a single day offline can be lethal to business relationships. Our clients would not appreciate being put in a position of telling their diners that 'fish is off the menu today, I'm afraid'. They would seek more trustworthy sources of supply. And once a chef's loyalty has been forfeited, regaining it can be a lengthy, if not futile, ordeal.

The DNA of any smokehouse is its kiln – or, in our cases, kilns. I had taken the opportunity of our forced relocation to upgrade our infrastructure. The performance of our previous British-made kiln had been frustratingly inconsistent, and its manufacturer support had been unreliable, so I had scoured Europe for a product that would serve our business for decades to come. After viewing a number of alternatives that had ticked some, but not all, of our requirements, my right-hand man and Director of Operations Lloyd Hardwick and I had chanced upon an intriguing system at the annual Brussels seafood convention.

At this point, I need to beg your warm-hearted indulgence. A high-performance kiln is the heart of a smooth-running smokehouse, and I can get quite passionate about the subject. Eyes do tend to glaze over when I'm on a roll about the latest smoking technologies. I recognise it's not a topic that necessarily obsesses people in other trades, and I guarantee this will not be a book about how to specify and procure a perfect kiln. Nevertheless, it is germane to the story of our reopening, and – with your permission – I'd like to spend just a minute or so describing why the 'Airmaster' blew us away.

The Airmaster was used throughout Europe for smoking meats, and it boasted a number of features that appealed to us. Traditionally, smokers use combustion and sawdust to generate smoke; by contrast, the Airmaster relied on the friction created by an uneven wheel spinning against an oak log, allowing for more precise control of the quantity of smoke. In addition, both Lloyd and I had been paranoid about sawdust since that had been the apparent cause of a factory fire some years ago. Next, the Airmaster had a state-of-the-art electronic control unit, so the user could identify and pre-programme the optimal settings for each stage of the drying and smoking process. The manufacturer offered a number of reassurances about maintenance, pointing out the regularity of short-haul flights into the nearby London City Airport. Finally, they could create something that would look gorgeous, rather than provide us with their standard design.

For most smokehouses, the aesthetics would be an irrelevance. However, I had a vision of Forman's as a tourist destination. If I was to commit over £1 million to the purchase and installation of new kit, it would be a terrible waste for it to be hidden from public display. In Marshgate Lane, the kilns were built into the wall, with only the steel doors on view. This time, I was keen for the kilns in their entirety to be the factory showpiece – free-standing, centrally positioned, like the clock tower in a Eastern European town, with glass doors so that visitors could view the salmon being smoked. I was so insistent on this point that the size and shape of the building had been architectured to suit the kilns rather than the other way around. The technical superiority meant the Airmaster was our preferred choice of replacement kilns. Their stunning visual impact was the clincher.

However, whilst the Airmaster had an enviable meat-smoking track record, its use in the fish trade was relatively scarce, and – whilst they assured us it would be possible to tailor all aspects of the smoking process – our due diligence needed to be robust before we could commit.

Shortly after the Brussels show, Lloyd and I spent two days at the Airmaster plant in Stuttgart inspecting every aspect of the manufacture and discussing potential refinements. Of course, the most important test had been to smoke some salmon, and we both agreed the taste had been exquisite.

Against all these positives, we had to weigh a single area of concern. Forman's had traditionally prided itself on its 'Buy British' policies. Yet, we'd be procuring the Airmaster smoking ovens not merely from abroad, but from Germany – the country of the Holocaust against the Jewish people from which my father had been a survivor. To make matters worse, the manufacturer went by the unfortunate name of 'Reich'. As one wit drily remarked at the official opening event for the Stour Road factory, 'I can see why you only bought two kilns. You couldn't have risked the Third Reich being found, alive and kicking, in the bowels of H. Forman & Son.'

Early on that Monday morning, René was yet to see the newly installed kilns, and I couldn't wait to unveil them in all their dramatic glory. I escorted her, hands clasped over her eyes, to a first-floor viewing platform, where the most impressive view was to be had, and whispered gently, 'You can look now.'

The kilns were even more magnificent in situ than in the Stuttgart plant. Built of stainless steel, they had been polished and re-polished until the metal came alive, light reflections creating a glistening effect on every surface. And, with their four chambers and two smoke generators, they were truly enormous. The visual impact was made more powerful by the various vents and chimneys atop the kilns. These 'inner workings' are usually concealed behind panelling, but I'd left them exposed to reinforce the sense of being inside an authentic, functioning factory. René took one look at the mammoth array, and exclaimed, 'I can hardly believe what I'm seeing. It's like being inside Willy Wonka's … Salmon … Factory. It's amazing, I can't wait to taste the fish.'

Ah yes, tasting the fish. That would be the highlight of René's 'day one' visit. The moment our triumph would be complete; when we finally laid behind us a decade of upheavals. With Stour Road up and running, producing the world's finest smoked salmon to London's most discerning gastronomes, it would be clear to all that Forman's lived on, fighting fit and equipped to seize the opportunities of the new millennium. Despite the setbacks, the lies, the cost, our business would re-emerge with our standards uncompromised and our integrity intact.

The reputation of smoked salmon in the UK has been sadly diminished during the past two decades, due to the shoddy practices of mass producers. Under pressure from the retailers, they cut corners throughout the curing and smoking process. Much of what is disingenuously labelled 'smoked salmon' now contains as much brine as flesh. The food-shopping public, in their hundreds of thousands, has been indoctrinated to believe that £2.99 for a few slivers of damp, salty, sugary and leathery fish is decent value. I despair that any right-minded producer could take the glorious fish that is the Scottish salmon and transform it into such garbage. It's like using lead crystal to manufacture a junkie's syringe, rather than upscale glassware.

When prepared properly, it takes a full forty-eight hours for smoked salmon to be ready for consumption. Due to the rushed weekend move, the salmon despatched on the morning of 15 October 2007 had been cured and smoked across two different locations. Having been cured in Marshgate Lane, the fish had been packed into chilled polystyrene boxes and transported across the River Lea to our new factory, where they had been stored in finely calibrated conditions. When Lloyd felt confident that the Airmaster was ready, the fish were set out on two-metre-high trolleys, which were then wheeled into the chambers. For eight hours, through a perfect combination of fan-drying and dehumidification, the machine's air flow system dried the fish, at which point the smoking could commence. As the temperature approaches

25 degrees, a thin crust called a pellicle, a millimetre or two in thickness, forms on the surface of the fish, preventing excess smoke from penetrating the flesh. The goal is to ensure the dominant taste is salmon, rather than water or salt or smoke. Whilst the naked eye can sometimes struggle to discern the difference between outstanding and mediocre salmon, all is revealed the moment the fish makes contact with the tongue.

Glowing with delight and awe, René asked Rita Law, one of our staff members (of whom much more later), to help her collect some champagne flutes and bottles of Chapel Down Brut Reserve from the back of my Land Rover. The moment that the first trolley emerged from the kilns should be marked with a hearty celebration. I felt the warm hands of my forefathers resting on my shoulders, four generations of Formans gathering for this moment of history. A tear had formed in the corner of my eye, and was now spooling over my eyelid. I wiped it away with the underside of my thumb and tapped the fork. To my side, Rita was unwinding the wire muselets around the champagne corks, and René was setting out the flutes on one of the work surfaces, ready to receive the silky liquid. We were both standing an inch taller than usual, puffed up with the thrill of the moment. I began: 'These few days have been truly momentous. I couldn't let them pass without saying a couple of words to mark our new beginning.'

Having delivered a number of speeches at public forums over the years, I was keen to keep my audience engaged. So, as I spoke, I looked around the factory floor, making eye contact with as many members of staff as possible. Which was how I noticed that Lloyd, usually the most stoical of my entire team, fidgeting nervously. But what can go wrong with a simple toast, first thing in the morning as I arrive for our first day?

I continued: 'You don't need me to remind you of the troubles we've faced. You've all been there with me and I thank you for that. But we've survived. And, I believe, come out stronger and better than ever. We also have our drop-dead-fabulous kilns. Lloyd and I looked at many alternatives, but in the end there was no doubt. Forman's never compromises on quality. They weren't cheap, I think you all know that, but they'll continue our reputation as the Rolls-Royce of salmon smokers, and so will be worth every single penny.'

Lloyd had been shifting uneasily throughout these remarks, and finally he could keep his counsel no longer. He stepped forward and interrupted me mid-flow: 'Lance, can I just have a couple of words, please?'

For a moment, I was irritated at this cack-handed intervention. But Lloyd and I had been inseparable for a decade, and I knew he wouldn't be disrupting my flow without just cause. That realisation sent an icy chill through my body.

'What is it, Lloyd?'

'I think you'd better come over here.' He directed me towards the slicing and trimming table, where a handful of sides were hanging from a rail.

'Lloyd, what is it?' I repeated. The icy chill had not yet dissipated.

He took the side from the rail and laid it on the stainless table, handed me a carving knife and invited me to slice a piece for tasting.

'It's not right, Lance,' he said. 'I'm not happy and you're not going to be either.'

I've eaten smoked salmon almost every day of my professional life. With a perfectly prepared slice, as the fish starts to interact with the tongue, there are a series of taste sensations. Firstly, the firm richness of the fish itself, then the release of the salt, and finally the subtle presence of the smoke, but never overpowering the salmon. Texture is a vital part of the experience. The cut should hold together rather than flake apart as soon as it's inside the mouth. And if it's so wet and slimy that it's sliding around the mouth, you've definitely got problems.

Sensing something was amiss, René had ditched her champagne duties and was standing by my side. She threaded her arm reassuringly around mine. 'You'll work it out. You always do.'

'I can't understand it,' said Lloyd.

It was wet, for sure. Slimy, without doubt. And, above all, there was a disgusting bitter aftertaste. So unpleasant and intense that I might need to gulp down the contents of both champagne bottles just to cleanse the palate. This was like that cheap supermarket smoked salmon that I despise ... only worse.

In quick succession, four nightmarish fears burst, unbidden and unwelcome, into my consciousness. Firstly, that I had just burned £1 million I didn't have on two kilns which, it seemed, couldn't perform the basic function of smoking a few Scottish salmon and, being built in to the factory, it would be impossible to replace them. Secondly, the very next day we had an advanced order for a gathering of dignitaries at the Berkeley Hotel in honour of former US Vice-President Al Gore, a job which was now in direct jeopardy. Thirdly, that my forefathers – if their spirits were drifting around the factory as I sometimes supposed – would now be debating the numerous inadequacies of 'the ignorant boy who bought kilns from Germany'. And, finally, that I now possessed even more compelling evidence that the ghastly month of October carried an undiminished, planet-sized grudge against east London's most hapless salmon smokehouse.

Suddenly, my mind was filled with images of every disaster suffered by Forman's – the entire macabre procession of flood, fire, fraud, compulsory purchase ... and now this. And this time, not the result of some freak external event, but the consequence of my own impulsive decision-making. Was I being punished for a terrible transgression committed in my youth? Or was the bloody-minded choice of a German manufacturer sufficient just cause? I was worried. And Lloyd was worried. And Lloyd doesn't worry. Which was worrying.

CHAPTER 2

FORESHADOWING

Dickens once wrote that the late eighteenth century was 'the best of times, the worst of times'. But for me, 200 years later was simply the strangest of times. Much of this was self-inflicted. I had somehow persuaded the admissions panel at Trinity College, Cambridge, that I'd be a useful addition to their economics intake (I suspect it was a mixture of desperation, perseverance and chutzpah), and spent three years surrounded by future leaders in the fields of politics, business and the arts. However, when I made my rite of passage in the first week to the University's Freshers' Fair – an enormous hall that teemed with a thousand societies soliciting for new members – I balked at any with a serious mission, and instead signed up with brio and relish for CURLS – the Cambridge University Raving Loony Society.

Toilet humour has always been popular amongst adolescents, and at CURLS we took that mantra literally. One icy cold Saturday, my fellow lunatics and I requisitioned a minibus and launched a dawn raid of our arch-rivals at Oxford University. Oxford, like Cambridge, was keen to ensure a modicum of hygiene amongst the undergraduate population, and every weekday a 'scout', typically an elderly domestic cleaner, would dust, tidy and replenish the essentials – which included toilet paper.

During the weekend, this created our opportunity for impishness. En route to Oxford, we made a brief stop at a general store and bought up the entire stock of black bin liners. With military precision over the next seven hours, we sneaked around the corridors and staircases of each of the university's halls of residence, filling the bags with every toilet roll in every cubicle in every communal facility in the wicked satisfaction that we would be leaving Oxford students bereft of supplies until the following Monday. We loaded up the back of our van with our treasure to lay witness to this great feat.

However, our deed did not go undetected. Reports spread around the town that skulduggery was at play, and suspicion inevitably alighted on the gang of persons unknown who had been spotted carrying bulky bin bags around college quads. Not long afterwards, we were approached by the fine fellows of the Oxford constabulary – clearly, crimes of violence must have been at a record low in Oxford that year for resources to be spared for an investigation such as this!

'Is this your minibus, sir?' asked the first. He almost spat out the final word, as if to symbolise his disgust at the obligation to be polite. 'Would you allow us to take a look inside?'

No sooner were the back doors unlocked, than they were forced ajar by the pressure of 1,000 rolls of Andrex Classic White, which toppled chaotically into the layby. I'll never forget the sight of three bulky law enforcement officers, standing on the verge, woefully unable to stifle their chortles. They weren't going to take any further action, but recommended we leave town right away and of course we obliged, fully loaded. It was on the Saturday night journey back that we debated where to offload the rolls and we sneaked into the architecturally iconic King's College Chapel around midnight, leaving one on every pew. It was quite a sight for the Sunday morning churchgoers.

Another jape hit the national press, but the culprit has never been revealed until now. High above the Trinity Great Gate is an imposing statue of Henry VIII, who had founded the college in the 1540s. Down the ages, the statue's resplendent sceptre had been replaced by a chair leg for reasons unknown. But I felt that a wooden pin didn't fully embody the personality of the student town. So, whilst the college slept, one night I free-climbed around the sides of the gate and replaced the chair leg with a bicycle pump. The college authorities apparently felt this was a heinous act and went to great trouble to return the statue to its previous state of grandeur. Not, hilariously, by returning Henry's sceptre, but by finding an unused chair and breaking off its leg to offer up to His Majesty.

Throughout my years at Cambridge, the words of John Smullen rang in my ears. John was the economics teacher at school who had sparked my interest in the subject and had cajoled me to chance an application. His advice was that I should 'never settle for the easy option'. 'You make progress', he added, 'by the brave choices.'

He used a vivid metaphor to reinforce his point. 'Imagine', he said, 'you're traversing a continent, and come upon a crossroads. The way ahead may seem fraught with risk and danger compared with standing still or turning back. However, it's only by pressing on that the mission will be complete.' John was a guru and visionary as well as a scholar, and we remained close for many years.

Around half the student population take out membership of the famous Cambridge Union Society, which runs a packed programme of debates, lectures and entertainment in a magnificent and historic building a short walk from the city centre. From my earliest days I was entranced. CURLS had been a hoot, but I lacked the stamina for three full years of pranks and mischief, so my interest waned. Instead, I set my sights on scaling the slippery rungs of the Union Society ladder, already the scene of jostling, betrayals, backroom deals and base politicking as every unscrupulous hack who fancied themselves as a future Chancellor of the Exchequer sought to eke out career advantage.

'And that, Mr President,' bellowed Cecil Parkinson, droplets of sweat appearing across his brow as he worked himself towards an impassioned crescendo, 'is why the gentleman opposite should never again be entrusted with power in this land.'

With this flourish, he returned to his place on the front benches of the Cambridge Union. The thunderous reception combined vitriolic jeers and deranged applause, with Parkinson clearly savouring the emotions he'd let loose. His eyes fixed with intensity on Peter Shore, who had leapt up without waiting for the noise to subside, and now leant over the despatch box opposite.

Theatrically, Shore flung his prepared notes aside. Dismissively, he made a cutting motion with his left hand. Then, he began. 'Mr President, let me tell you why the future for this country must be a Labour future.'

I was absorbed in the spectacle of these political colossi engaged in unrestrained combat. Parkinson was Party Chairman in the Thatcher Cabinet, and widely touted as her preferred choice of successor. Shore was shadow Chancellor of the Exchequer, an opponent of Britain's membership of the Common Market and a formidable orator who mixed precise facts with florid expression into a unique rhetorical tapestry. Never had I been so close to gladiators of such accomplishment and skill.

Emboldened by the Parkinson/Shore clash, I set my sights on the presidential prize. My foremost foe was a canny Scot, Clive Blackwood, whose trajectory towards Downing Street suffered a slight relapse when he confessed on tape to rigging elections to CUCA, the University's Conservative Association. But not everyone at the Union was a treacherous scoundrel. I met Simon Sebag Montefiore, who later served on my committee, and Andrew Roberts, both now renowned historians, as well as Simon Milton, who later, knighted, served as deputy London Mayor under Boris Johnson, and my friend and mentor Dean Godson, who now runs the influential government think tank Policy Exchange.

Bewitched by the brilliance and intrigue, I found myself spending more time around the Union, where I came to the attention of my peers not so much due to my rhetorical prowess, but because of my flamboyant dress sense. I had acquired a canary-yellow, raw silk dinner jacket, and wore it whenever I was due to speak from the despatch box. Remarkably, I benefited from this unconventional approach to getting noticed, and rose through the ranks. In the middle of my third year, I was elected to serve as President for the Lent term of 1985, without doubt the proudest moment of my life to that point.

René and I were already close, and she visited Cambridge regularly and often sprinkled stardust on my campaign. She had been a child actress of some note, cast as one of the leading characters in the long-running series *Grange Hill*, and also appearing alongside Sting, Andy Summers and Stewart Copeland in the video of the Police's number-one hit 'Don't Stand So Close To Me' (she was the schoolgirl over whom the band was drooling, a topic which rock stars might be uncomfortable addressing in today's more alarmist climate). As I spent more time preoccupied with Union affairs, René offered to attend lectures and take notes on my behalf. She pitched herself amongst the budding economists as the brilliant Frank Hahn expounded on general equilibrium theory and monetarism. Hahn was wont to select members of his audience at random to provide a pithy summary of his preceding words. 'Yes, professor!' he would shout, teasingly. 'Explain what I just said!' René's stage school training was never going to be good enough to act her way through that, but her improvisational dance moves meant that she could fold her body under the row of desks in an instant.

My presidential term coincided with the 1980s miners' strike, when militant unions under the leadership of extreme demagogue Arthur Scargill campaigned to overthrow the Thatcher government on the pretext that she was shutting down collieries out of political spite, devastating families and laying waste to an industry. I couldn't ignore the opportunity to stir up trouble, and invited Scargill to debate at the Cambridge Union against Ian McGregor, the Chairman of the National Coal Board, and a man Scargill had described as 'the American butcher of British industry'. It was quite a coup when both accepted, and plans for a huge media occasion were kicked into motion. I could barely sleep with excitement. Then, at the eleventh hour, Scargill executed a volte face on the grounds that he would never share a platform with his bitter foe. I soon realised I was victim of an organised boycott when, as I searched for an emergency stand-in, every other major trade union leader blew a similar raspberry in my direction. A problem was mushrooming into a crisis.

Desperate to salvage something, I switched the event from a debate to a lecture, provoking a full-on media storm that was displaying outrageous political bias. On the day of the lecture, I reported a string of death threats from the Socialist Workers Party and their chums to the authorities, and was rewarded with police protection. From dawn, anarchists and activists had gathered outside the Union, waving placards and chanting into loudspeakers to denounce McGregor's works and condemn his very soul. In the event, his travel arrangements were, perhaps fortuitously, disrupted by an unusually heavy snowfall, and the lecture did not proceed. But I'd learnt an instructive lesson in the feral power of the press.

Fortunately, such cancellations were rarities, and the weather had cleared by the following week for the highlight of my presidential term: a debate on the motion 'This House reigns supreme', the first inter-Varsity debate, between Cambridge and Oxford, in around a half century. The Oxford team was led by Roland Rudd, later a leading figure in the campaign to keep the United Kingdom in the EU; however, they had set out from Oxford with two large crates of fine wine ('The only good thing to have come out of Oxford is the road to Cambridge'), and had consumed every last drop by the time of their arrival. The debate rapidly descended into a vortex of insults, with food and drink thrown across the chamber, and every point of order raised by the Chair routinely ignored. Once again, I found myself in the eye of a saga being leaked to the world's press. I spent the next morning fending off enquiries from as far afield as Chicago and Johannesburg about the depravity and sloth of modern youth.

The final appearance of my yellow jacket was when I opened the last debate of term. For weeks, I'd be inseparable from the presidential telephone to assemble a slew of 1980s household names to hold forth on the motion: 'The British lack style'. The line-up included Leslie Crowther (of *Crackerjack* fame), Chris Serle (*That's Life*), and Paul Gambaccini (Radio 1) – all masters of the craft of telling a lame joke with such verve and timing that their audience is like putty. My nemesis, Blackwood, led the opposition. His opening remarks in broad Glaswegian, aimed in my direction, 'I like ye style, but I na' like ye,' summed up the petty-mindedness of this blustering schemer, whose political career – fortunately for our nation's well-being – never fulfilled his wild cravings.

The liberty of the individual has always been at the core of my worldview. I have an innate suspicion of over-mighty government, and believe the instinctive tendencies of those in authority is to bully, stifle and interfere – creating ineffective laws that they can administer, and levying penal taxes that they can waste. At Cambridge, this outlook found its voice in the establishment of a new group called The Libertarians, with two like-minded fellow students, Andrew Fox and Rory Maw. Our motto – 'Extremism in the defence of liberty is no vice, moderation in the pursuit of justice is no virtue' – is a creed to which I hold true to this day.

After three unpredictable years in England's most beautiful county town, I graduated without a degree. I was struck with acute appendicitis for the week of final exams, and – after being visited in Addenbrooke's Hospital by a team of humourless academics sent to determine whether this was some feeble excuse to avoid the unpleasant consequences of neglecting my studies – I was granted an aegrotat degree, an unclassified qualification awarded in exceptional circumstances where the authorities are persuaded a student would have passed, but are unable to fathom at which level. I was told that aegrotat degree certificates have the word 'appended', which was not the most spirit-lifting description in the circumstances. To the end, my time at Cambridge had been marked by the unorthodox and bizarre.

* * *

After graduation, I joined the accountancy firm Price Waterhouse, to train as a chartered accountant, probably for no better reason than the malign effects on my subconscious from twenty years of overhearing Jewish parents imploring their offspring to become 'a doctor, or a lawyer, or an accountant'. From the first day, I wondered whether my choice of career had been catastrophically wrong, or simply woefully misguided. After the heights of student politics, my days were now spent deciding which coloured pencil to use to check off a bank statement. I learnt the fine art of wandering around the corridors with a clipboard looking busy, but that too grew monotonous after a while. I spent an increasing number of days in a small office with the blinds down, playing chess with my friend and colleague Simon Leary. (Simon is now a partner at the firm, so I'm hoping his career isn't blighted by this revelation, and also that he's too busy to retaliate in kind.)

Luckily for my sanity, the tedium was not to last my full six years at PW. Having demonstrated by boundless competence in making perfectly brewed cups of tea for partners, and operating the more obscure photocopier controls, I tentatively began to explore opportunities outside the firm. This changed as a result of a chance meeting with dynamic partner Howard Hyman, who had set up a specialist Privatisations Unit, and invited me to join it.

By the late 1980s, the Thatcher government had already sold the majority of state-owned industries to private investors, and the Privatisations Unit was spreading its wings abroad, and in particular to Eastern Europe, where the first stirrings of market-oriented policies could be detected. My father's wartime experiences meant the land beyond the Berlin Wall held great significance for me and my family, so my sense of adventure was piqued. I spent much of the next twelve months holed up in Warsaw's LIM tower, a joint venture hotel between the Polish airline LOT, Ilbau, the Austrian contractor, and Marriott, which was an oasis amongst a mass of grey. Every month I returned I would notice more signs of Western influence. Trying to figure out how on earth to put a fair valuation on a car production industry that was still technically functioning under state planning, I converted the car firm's books into a set of accounts that would be recognisable under international accounting standards. I wouldn't normally draw attention to such matters unless I was making a deliberate attempt to lose readers. However, I do believe this was the first occasion that Polish accounts underwent such a conversion. Probably not enough to merit a footnote in history, but possibly a footnote to a footnote.

As we were nearing the end of the project, we were asked to share an indicative valuation with the Director of the company, who was also a member of the Polish Parliament. We met on the twentieth storey of the hotel in their fine-dining restaurant – 'fine' in the sense you could order, and be served, more than a boiled egg and some dry bread. It was a delicate situation; we needed to be confident of finding buyers, but were wary of setting such a low price that our host would take offence. This was the firm's first piece of work in Eastern Europe and the region's first ever privatisation, so there was immense pressure to get it right. The Director's face dropped when we shared our strategically optimistic view that 'around six' would be fair and reasonable. Only after fifteen minutes of nervous explanation whilst he grimaced and glowered did we realise we'd committed a schoolboy error in cross-cultural communication. He'd interpreted our suggestion of a $600 million sales price as meaning just $6 million. The vodka flowed more freely when the truth finally dawned on all.

Vodka was an omnipresent fellow traveller during those years. Having earnt our spurs for handling a delicate privatisation professionally and reliably, we were in demand throughout the rest of the bloc. A few months later, we found ourselves in the small Baltic state of Estonia, where the President was keen to use the private sector to turbocharge the economy, but equally keen not to alert the Kremlin to his intent. PW decided it was crash-or-burn time and fielded a small team of economists, privatisation experts, currency specialists, tax advisors and so forth. The mission was to advise on the economic consequences of independence from the Soviet Union, such as the launch of a new currency. Mundane matters like that.

The bulk of the week was spent engaged in the usual advisory routines, such as meetings with party officials and visits to state-run enterprises. On the final day, our team was invited to the President's dacha for a 'celebratory banquet'. Our motorcade made the hour-long trip from Tallinn along near-deserted woodland roads, which we later learnt sometimes doubled as military landing strips. On arrival at the dacha, we were treated to a 'magnificent' feast in the ornate banqueting hall. At least, I was told by my colleagues that the catering was magnificent: virtually everything on offer was non-kosher, and I spent three hours indulging only in bread rolls and vodka.

During the week, we had often heard the word 'terviseks' used when toasts were being proposed. We had even picked up that the 'tervi' means 'healthy', but debate raged as to whether the compound word meant 'good health' or 'healthy seks'. Our suspicions were further stirred when the President, rising to offer some closing thoughts, peppered his remarks with a word that sounded unnervingly like *sauna.* We smiled politely whilst noting widening smirks on the Estonian side.

The President led a series of toasts and then slammed his glass onto the table, at which point the palace butlers ushered all the male members to one door in the corner of the room and the females into another corner. The men were 'asked' to disrobe fully as we were now about to enjoy the full Estonian hospitality package of a post-dinner sauna. It's not the customary conclusion to a professional meeting and, despite feeling a certain trepidation, we had no desire to offend our hosts and, fortified by the vodka, stripped off. 'I wonder what'll happen to the girls,' I mused, but it would not be long until the answer revealed itself. Although we were guided out through separate doors, we emerged into the exact same sauna on the far side. Double entry accounting has never been the same for me since.

Perhaps this was not a high-level consultancy delegation after all. Perhaps I was trapped in a surreal fantasy dimension. And, as if to prove the second theory, the former Chair of Moscow Narodny Bank was now beating my back with birch sticks, before inviting me to do likewise to Bruce Edwards, the global head of Price Waterhouse, on the grounds that 'this is the way to enjoy a sauna the best'. Maybe so, but not a course I would recommend to any newly arrived graduates considering the routes for career advancement.

And then… I remember nothing until I awoke in my hotel room, birch leaves scattered across the bed, with no idea how I'd made the hour-long return journey from the dacha. And I could hardly ask my colleagues for enlightenment: breakfast was notable only for the dozens of sheepishly averted eyes and total absence of conversation.

I relished my travels to Eastern Europe and thoughts of joining the family business waned. For a while, I tried to stimulate PW to make a more whole-hearted commitment in the region, but their focus was auditing and tax. I felt this was missing the big prize; the collapse of communism was literally a once-in-a-lifetime opportunity, and fortune would favour the earliest pioneers. When Western Europe had emerged from its own horrors in the middle of the century, some of the greatest returns had been in the real estate sector. I reasoned that ex-communist states would follow a similar trajectory, and hence I needed to brush up my Eastern European Rolodex.

It was time to network like fury! Conferences, exhibitions, book launches – if it was related to Eastern Europe, you can bet I'd wangled myself onto the invite list. Which was how I came into contact with architectural association scholar extraordinaire Phil Hudson. We clicked immediately; we'd each finally found somebody with whom we could unburden our excitement and passion for the lands out east. We agreed a Faustian pact: we would abandon the security of employment with big-balance-sheet firms and launch out independently.

As with buses, opportunities never arrive one at a time. Within a week of leaving the firm, I learnt that Norman Lamont, the Chancellor of the Exchequer, was seeking a new special advisor, and Dr Madsen Pirie of the free-market Adam Smith Institute had nominated me for consideration. Although I did not secure the appointment (it was awarded to the former Director of the Institute for Fiscal Studies, Bill Robinson), the Treasury recommended me to the Department of Trade and Industry, where I became special advisor to the Rt Hon. Peter Lilley MP, then a member of John Major's Cabinet. The role of special advisor, as I learnt, meant living the life of a Cabinet minister, but without the prestige, press intrusion or constituents. As ministers would meet at No. 10 for weekly Cabinet meetings, special advisors would be in the adjoining room, discussing the same issues but without the scrutiny. Phil could see the benefit of my leaving him only days after joining, and we agreed that the experience and connections I would gain at the heart of government could be invaluable later for our new business venture.

I often accompanied Lilley to media training events where PR professionals would spend a fruitless hour trying to teach him the dark arts of obfuscation, distraction and sound bites. Lilley was impervious to such superficialities, however, and insisted on answering fair questions directly and with integrity. I recall his responses during one mock interview with a hard-nosed and cynical media trainer.

INTERVIEWER: 'Secretary of State, unemployment is up for the sixth month in succession. Isn't that a failure of government policy?'

LILLEY: 'If you look at the underlying statistical trends, on a seasonally adjusted basis, the rise is within a 75 per cent tolerance.'

INTERVIEWER: 'You've forgotten what I've been telling you! You don't need to answer my questions directly. You have a fifteen-second window to articulate the key messages on your index card to the listening public. Remember, air time is scarce. Let's try again. Secretary of State, what would you say to the families affected by this failure of government policy?'

LILLEY: 'I'd say they need to evaluate the underlying statistical tolerance before reaching a conclusion.'

Peter Lilley was too honest to be a spin doctor's puppet. His instinct was to answer the question that had been put to him without twisting it into a recital of government success stories. He was also one of the few Cabinet members with the intellectual dexterity to provide a coherent and direct answer to almost any unanticipated question. The public often tell pollsters they want their politicians to be less pre-packaged, but the public can be two-faced, and Lilley's honesty dropped him in hot water on a number of occasions. If he'd been more calculating, he would have quickly graced one of the top half-dozen Cabinet positions. But that was not a compromise Lilley was prepared to make.

In our Victoria Street offices, we'd indulge a depressing litany of businessmen stretching out their begging bowls for government support or largesse, wilfully impervious to Lilley's (and my) non-interventionist instincts. Sir Denys Henderson, the Chairman of ICI, was like a quivering, trembling wreck of a schoolboy when he implored us to 'do something' about the shareholding being built up in his company by legendary asset-stripper Lord Hanson. Having listened to Henderson's pleas, we felt that in the interests of due process we should offer the chance of a similar hearing to Hanson himself.

The contrast could not have been greater. Oozing magnetic charisma, Hanson gave a polished, urbane performance, whilst noting with the slightest glint in his eye that surely such important people as the staff at the Department of Trade and Industry had great matters of state with which to preoccupy themselves, rather than the petty triflings of cross-shareholdings between conglomerates. As Hanson batted aside a couple of half-hearted questions from Lilley's officials, I was struck by the sublime gauntlet cuffs of his well-cut suit. From that day to this, I have worn my cuffs in an identical gauntlet style. The man knew how to make an impact.

Strangely, my path kept crossing with that of former Olympics middle-distance medallist Sebastian Coe. People even thought I looked like him. At Cambridge, he had attempted the Trinity Great Court Run, racing around the perimeter of the quad whilst the clock chimed for midday, as used for a seminal scene in the film *Chariots of Fire*, and had graciously signed my programme. Then, whilst working with Lilley, Coe was amongst the MPs and candidates I briefed about trade and industry matters. If I'd known then what was in store, I might not have executed the task with quite so much diligence.

* * *

After the 1992 election, Lilley moved to the Department of Social Security, and I decided that two years amidst mandarins and time-servers was probably sufficient. I felt that Eastern Europe remained a half-finished part of my life and I teamed up full-time with Phil.

We set up a real estate company, called East8, originally operating out of London. For the first time in my professional life, I didn't need to await the lethargic decisions of faceless and risk-averse committees if I wanted to use my initiative. When Phil and I felt the urge to pursue a particular strategy, we needed to convince nobody but each other. If an idea caught our fancy, or we needed to respond fast to a sudden opportunity, the only limiting factor was our own energy and stamina. The first priority was to raise our profile. We published reports, struck innovative marketing deals with Eastern European airlines and organised conferences. One of these, held in the London Docklands, revolved around the theme of urban regeneration, and was attended by ambassadors and city Mayors from most of the countries in the region. Václav Havel, the first President of the Czech Republic, introduced our event by video. We set about to explain how the regeneration of the Docklands and Canary Wharf could be a model for the capital cities of central and Eastern Europe. The Chair of the Corporation of London, Michael Cassidy, allowed us use of the Guildhall for our closing gala dinner. They were heady times.

An increasing amount of our time was being spent nurturing opportunities which would pass muster with serious investors. In the early days, we wasted many frustrating hours on projects of dubious merit, but also completed a smattering of mid-sized deals. But we were yet to hit the big time. Eventually we opened an office in Kiev. Ukraine had been one of the later Soviet-controlled states to fall, and whilst Western pioneers had started their descent en masse into the 'obvious' central European capitals such as Warsaw, Budapest and Prague, we gambled that Kiev was not yet on the radar.

As our track record grew, we found ourselves involved in more significant transactions, and in late 1993 won a design competition that provided us rights to develop a hotel in the centre of Kiev directly opposite the sumptuous Opera House. We reached out to, amongst others, Lebanese billionaire Albert Abela, who had an eclectic range of catering and hospitality interests throughout Europe, but was certainly adventurous enough to put his money into this uncharted territory. As we enjoyed tea in his Hampstead home, he startled us both by brushing aside the development drawings to talk politics.

'I wish that Stalin was still alive,' he smirked.

I sat open-mouthed and glanced over to Phil. He was thinking what I was thinking, which was, 'Who on earth is this we are getting into bed with?'

Abela glared straight into my eyes with a look that engendered fear, and asked, 'You know why?'

'No, Mr Abela. Why?' I responded.

'I wish he was alive,' he repeated, slapping his palms triumphantly against his thighs, 'because I'd like to see him killed!' A toothy grin spread across his face and he aimed an imaginary gun towards my head as if I was target practice for when the evil dictator stood, reincarnated, in his sights. Abela was an early investor in this project, only to have the Ukrainian local authorities withdraw the development rights and pass them in another direction. For many long years, the site remained undeveloped.

My adventures in Eastern Europe meant I was spending less time with my family than was ideal. René and I had married in 1987, on a sweltering Sunday in July that was noteworthy as both the hottest of the year and the date that Pat Cash beat Ivan Lendl in the Wimbledon men's singles final ('Cash is better than a Czech,' I noted in my groom's speech, as I thanked the guests for their kind gifts). With the increasing range of her family commitments, René had left behind the world of the theatre and was running a medical recruitment agency. This had been a bittersweet development for me – partly because performing before an audience had for so long been her passion, but also, I confess, because I'd miss the many evenings I spent as her 'other half', waiting behind stage as she enchanted the crowds, whilst before my eyes, and oblivious to my presence, swarms of young actresses raced through their costume changes. (To date I have had no enquiries from Nottingham or Leatherhead law enforcement.)

The next generation of the Forman household was taking shape. Our firstborn, Matthew, was soon followed by Oliver, and, after a gap, by Annabel. Annabel was named after the scene of our first date, the famous private club in London's Berkeley Square. Of course, under Mark Birley's ownership, Forman's smoked salmon was prominent amongst Annabel's remarkable array of fine cuisine; I doubt my father would have permitted us within 100 feet of its entrance otherwise, although neither he nor I would claim that the calibre of the club's smoked salmon option is the sole cause behind its unparalleled reputation amongst the glitterati for elegance and indulgence. In any event, our reason for naming Annabel as we did has been the cause of much jocularity through the years. I wish I'd had a fiver for every time some joker has remarked: 'Thank goodness your first date wasn't at Tramp!'

CHAPTER 3

FOREBEARS

Scientists have labelled 1905 the 'miracle year' due the remarkable breakthroughs in theoretical physics made by the future Nobel prize-winner Albert Einstein. He published a series of papers on $E=mc^2$ as part of his exploration of the theory of special relativity and completed a landmark dissertation on Brownian motion. It was an unforgettable era of scientific discovery and adventure.

However, Einstein's ground-breaking insights are not the primary reason that I regard 1905 as a time of miracles. For me, even more significant was the opening of H. Forman & Son in London's East End by my great-grandfather, Aaron – colloquially known as Harry.

There are a number of professions that claim to be the 'oldest on the planet', including some that are less than reputable. But fishing certainly makes a strong case. Isotopic analysis of skeletal remains from the Palaeolithic period of history show that, 40,000 years ago, freshwater fish were being caught and consumed by early man. And, a few millennia later, dried fish was a staple for the Egyptian communities that congregated around the Nile, as revealed by papyrus scrolls and hieroglyphics in the Luxor tombs. For thousands of years, the practice of farming persisted, with only occasional refinements to methods of preservation and preparation, such as when the nineteenth-century East Europeans used pickling and smoking to extend shelf-life, and the Scandinavians buried fresh salmon in salt, giving rise to the term 'gravadlax' ('grav' meaning to bury, as in a grave; 'lax' meaning salmon).

Fish has long held an important role in Jewish culture, being associated with fertility (Jacob encouraged his children to multiply 'like fish in the seas') and eaten on the Sabbath by way of custom. Yet, whilst the Jewish influence on salmon curing and smoking is relatively well known, it's perhaps surprising that the same applies to the dish usually considered a 'British staple': fish and chips. The Portuguese Marrano Jews were the first to import the concept of dipping fish in egg and flour and then frying in breadcrumbs until a golden batter forms. That was in the sixteenth century, but it would be another 300 years before Jewish immigrant Joseph Malin coupled the battered fish with chips to create a striking combination. His outlet on Cleveland Street, within the sound of Bow Bells, which opened for business in 1860, was arguably the world's first chippie. It, and its many imitators, became hugely popular with the local working classes who for the first time were able to dine in restaurant-like surroundings (a carpeted floor no less!) that had hitherto been exclusively available to the well-heeled.

It was around those times that the phrase 'Jewish East End' came to be applied to the small area, around two square miles, in Whitechapel and Stepney, where the thousands fleeing from Poland, Romania and Russia would arrive by ship and make a temporary home. As they settled, they made a conscious effort to integrate, learning English, turning themselves into 'proper Englishmen', and plying whatever trades enabled them to make a living and survive as a self-sufficient community. As they grew in confidence, the narrow streets would heave with the bustle and noise of constant activity. Yiddish theatre became popular, not only amongst the immigrants but amongst the curious indigenous population, and living conditions were often so cramped that young actors would rehearse their lines on street corners. But the main preoccupations were trading, making things and – of course – food. Merchants would haul wooden carts around the cobbled streets shouting out prices in Yiddish and English, motivated by the lure of having sufficient funds to open a 'proper shop'. Small businesses thrived – cabinet makers, tailors, shoesmiths, cigarette makers – wherever there was a profit to be turned. But food was where the community found its heart. It was the excuse to gather, to gossip, to scheme, to share. Grocery shops were never short of custom, and would stay open until midnight or later supplying groups of twos or threes who suddenly felt compelled to solve the world's problems and needed a few piled-high plates to fuel their discourse. The smells were glorious and intoxicating. With so many different businesses crammed in such close proximity, a dozen aromas would waft through the streets, mingling to create a tantalising and unmistakable blend – schmaltz herring, smoked salmon, rye bread, onion bagels, potato latkes, chopped liver, kishka. It was not long before non-Jewish neighbours were tempted to try this 'heimishe' cuisine, recipes originally from the shtetls and villages of the 'homeland', and its popularity started to grow.

The method of curing fish and then applying cold-smoking had initially been underpinned by the need to preserve summer fish for consumption around the calendar at a time when refrigeration methods were very basic. As Jewish fish smokers started to flourish around Spitalfields and the Thames, not even realising there was a salmon native to their new home, they initially imported fish from the Baltic; the salmon they knew. But before long they discovered sumptuous fresh Scottish salmon coming down to Billingsgate each summer, and the fish was perfect for their needs. When they applied their smoking methods to these fresher fish – fish that hadn't been left in barrels of brine for three months on their journey over – the results were majestic. The marriage of Scottish salmon and London curing delivered a magical result. As the Jewish smokers plied their ideas with increasing confidence and verve, they established the salmon as the undisputed King of Fish. Smoked salmon was on its way to becoming Britain's first ever home-grown gourmet food, and – alongside caviar and foie gras – one of the world's most popular gourmet choices during the decades ahead.

My great-grandfather Harry was an émigré from Russia, and had been dabbling around the edges of the London fish trade. But it would not take much more than a few years before his young son Louis also had an important role as primogenitor of the firm. Whilst accompanying my great-grandfather on various errands one morning, they started chatting about a newly opened smokehouse. Louis's stream of questions fired Harry's imagination and a few months later H. Forman & Son opened for business. In light of the young Louis's inquisitive streak, it was perhaps inevitable that both 'Harry' and 'son' were separately acknowledged in the business' brand name, a choice that has stood the test of a century.

In those rumbustious times, it was still possible for somebody with a great idea to take his new concept from drawing board to profitability in a matter of months, without the lifeblood being drained by the dead hand of state regulation. By the late 1920s, H. Forman & Son was thriving. Harry and Louis became a double act as effective as Bonnie and Clyde or Rogers and Hammerstein – whenever the business faced a choice, they would thrash out the pros and cons and reach a decision that was implemented without delay. It was a partnership that enabled Forman's to be fast, mobile and opportunistic – the characteristic most cherished by legendary entrepreneurs. Working together, Harry and Louis's instinct was to take the product upmarket, and they made appointments at London's foremost culinary establishments.

The reception was euphoric, and soon Forman's clientele included Fortnum & Mason, Harrods, Selfridges, the Ivy and Mirabelle. Smoked salmon was now seen as a delicacy, and its enjoyment as a sign of culinary refinement.

My grandfather found he had a knack for sourcing the best quality fish at the best price and introducing it to the most prestigious customers before any of the rival smokehouses had woken to the opportunity. But, despite the Formans' skill and acumen, they did make an error of such monstrous proportions that it has haunted the family down the decades. My grandfather was friendly with an East End barrow boy who was one of life's inveterate hawkers and hasslers, constantly blagging a few coins from shoppers at the local market for some piece of junk he'd found lying in the gutter a few hours before. In his teens, the barrow boy decided he wanted to expand, and my grandfather offered him five pounds to finance his growth. Tragically, the deal was structured as loan finance rather than as an equity injection. The barrow boy was Jack Cohen, who set up his stall in Well Street Market in 1919 and whose business became known as Tesco. If Harry had been entitled to, say, 50 per cent of the share capital, you could be reading a very different type of book right now.

From the River Tweed in the Scottish Borders to Strathy in the far north, Scotland has long been home to some of the finest fishing in the world. This was due partly to the picturesque locations, such as the grounds of the royal estates and medieval castles, and partly the variety of large and healthy salmon, seatrout and other fish types. Until the turn of the last century, salmon was caught for either sport or personal consumption, and whilst some rudimentary smoking techniques had been developed by the Scots, for example to make kippers from herrings, the results were not considered gourmet at that time. The smoking was heavy – their level of expertise didn't allow for the very subtle use of smoke, and so chefs were reluctant to serve the fish as part of a fine banquet. As demand grew from the smokers of London for a reliable supply of fresh salmon, the various fisheries realised it would be in their interest to get professionally organised. The Salmon Net Fishing Association of Scotland was established in Aberdeen in 1906 by the owners and lessees of salmon fishing destinations on Scotland's east coast.

The turn-of-the-century smokehouses were literally that. Today, the centrepiece of most smoked salmon factories is a gigantic, computer-controlled kiln manufactured from the finest stainless steel. But in the early 1900s, the smoking took place in a smoke hole, a brick chamber perhaps five feet wide and deep, and twelve feet high, in which sawdust would be strewn. Inevitably, it was not possible to replicate every variable with precision from one day to the next, and so there could be considerable variability in the taste of the salmon depending on the weather conditions, with smoked salmon being produced on a cold crisp February morning generally superior to that smoked on a warm and humid summer's day.

For the next seventy years, smoked salmon production prospered in the East End. London curing techniques came to be admired and its smoked salmon became one of the most popular gourmet foods across the Western world. But the sector could not forever stand against the merciless onslaught of industrialisation and mass production. The late 1970s witnessed government grants alongside private sector capital investment pouring into salmon farming to create jobs in the Highlands and Islands where traditional industries were dying. With grant funding and the onset of new innovations in fish processing technology, the traditional smokehouses struggled to compete. By that time, these large-scale smokehouses had huge capacity and needed to fill it, so introduced smoked salmon to supermarkets at a mass-market price point. Inevitably, this strategy entailed slashing cost out of every stage of the curing and smoking process. Cutting corners, rather than slicing salmon, was the obsession. Traditional curing methods were damned as curious, antiquated anomalies – out of tune with the modern world. Brine was used to bulk up the fish, and the salt content raised by around 30 per cent in order to lengthen the supermarket shelf life of the fish. Other preservatives such as sugar were pumped into the product. It became almost impossible to taste the actual fish amidst this unwholesome concoction of artificial additives.

Tragically, a number of East End smokehouses sought to do battle with these behemoths on their own terms. One by one, their adventures proved ill-fated, and their operations collapsed. In at least one case, that of Barnett's of Frying Pan Alley, the owners crossed the street to join the Forman's payroll. As a result of this merciless rationalisation, Forman's today is the oldest commercial salmon smoker, not just in London, but across the four corners of the globe.

In time, Louis took over the reins at Forman's, and ran the business until his early death in his mid-fifties. He remains the star of Forman's most iconic photograph, standing proudly in his trademark Homberg hat alongside the largest Atlantic salmon caught in 1935, an image which to this day graces the main staircase in our building. The 74lb salmon was sold for two shillings and ten pence per lb, a premium over the regular price of two shillings and thruppence (at less than twenty-five pence a kilo, both were around one-hundredth of today's price), Louis smoked this beast and it was shipped to Selfridges deli counter. The stories of his generosity are legion, although this was often abused by relatives. My mother tells of occasions when, checking out of a hotel, he'd be presented with a rather longer bill than expected, on account of the number of 'extras' that other family members in the group had asked to be 'charged to Louis's room'. He always obliged, though, no questions asked.

Louis was ahead of his time in one particular way. Long before the nutritional benefits of smoked salmon were generally appreciated, he intimated about such qualities with humour and self-mocking charm. His catch-phrase was: 'If you eat of a slice of Forman's every day till you're 100, you'll live to be very old.' Although this spoke to a deeper truth, it sadly didn't apply to Louis himself. He passed away a fortnight before I was born, aged fifty-seven.

After nearly six decades in the hands of either father or son, Louis's boots were filled in 1962 by his son-in-law, my father Marcel. It was my father's clarity of vision that ensured Forman's resisted the temptations of mass production. He was obsessive about quality and would simmer irritably if he found a single slice leaving the factory which, in his view, fell short of total freshness. He was not averse to any form of modernisation, and oversaw the installation at Forman's of the first actual kilns, but he was instinctively sceptical of sharp-suited salesmen and rejected far more overtures to install new-fangled gadgets than he accepted. His first, second and final challenge was whether any change posed a risk to product quality. Any suggestion that taste or texture might be compromised in the search for economy, and the proponent would be quickly ushered through the exit door.

From an early age, my father was keen to involve me with ad hoc work at the factory, and would often spend family mealtimes sharing anecdotes from the factory floor. But during my teen years, becoming a salmon smoker had negligible appeal. A long day in a salmon factory inevitably meant Marcel returned home reeking of the pungent smell of smoked fish, a stench that tended to linger no matter how many remedial actions my mother took – including the purchase of a separate closet for his clothes. At school, something of a black market developed for the contents of my lunchbox. Even the most ardent enthusiast for the London Cure occasionally craves variety, and yet every day I would be packed off with the identical fare: four generously filled smoked salmon sandwiches. By the end of the week, I'd be desperate to offload them for anything with a different taste – an apple, a Mars bar, a slice of cake – anything that wasn't coloured pink and had begun life north of Hadrian's Wall.

The obligation to keep the faintest whiff of salmon far from the family home has been an ever-present ordeal down the years, and I'm often just one oversight away from calamity. Shortly after joining the business, and having promised René faithfully to keep our bedroom 100 per cent devoid of any fishy aroma, I had as usual scrubbed my skin until it was raw and jumped into bed, only to be told by my wife that she could still detect a faint trace. After a probe of CSI intensity, the culprit stood revealed: the hard-to-remove smell of smoke clinging stubbornly to the rim of my spectacles.

The connections between soap and salmon weren't limited to my shower cubicle. When, as a child, I was driven by my father to the factory, the aroma of perfume and soap would often be overpowering on the final approach. This was not because of a legion of factory workers trying to scrub the last traces of salmon from their pores, but because the world-famous brand Yardley & Co was located a couple of minutes away. Lavender, sweetgrass, pine woods, peppermint, honey citrus – plenty to spur the marketing boys into dizziness and delight as they plucked exotic and evocative adjectives to describe the 'complex blends' and 'uplifting balm' of a good old-fashioned bar of soap.

Working in a smokehouse, one would become inured to the fishy aroma, but be reminded of it very quickly when re-encountering the outside world. I recall numerous occasions when, returning from a half-day in the factory as a teenager, the person sitting by my side on the Underground would discreetly reposition themselves to the far end of the carriage. However, for sheer all-round embarrassment, nothing surpasses a recent incident at Tiffany's in Bond Street when I was browsing for an anniversary gift for René on my way home from work. I noticed the nose of the section supervisor was twitching feverishly, and she was squinting as if to figure out a problematic crossword clue.

Eventually, she could bear the frustration no longer and called to her colleague across the aisle: 'Tamsin, could you get somebody to take a look at the air conditioning? I think it must be faulty because of the terrible smell.'

Her voice was pure cut glass but she reddened rapidly when I exclaimed loudly: 'It's me, not the AC. I work in a fish factory!'

* * *

'Come on, Lance,' my father would enthuse at the start of the school holidays. 'You're coming with me to the factory for a few days. You're not staying in bed all day.'

Getting up at 4 a.m. filled me with dread. It was the outrageous unsocial hours. For a sixteen-year-old who has spent weeks without rest cramming for O levels, the prospect of being at Billingsgate Market at four in the morning is tantamount to torture by medieval thumbscrews. But, whether from filial devotion or from fear that any resistance would provoke dire consequences, I eventually acquiesced. In the summer of 1979, I collected my first weekly wage cheque from H. Forman & Son. And it was barely enough to cover the cost of a fledging date at the local cinema. My father was adamant that I needed to earn the respect of his staff. I must ask no favours as the boss's son, he said, 'For be in no doubt, none will be granted!'

During those first weeks, my constant companion was a twenty-stone scallywag named Peter Chiswick. He was one of my father's drivers. You'd expect a driver to be well-presented and fit, having to carry boxes through tight corridors and down narrow staircases, beneath the pavements, into London's restaurant kitchens. Peter defied every aspect of this caricature, but he hadn't been short of ways to make himself invaluable. I used to accompany him on his early-morning delivery rounds, and saw how he tooted and waved at theatre managers as we drove along Shaftesbury Avenue. I imagine part of the reason for his recruitment was his ability to obtain tickets – and usually the best seat – to any show in town.

In today's London, with a traffic camera on every street corner, he would be banned from his duties within a few hours. He regarded pavements as parking spaces, red lights as advisory rather than mandatory, and the humble zebra-crossing as the ideal spot for executing a hasty U-turn. In those pre-PC times, he would also toot whenever his eye was caught by a woman in a particularly fetching mini-skirt, stretching his head out the window with a gruff ''allo, luv' or 'o'right, darlin'' – quite an eye-opener for a middle-class teen. He would also park up and tell me he was going to have a shut-eye and I would sit, for an hour sometimes, reading his *Sun* whilst he laid back and snored, not knowing whether I should report such behaviour back to my father on my return. I never did (until now, at least). Peter trusted me, and if my dad was happy, why should I interfere?

By the second day, Peter was already involving me as an accomplice in all his wiles and ruses. He had parked the delivery van at a sharp angle, directly alongside the loading doors at the side of the Dorchester Hotel, and left me alone whilst he finished offloading supplies. I was getting fidgety; he had been absent for longer than the promised 'couple of minutes', and I wasn't confident I'd be able to handle the situation should the hotel authorities turn up, irate at the obstruction we'd caused. Suddenly, with a chuckle, he reappeared, his arms laden with snacks. 'Have a roll,' he said. It was a statement, not a question. I was ravenous after my early start, and tore greedily into the bread.

'Thanks for getting these,' I said. 'Where did you find them?'

'On the breakfast trolleys left outside the guest rooms,' he said. 'Don't worry, by the time they've woken up, we'll be the other side of Tower Bridge.'

After a few days on delivery duties, my father felt it would benefit my salmon education if I was exposed to the fish merchant's holy temple – Billingsgate Market itself. We arrived and parked up the cobbled streets by Monument. We were at the main gates an hour before dawn, and already it was abuzz. To my untutored eyes, all seemed chaos; thousands of workers darting around shouting the same three or four words in broad cockney – 'Mind your backs', 'Up the 'ill' – as they pushed and pulled their barrows up the street to load fishmongers' vans with the catches of the day, as if a stylus was stuck in the groove of an LP. But, during the rest of the summer, I learnt that the hubbub and commotion was as well-orchestrated as the most sophisticated military manoeuvring.

The men striding purposefully with an array of sharp and intimidating instruments were responsible for cracking open the newly arrived wooden coffins chock-full with what the Billingsgate denizens called 'stiff alive silver bars', an affectionate term for the stunning collection of Scottish salmon that would glisten in the ice as soon as the tops were lifted away. Under my father's tutelage, I learnt a few tricks to determine the freshness or otherwise of a fish. One technique made a particular impact: he explained that a myriad of sea lice on the belly and tail of a salmon is a cause for celebration, not castigation. As benign parasites, it's when the sea lice start dropping away from the fish's skin that suspicions about the freshness of the host's body are most likely to prove justified.

Business would often wind down at Forman's in the early afternoon, but my father would still have a tray full of paperwork. So I often took advantage of some free time to wander around the warren of backstreets and alleyways surrounding our factory. In the early 1970s, Marcel had relocated the factory from Dalston's famous Ridley Road market to a modern, purpose-built 6,000 sq. ft factory in Hackney Wick, a vast thriving community of traditional East End businesses for which the phrase 'salt of the earth' could have been invented. Within a few minutes' walk were a veritable mash-up of colourful businesses –

tile wholesaling, glass bending, TV repairing, chocolate making, textile weaving and soap manufacturing. It was like witnessing a microcosm of your entire life. Almost every product you needed to get through the typical week could, perchance, have had its origins in the city-within-a-city that was 1970s Hackney Wick.

Having spent most of my summers and Christmas school holidays at Forman's during my teens, for the next decade my attention was focused in other directions – university, Price Waterhouse, politics, Ukraine. But the lure of the family business was never far from my consciousness. At the same time, my father's thoughts were turning towards retirement. He was approaching his sixties and wanted to spend more time on the pleasures of life that, working a sixty-hour week, had long been denied him. I agreed with Phil Hudson that my role within East8 would transition from active co-manager to silent partner. Although I discussed this change in career direction with my father, I felt I would get a better and more balanced assessment of the state of the business if I spoke with his trusted General Manager, Stuart Meachin.

Meachin had been an occasional acquaintance over the years, and I was keen to make a positive impression so that nobody within the firm could accuse me of being the dilettante son, parachuted in through patronage not merit. I trusted and believed that Meachin would be an inseparable colleague during the next decade. Together, he and I would take Forman's into a rich and flourishing future.

So, imagine my astonishment when, after exchanging a few bland pleasantries, he hit me with his devastating diagnosis of Forman's ailing business model and the gruesome times ahead.

'Smoked salmon is becoming a commodity product,' he said, shaking his head dismissively. 'Most of the other London smokers are gone now and I can't imagine we will survive another ten years. It's all being mass-produced in Scotland with new machinery and there's no way we can compete with that down here.'

I looked on in astonishment as he enumerated the threats that, according to his worldview, were now encircling the business like sharks around a leaking dinghy. I noticed he was going to considerable effort to avoid eye contact – boiling a kettle, making a couple of coffees, stirring the drinks. Even when he passed one of the mugs to me, his gaze was fixated on the partition wall beyond.

'Don't worry though,' he continued. 'I'll manage the decline for the family.'

CHAPTER 4

FORMULATIONS

It's a wonder that business was ever done before the invention of computers.

My father and I were agreed that I should learn about Forman's 'from the bottom up'. From my time alongside Peter Chiswick on his rounds, I already had an inkling about delivery and distribution, albeit some years prior and acknowledging that Peter's approach was not necessarily representative of 'best practice', but the factory floor was still a foreign land to me. I made it my priority to secure a working knowledge of the jobs of everyone in the organisation so that I could never be outfoxed by spurious assertions or invented facts. In my head, this aim made perfect sense, but it worked better as a laudable intent than an executable pledge. I quickly realised that a university degree, albeit ungraded, and a few years pushing paperwork in the City and Westminster counted for nothing when faced with the pressure of a fast-turnaround factory operation.

One of the complications in smoked salmon preparation is that the product is, of course, natural. The fish, even once cured and smoked, are far (far, far) from uniform. Wild salmon is more likely to display bruises and bloodspots; certain salmon will have a silkier sheen; others will reveal a slightly higher fat content. Chefs worth their salt are aware of these differences, and many have specific predilections ('wild, silky, not too much fat'), for which they are prepared to negotiate a bespoke price. In the mid-1990s, Forman's had around 150 regular trade customers, typically carrying five or more price points each – far more pricing information than anyone could reasonably carry around in his head. Except that, by '*anyone*', I mean *me*. My father managed it, Meachin managed it, my immediate colleagues managed it. I soon realised that perhaps half the workforce had the information seared into their consciousness; information which my mind was incapable of retaining.

'Where are the spreadsheets?' I asked.

'A what?'

'A spreadsheet. Like you have on a computer. Where you record numbers and do calculations.'

'Can't see the point in that. Isn't that why we were given brains in our heads?'

It was a humbling experience.

The knowledge was also mission critical for one of my early roles. I was responsible for filling out the pricing slip to accompany despatched orders. Somebody else would be weighing the fish and shouting out the weight, and I had to scribble – for example – '22 lbs @ £** per lb = £**'. If it took me longer than a few seconds, a serious backlog would build up and the drivers would be late for their delivery rounds. A well-oiled machine would start to clog. If I inserted an incorrect price, either we'd face an irate customer call a few hours later accusing us of sharp dealings, or we'd be eating into our profit margin. After a disastrous couple of weeks, I took to revising the price list – the hardest period of intense study since sitting my accountancy exams. Yet, despite these plucky efforts, the typical conversation at 5.30 a.m. would flow as follows:

Me: 'Ah, Wiltons, the price they pay is... (hoping somebody would shout it out) ... anybody? Wiltons price? Any idea?'

Meachin: 'What have you forgotten now?'

Me: 'No, it's £6.50 ... isn't it? Aren't they the ones who pay in pounds not kilos?'

(Meachin deadpans whilst my face contorts.)

Me: '£6.50...?' (hoping Meachin will let slip)

Me: 'So... £6.50?'

Me: 'Come on, Stuart, I give up. Help me out here. This is ridiculous. There are better ways...'

Meachin (bellowing across the factory floor): 'Mr Forman, sir! He's gone and forgotten it all again!'

In addition to the constant niggling, every day provided more evidence that Stuart's vision for Forman's was diametrically opposed to my own. It was as if I'd scribbled my own priorities on a sheet of paper, and he'd gone down the list writing 'not a chance' next to each one. In joining the firm, I had a single-minded intent. I would devise the most audacious, outrageous, ambitious growth strategy, and then rush full-pelt to see it delivered. This was not a time for backsliding or sowing the seeds of doubt.

Our historic smokehouse competitors were falling by the wayside as they tried and failed to match the mass-production methods of the new industrial giants in the sector. Yet we still had a client list that read like a Who's Who of London's finest kitchens, and our salmon remained distinctive and loved. There were channels we'd barely touched, such as the retail sector, and direct-to-consumer distribution. I also had a gut feeling that our brand was woefully under-exploited, and that some inexpensive and innovative creativity would forge lasting cut-through with consumers. It was time to unleash potential and mould destiny, without carping from the sidelines about 'managing decline'.

To this day, I'm uncertain whether Meachin's analysis was genuine or a clumsy effort to deter me from hands-on involvement so that the business could fall into his lap as my father retired. I suspected the latter, since he was making my life a misery, clearly believing I lacked the stamina to thwart such adversity. In addition to my defective memory, he revelled whenever one of my pet projects backfired. There was a time when, attempting to add a dash of panache to our label designs, I had arranged for a few thousand to be printed in readiness for a huge Harrods Christmas order. Stuart glanced at the labels and then mobilised the team to unpeel and adhere them to the boxes. After three painstaking, laborious hours, Stuart let out a shriek straight from the Casting Central room of a Z-grade horror movie – effing and blinding with my name appended to each expletive. Apparently I had omitted to change the year in the 'sell by' section of the labels, meaning that every single one had to be manually replaced. The glint in his eye betrayed that he was rejoicing in my humiliation.

I could not afford to suffer 'noises off' as I set the business on a new direction. My first 'official' day in the hot seat was Monday 9 May 1994, and within six months Meachin was gone, relieved of his duties. It was him or me and I think it finally dawned on him that the prodigal son was in for the long haul.

My father was still fairly active in the business, but slowing down, and as I prepared to take over the reins I knew it would be crucial to simplify the family shareholding arrangements. I had three sisters, meaning we were each entitled to a one-quarter share as my parents handed Forman's to the next generation. I feared such a share arrangement would be a recipe for paralysis and inertia. Even if my siblings agreed on my strategy now, who knows how they may feel ten or twenty years down the line. The prospect of needing to command a supermajority vote before embarking on any strategic initiative was a concern.

I consulted Peter Leach, partner at Stoy Hayward (as was), and one of the world's most renowned authorities on the subject of the family-owned business. He gave me his book on family businesses and some of the comments were so pithy and apt, I wondered whether he'd been bugging our living room. He assured me that all family businesses are the same, whether it's a corner shop or a multinational, and the key to the success is to remove family issues from business decisions. I needed to have the business valued, buy out my sisters' stakes, and then 'sink or swim' depending on my own judgement and management ability. After some eleventh-hour haggling (a routine part of such negotiations, I was blithely assured), a deal was hammered out that all four of us felt was honourable, the paperwork was signed and the restructuring completed. The next morning, I sat with renewed authority in my 'CEO chair'.

It was still the same rickety chair I'd been perched on the previous day. The faux leather was peeling away, the chrome armrests were showing signs of rust, and one of the tiny wheels on the star base was coming loose. But now I had control of the business, and could forge its destiny without deferral to others. I looked around the operation with an unprecedented level of confidence.

Like (I'd imagine) a newly elected Prime Minister when he first crosses the threshold into Downing Street, I felt a tinge of apprehension about the challenges ahead. A family business with just twenty staff competing in a food industry worth billions: would we really be able to avoid being squeezed out of business? But these concerns were dwarfed by a sense of pride. Pride that it was now my responsibility to keep the company alive after ninety years in the hands of my forebears. And pride, deeply felt, that all the ingredients were now in place to achieve something truly exceptional.

My ego was still a tad battered at my lacklustre attempts to commit the best part of 1,000 price points to memory, and so my first investment once I assumed control was to introduce – you guessed it – spreadsheets, as the first stage in a broader project of automation. Computers started appearing on the desks of our accounts team. Email was introduced. Our telex and fax machines, which had once provided a continual hum around the clock, were being used less frequently –

a few times a day, then once a day, then once or twice a week – and as they fell out of favour they were progressively shifted a few feet further into the dim recesses of a corner office, making way for 'modern' equipment, such as a bulk printer and a photocopier.

I felt like Steve Jobs on steroids as various network installers taped cables to the undersides of desks, and software engineers loaded the latest packages onto the desktops. Comprehensive pricing schedules were soon available at a touch of a button. I simply needed to master the art of a sneaky sideways glance at the on-screen display and I'd never be shown up for pettifogging ignorance ever again.

Truth be told, it was not all the white heat of technology. There was one humble item that had been the mainstay of our ordering system for a decade or longer, and it resisted every attempt to put it out to pasture. This was our ancient-as-the-hills answering machine. For anybody under the age of thirty-five reading this narrative, I should explain that – once upon a time – telephone technology did not allow messages to be left on the device itself, or on a messaging system in cyberspace. Instead, if you wanted to allow callers to leave messages, it was necessary to plug an unwieldy contraption the size of a toilet seat into the side of your phone. When an incoming call wasn't answered, the machine would play a short taped message, and then invite the caller to leave a message on the self-same tape.

Oftentimes there would be a frustrating delay whilst the tape rewound to the appropriate place, and it was not uncommon for the tape to snap, get entangled with the answerphone's inner workings, or simply fail to make an audible recording. But, for all these hilarious defects, the wretched thing was actually quite efficient. Not only that, it was vital to the integrity of our operations. Many chefs would only realise they were low on their salmon supplies when their kitchens were being closed long past midnight. To this day, long after the invention of email, the last thing they want to do at an ungodly hour is to fire up a computer and compose a note in Outlook. Far simpler to leave a message on the Forman's answering machine and head home confident that the issue is in someone else's hands. Often, the day's most valuable orders would be left at one or two in the morning in a harassed and exhausted tone, with crucial information – such as the chef's name – mumbled or entirely absent. Any member of staff who proved adept at deciphering near-incomprehensible answerphone messages had virtually guaranteed themselves a job for life.

Sorting out the technology was a necessary chore, but by itself didn't win a single new piece of business. With the office computerised, it was time to turn my focus to Forman's marketing activity – which, up to that point, had been non-existent. My father was blunt: he couldn't see the point. He knew the chefs personally, they trusted him to source and smoke the finest salmon, and spending money telling people his name was Forman seemed a sure-fire way from riches to rags. He was never impressed by companies that spent a fortune promoting their wares during ad breaks: 'Why would anyone buy a widget because Sean Connery or John Cleese claim they like it?' he scoffed. 'Can't people make up their own minds?'

His disdain for anything other than superb-calibre fish was evidenced in the packaging we used. To save a few pence, he'd task his drivers with hoovering up used cardboard boxes left on London's pavements for collection by the early-morning refuse trucks. 'It's called recycling,' he said in justification. 'Isn't that meant to be a good thing?' This meant that Forman's finest salmon would often be delivered to swanky hotels and restaurants in battered, second-hand cardboard boxes with the names of entirely different products – 'apples', or 'cheesecake', or 'napkins' – emblazoned across the sides. On rare occasions, he'd push the boat out and organise a bit of token gold packaging for corporate gifts. And that, basically, was Forman's branding strategy from 1962 to 1995.

As part of a brand refresh, I momentarily contemplated whether to simplify our name – reducing H. Forman & Son to the more streamlined 'Forman's', which was how most people colloquially knew us. But it was too much of a wrench. The only reason I was in charge of a working smokehouse with a loyal client base was because of the vision and work ethic of my forebears. If I cast away that heritage, I might as well renounce my soul. Besides, staying true to the business' near-century-old name gave me the liberty to be more innovative in other areas that were in greater need of an overhaul.

I collected the packaging from dozens of other smokehouses to open my mind about design possibilities. Surprisingly, despite analysing examples from numerous countries and food types, the same three ideas kept recurring. Firstly, there were designs that reflected the country of origin – in the case of salmon, this was often a tartan pattern. To me, this seems a strange choice – consumers aren't buying a *country*; they may never have been to that country; they may even have reasons to *dislike* that country. My emotional response to this style of packaging was lukewarm verging on apathy. 'I just don't care,' said my inner voice. In addition, I was keen to raise awareness that gourmet salmon smoking is a London, not a Scottish, tradition (hence trademarking the London Cure logo a few years later). The second batch fell into the bucket entitled: 'Let's show them the animal they're eating.' Surely not, I thought. A gastronomic experience is about the ambience and the taste, not the hunter/gatherer instinct. And, finally, there were many examples where the wraparound was no more than a huge cellophane window, with the merest sliver of a cardboard perimeter on which to provide some text. I wasn't keen on this either. The bulk of our business came from repeat customers, who knew exactly what a few slices of smoked salmon should look like. Whilst a modest window had much to commend it, I didn't want to sacrifice valuable space on the packaging which could otherwise be used to speak directly to the customer.

The glory of smoked salmon, I reasoned, is in its consumption – not its country of origin nor its appearance through a cellophane window. I had neither the time nor the patience to scour Madison Avenue for my very own Don Draper to breathe life into this thought, however. Luckily, I needed look no further than a building across Queen's Yard, the HQ of a wonderful design and print firm called Quadrographics. They 'got' my idea immediately. Together we conceived the phrase 'the discerning gastronome'. This nomenclature, we felt, conveyed the worldview and temperament of a diner who actively seeks out Forman's smoked salmon as food worth savouring. It also carried a tinge of refinement and a hint of exclusivity. But, above all, it encapsulated the conviction that fine food is one of life's greatest pleasures and isn't there to be gulped, wolfed or rushed. With the personality of our figurehead agreed, we next gave him an identity, through a stylised drawing of the gastronome himself, seated at a small round restaurant table, enraptured by the taste of his meal and the accompanying refreshments.

As soon as Quadrographics presented their visuals, I was hooked. It was unlike anything I'd seen before – not just on smoked salmon packaging, but on that of any other food product. It was quirky without being facetious; irreverent without being anarchic; light-hearted without straying into camp or comedy. The picture was the centrepiece of our redesigned packaging, alongside a new H. Forman & Son crest whose every curve and corner was laden with symbolism, and the use of black as the backdrop, which I felt best served to accentuate the pink of the salmon (I didn't entirely lose the window; I simply reduced it to a more discreet size and position).

The new packaging was scarcely on the vans when friends and colleagues started calling me to enthuse about the gastronome concept. It was, they said, so distinctive, so compelling, that surely it had the legs to stretch into other media. I raced back to Quadrographics, summoning their best people for a full-on brainstorm. And that was the origin of the annual Forman's wall calendar, a poster-sized celebration of everything that's discerning and all that's gastronomic. In my first winter in charge, a calendar was despatched to every one of our loyal chefs in which the now-iconic image of our gastronome is looking towards the side of the poster, where the days of the year were laid out month-by-month. I thought a few of our customers might chuckle at our élan, but I wasn't expecting much more. Yet, much more duly happened! By midday on 2 January, reports started arriving via my drivers that our calendar was being granted pride of place on the walls of London's busiest kitchens.

The pressure was now 'on'; this could be no singular triumph. By May, we were being asked by our regulars what we planned for an encore, and these inquiries could not wilfully be ignored. And lo, twenty years later, Quadrographics (now rebranded 'Design & Print'), retains the contract to take the discerning gastronome calendar annually into ever-more daring, subversive directions. Over two decades, the gastronome has requested another helping please, been joined by companions of various stripes, and been censored by the Olympic brand police (all references to 'London' or '2012' or '20' or '12' deleted from the 2012 calendar). His presence has solidified Forman's reputation as a firm concerned principally with the enjoyment of our product, and only secondarily about the financial benefits. If we cut corners to make a short-term buck (which, of course, we never would), we'd be red-carded by the gastronome, who would take his custom elsewhere. And implicit in this narrative was a message to restaurateurs and hoteliers: they too should covet the patronage of the most discerning of gastronomes. Forman's smoked salmon on the menu is one of their most indispensable tools in such a quest.

With a consumer brand came the need for a consumer strategy. In the mid-1990s, around two-thirds of our sales were to hotels, primarily in London and Hong Kong, and I'd lost a few sleepless nights when hucksters tried to persuade a few of my loyal chefs to invest in technology that jeopardised our business model. The most worrisome was a kitchen-sized curing and smoking contraption which allowed chefs to prepare the whole shooting match themselves – all they needed from us was the raw salmon, salt and woodchips, and even those could be procured from many other vendors. If this gained traction, our small niche would vanish into near nothingness, like a collapsing star. Blink, and we'd go the way of the neighbourhood milkman.

In this instance, we muddled through. The machines weren't industrial grade, and in any event the kitchen staff struggled to master the controls. Never have I felt so much quiet joy at the crushed dreams of others! But my close brush with forfeiting one or two long-standing accounts left its mark. In business, as in politics, a '1 per cent' strategy has its limitations. I didn't want to spend my next two decades vulnerable to the whims of a few decision-makers at a handful of venues. My blood pressure couldn't stand it. The new brand identity opened up the opportunity to broaden our distribution. It was time for the name of H. Forman & Son to filter into the collective public consciousness.

'Do you really think it can work?' asked René.

'Here's how we'll measure success,' I said. 'One day, we'll be sitting down at dinner with people we've never met before. They'll tell me they're in the media business or whatever. I'll say I'm in the smoked salmon trade. And they'll say, "Oh, you mean like that company Forman's. We never leave Waitrose without some."'

In the short term, I reduced our dependency on the hotel trade by paying more attention to the retail channels that were already active. I set up regular meetings with the buyers at Harrods, Selfridges, Fortnum & Mason and Harvey Nichols, in which we discussed simple ways to raise the profile of the product on the shop floor. In-store tastings, more creative displays and product information boards were all found to provide a revenue lift. We even launched with Fortnum's a Wild

Salmon Race, where prizes were awarded to the first people to catch a wild salmon when the rivers opened for the season.

There were downsides in approaching the major British supermarkets such as Tesco, Waitrose, Sainsbury's, and so forth. They are notorious for 'tough' supplier negotiations. I needed to figure out a price that worked for us, and never waver nor falter when negotiations reached the proverbial 'thumbscrew tightening' stage. Concern had also been expressed in some quarters that we'd be 'diluting the brand'; that our bond with top chefs would be diminished the moment they spotted the Forman's discerning gastronome sharing shelf space with the mass-produced and own-label gunk that we were forever decrying. I was sanguine about this risk; we were entering the era of the celebrity chef. How could they cast aspersions on my retail strategy when I'd be crossing paths with them at the same supermarket HQs as we haggled over our respective deals? These issues were challenges to be overcome, not reasons to avoid the opportunity. What I hadn't appreciated was the intense scrutiny. Securing a short-term pilot was no big deal; the retail mindset is to be forever on the lookout – experimenting, trialling, testing, studying. But, as the saying goes: there's only one opportunity to make a first impression. By the end of the weekend, if a dozen packs of the finest from Forman's remain untouched and unloved, it's time to make way for something, anything, that will be a more productive SKU (stock keeping unit). The supermarket operator is agnostic whether shelf space is being occupied by confectionary, clothing or Christmas decorations. What counts is yield per square foot, and if a specific product falls short, you can forget your rapport with the buying team, the iconoclastic tone of your calendar, or your claims about nutritional value and supporting family businesses. If the numbers don't add up, it's time to be O-U-T the back door. And never does the spotlight shine as fiercely as in those trial days.

I was acutely conscious that the slightest question mark over Forman's retail potential during the trial period could be terminal to our chances of renewal, and even took a couple of detours to check out branches that had been nominated for the pilot scheme. On one early foray, I was lurking at the end of the aisle as a housewife picked up a pack of Forman's, smiled at the gastronome image, and was about to drop it into her trolley, when her rascal of a daughter shrieked out 'ice cream, Mummy!' As the mother trundled away to do the bidding of this troublesome creature, I was so mortified that I opened my wallet and bought the pack myself!

Retail has grown year-on-year as a proportion of Forman's sales. On balance, it has been a sound strategy, though not without its frustrations. The mega firms have a propensity for wanting on-file copies of all their suppliers' 'policies and procedure'. There must be a special place in hell for whoever coined the dreaded term 'procedures manual', guaranteed to turn any small business into a quivering mass of nerves.

'I don't have a team of thirty-five people dealing with policies and procedures,' I'd plead. 'I could recruit them, but are you willing to see my prices shoot up by about a third?'

'I'm sorry, Mr Forman. It says on page 18 of our supplier verification form that we need to see your disaster recovery plan. Otherwise how can we be confident you'll stick to your delivery schedule if you encounter a problem?'

The most recent time that happened, I emailed the complainant, with his Chief Executive on copy, attaching a list of every catastrophe and debacle to have befallen Forman's in recent years (see Chapters 5–19 for further information), with the pithy comment that 'I think we'll be alright.' There was no further mention of disaster recovery plans but if the subject rears its head ever again, I shall present a personally signed copy of this book to the culprit and ask them not to come back until they've read it.

Despite the steady progress of our retail initiative, I was still troubled and uneasy. Our presence on the fish section shelves was a boon for our public recognition, and extended our footprint far beyond the M25, but still left us dependent on third parties who could switch us off on a whim. I was convinced that we needed to supplement our multi-channel strategy with an ability to deliver our salmon direct to the consumer. The operational side of this was straightforward – all we needed was to open a UPS account. But building it into a commercially viable business line was a far trickier matter, since I could probably count on one hand the number of people who would be prepared to place an order for salmon alone (most of whom would have the surname Forman). If this was a serious initiative, we needed wider product availability. And therein lay the rub, because we were basically a salmon smokehouse. I needed a cunning plan to broaden our gourmet range.

Needless to say, my every plan was inoperable. Dead on arrival. (Planning has never been my strong suit. Remember the Yiddish proverb I quoted in Chapter 1 about how God finds hysterically funny our forlorn attempts to plan, to persuade others we can exert a modicum of control over our destinies? I've become increasingly outspoken on this topic, and even lecture occasionally at London Business School about the futility of planning. That tends to be received with mixed emotions by students who've just invested the cost of a semi-detached house – or a broom-cupboard in Knightsbridge – to learn the secret ingredients to a sure-fire winning plan.)

Yet Forman's does, today, have a direct distribution mail-order business. The genesis, far from being effective planning, was a fortuitous blend of luck, opportunism and an old-fashioned nose for a deal. I won't test your patience with a blow-by-blow account of the shenanigans and horse-trading, but suffice it to say that an outstanding business had been the victim of its own success. Word-of-mouth and a commitment to quality and value had delivered a vast Christmas season order book which now needed to be honoured. And would have been honoured, but for the horror-inducing, panic-prompting, terror-activated words 'computer glitch', uttered one morning by an agitated Head of IT. Ironically, having championed computerisation at Forman's, I was now to be the beneficiary of a computer failure elsewhere in the sector.

A few big corporate leviathans were circling around for any scraps, but the vultures were preoccupied with undertaking due diligence, instructing lawyers and drawing up watertight contracts. Whilst they were holding conference calls and signing off on the minutes of investment committee meetings, Forman's had already pounced. Our speed to act and flexibility of strategy meant we now had our very own mail order service, able to ship wondrous hampers packed with glorious products to a database of prized customers around the country.

The new business was called Forman & Field – not because I was suddenly a joint venture partner with a 'Mr Field', but (I confess) because it seemed an apt name from a branding perspective. It was alliterative, it provided a neat contrast to Forman's association with the sea, and it enabled me to blame the imaginary Mr Field if any of my retail contacts objected to our opening of a direct to consumer channel. Take a bow, Mr Field – as a convenient scapegoat, your talents are unsurpassed!

CHAPTER 5

FORGING AHEAD

It is one of life's oddities that so many high-profile figures are graced with the initials 'JC': Julius Caesar, Jaspar Conran, John Cleese, James Caan, Jeremy Clarkson, James Callaghan, Joan Collins, James Cagney, Jim Carrey, Jimmy Carter, and of course a preacher of some renown who wandered around Jerusalem a couple of millennia ago. So I figured I might have struck gold when I recruited as the new Forman's General Manager, replacing Stuart Meachin, a pugnacious, church-going Scot named John Cherrie. John possessed an encyclopaedic knowledge of obscure routes around the Scottish coastline (which proved invaluable for our regular forays to visit Scotland's wild salmon suppliers) and a tendency to dress in the style of a traditional livestock farmer, complete with loud check shirts, Barbour jackets and corduroy trousers.

For two years, Cherrie and I were inseparable as a management team. Trusting him to run the factory operations and deal with the staff freed me up to knock on doors chasing new business opportunities. In our first year together, sales grew by nearly 25 per cent, a pattern that was repeated in the following year. I could now talk about Forman's heritage, and the new initiatives I had been championing since taking over from my father, before moving on to our day-to-day customer service commitments.

Our business took on an increasingly international hue. We were sending regular shipments to both Hong Kong (half a dozen time zones ahead) and the US (half a dozen behind). This meant my working day was extended at both ends with queries from clearing agents and import authorities. But I was a glutton for punishment, and so – even with around four hours' sleep every night – still couldn't switch off my sales button. Whenever I took a family holiday overseas, I'd be on the lookout to wangle a meeting with the hotel's executive chef, during which I could parade the endless virtues of the Forman's range. I'm sure I must have been blacklisted by some destinations, who feared their kitchen staff wouldn't get a moment's peace with 'the smoked salmon man' in residence.

Over the years, leading international hoteliers have sometimes sought us out when passing through London, often with bizarre results. On a balmy Spring day in the mid-2000s, Grant Macpherson – a world-renowned chef whom I'd first met when he worked for Raffles in Singapore, then at Las Vegas's Bellagio Hotel, the strip's most-photographed venue due to its well-known frontage of dancing fountains – was sitting in my office talking about his new role at the Wynn Hotel, where the vision was to push even further the boundaries of excess and indulgence. He spotted a pack of roasted cashews with cumin on a side table, which I'd been sent speculatively by a husband-and-wife team who prepared them on their kitchen table as a pastime. I often received samples on a speculative basis from small and micro enterprises asking me to consider their product as a possible addition to our Forman & Field catalogue. I tried to help wherever possible, since we were establishing something of a reputation as a champion of gourmet British foods from niche producers, and for a start-up even a handful of incremental sales can be a valued boost to credibility and cash flow.

Macpherson and I split open the bag and munched absent-mindedly on the nuts whilst chatting about the vast quantities of salmon and live langoustine we would soon be flying over each week. I had only a hazy recollection of all this when, a few days later, back in Las Vegas, he called me to place an order for 1,600 packets of nuts … on the condition that they were delivered within five days flat so they could be used as complimentary in-room gifts, courtesy of Steve Wynn's wife, for all the guests attending the spectacular, multi-million-dollar opening of the Wynn's new extension. Fortunately, I hadn't yet disposed of the introduction letter with the husband and wife's contact details, despite having no interest in including their product in our range for our catalogue, and I phoned through. It was one of those 'do you want the good news or the bad news?' calls, and somehow – I have absolutely no idea how, but I imagine it involved an open-house invitation to the entire village – they were able to rise to the challenge. Sixteen hundred packets were crammed into corrugated boxes and air-freighted direct to the Wynn's party war room. I think even Macpherson was astonished by the turnaround.

Cherrie was becoming an ever-closer confidante and sounding board for every stray marketing idea that came into my head. He also displayed an infectious enthusiasm about getting to know the details of the operation and was happy for me to be out and about generating new leads, whilst he ensured the new orders were successfully fulfilled. The proof that our strategy was yielding results came when we realised we'd need to expand our footprint. Our existing 6,000 sq. ft simply couldn't accommodate the numbers of carvers and packers, let alone provide space for our growing fleet of delivery vehicles to be docked and loaded. We made an offer on adjacent premises which no longer suited the existing tenant and, six months later, the expanded Forman's factory was open for business, with government food minister Angela Browning in attendance. New customers, better facilities, official approval – how much better could business get?

* * *

I should have known what would happen next from a thousand clichéd Hollywood scripts. When the sun is shining and the roses are blooming, it's the moment to beware disaster. Plus, it was October, so time for the first in our legion of calamities.

The Friday evening, 2 October, had passed in a nondescript way, with a traditional family meal enjoyed by three generations of Formans, and the usual over-indulgence on chopped liver, chicken soup, roast chicken and chocolate mousse. Much of the dinner conversation focused on Matthew having just started his new prep school, Haberdashers', where I had been myself, some thirty years earlier. With my eyes closing at the dinner table, I excused myself and crashed out well before midnight, fully expecting a slightly longer than customary four to five hours of sleep. There was no reason to expect a call from Hong Kong, where shipments never arrived on a Friday night, nor from Las Vegas, as the Bellagio had only just replenished. So far, so predictable. I slept soundly until my reverie was interrupted by the din of my hyperactive alarm clock at around 3.40 a.m. or so, in my fog of half-sleep, I assumed. Only after the third ring did I realise the alarm clock, strategically placed a walking distance from the bed, was actually the telephone on my bedside table, and the time was still only two.

'Lance. It's John.'

Cherrie? He never called me during the night. Not once during our two years together. Was he sick perhaps? This must be serious. Not puncture-on-a-van serious. But deeply serious.

'You need to get down to the factory fast. There's been a fire.'

'What do you mean, fire?'

'I mean fire. I'm here now, but you need to come.'

Dressed in less than a minute and careering across London, my mind was filled with images from the movie *Towering Inferno*, of flames licking the heavens as an entire structure burns out of control. Surely Cherrie hadn't meant *fire* like that. As I raced down the Archway Road, I could see dark grey clouds billowing into the sky five miles distant – my new expanded factory in ruins. From three blocks away, I could already see the tinge of orange flames bursting out from the top of the building and hear the wailing of twenty fire engines that were wedged into Queen's Yard.

I parked in an alleyway close to the factory. Already, scores of neighbours had gathered to watch the devastation unfold. One of the fire officers – I assume, the man in charge on account of his loudspeaker – was bellowing orders to the crew about tackling the blaze. Their priority, it seemed, was to contain it to the sections of the factory – about two-thirds of the total – where it had been raging most fiercely. If the fire was allowed to engulf the other properties in the square, or even spread beyond into residential areas, Forman's legacy could be as the twentieth century's Pudding Lane – the scene of the genesis of the second Great Fire of London.

Jets of water were arching from every direction to calm the blaze, and whilst the flames were subsiding, it would be at least another couple of hours before the mushroom clouds changed from cauliflower heads to florets. Coughing as my lungs filled with smoke, I wondered, what next?

John had arrived with a group of his friends from church. With the permission of the fire brigade, they had taken a brave decision to enter a maximum of five metres into the building, so they could salvage the contents of a walk-in fridge. This was good thinking on John's part. With the stock moved to one of our refrigerated vans, we had enough smoked salmon to deliver to customers the following morning, which would buy us the rest of the weekend to work out a game plan.

The only problem was how would we know what to deliver. The order book, and the answerphone, were located in the offices upstairs where the smoke was still thick.

Instinctively, I headed straight towards the main door, but my path was blocked by a gruff fire officer with his arms outstretched, no longer letting anyone past the threshold.

'That's enough,' he said. 'No closer.'

'It's my building,' I pleaded. 'You've got to let me through.'

'It won't do your building any good if you're fried as well,' he yelled above the noise of the commotion. 'I insist – no closer!'

In retrospect, his order was probably for the best. Parts of the factory were already crumbling under the onslaught, girders and beams collapsing into an abyss. Yes, on balance, probably wise that I didn't play the hero on this occasion.

Suddenly, it dawned on me that one of our most prized possessions might have fallen victim to the fire, and all worries about the impact of the fire on Forman's long-term survival vanished from my mind. The single word *answerphone* was pummelling through my brain as if there was no other term left in the lexicon. Within the next few hours, dawn would be breaking across the capital and our vans would be tasked with delivering the right quantities of smoked salmon to the right destinations so that top kitchens could delight every discerning gastronome who happens to walk through their doors. Unless I acted fast, that entire operation was in jeopardy. Now, we ran the risk of never knowing the *right quantities.* Because the Forman's promise, 100 per cent reliability and efficiency, was largely rooted in the fact that, every morning without fail, the messages left on the answerphone were faithfully transcribed and passed to despatch. How to uphold our guarantee if our prized answerphone was a mess of melted plastic and seared metal? Forget our accounting records, our trademark notices, the photographs in my office – just give me my answerphone, I thought, and all will be well.

'Can I?' I said to the gruff officer. He was in urgent dialogue with one of his colleagues, and waved me away.

'This is actually important.'

Another wave.

'Just a quick question—'

'Please step back, sir!'

'I need your help. There's something very important I need to get, just at the top of the staircase.'

'And who are you, sir?'

'It's my factory. Can we get in? I really need to get in. Just to the office at the top of the stairs, just for five seconds.'

'Sorry, sir, there's no way anyone's getting in here for at least twenty-four hours. It's not safe, the whole floor could collapse on your head and that's not going to help anyone, is it, sir?

Sometimes in business I've learnt to be cunning. Sometimes to be angry. Sometimes to be assertive. On this occasion, I was begging. If they'd asked me to kneel on the tarmac and lick the ashes off the soles of their shoes, my compliance would've been total – with no attempts at negotiation, or moments of hesitation, I would've taken to the task with aplomb. Because, when in a fix, begging can be the only recourse available.

John overheard this discussion and volunteered to join the mission. As soon as they were suitably attired in headgear and masks, the fire officer and John raced in through the front door and up the stairs. Their twenty-second disappearance seemed to last for ever. Would they be able to salvage enough to keep us operational for the morning's deliveries, which we needed to despatch in a couple of hours? Then, out of the smoke, I saw the two running back down the stairs, spluttering and breathless but with the machine held tightly in John's arms, like a baby. But with the baby saved, was it still alive? We laid it on the bonnet of a van, wiped away the black film that had entirely coated the machine and pressed the rewind button. It worked. Deep breath. But now the message button.

'Hello, Forman's, Connaught Hotel. Six sides of your best for the morning.' Bleep.

'Crockfords, three sides please.' Bleep.

Yes. We're in business – but only for one more morning.

Amidst the chaos, dozens of strangers, neighbours, onlookers, early-rising busy-bodies and fire officers, the last thing I expected to see was a man in a smart suit, wearing a smart tie and heading over in my direction, briefcase in hand. Indeed, there were two of them approaching me from different directions and, as one picked up pace, the other seemed to speed up too.

'Are you Mr Forman?' enquired the first.

'Yes. Who are you?'

'Balcombe,' said one. 'Nick Balcombe.'

'Harris,' said the other, forcing a business card into my hand.

'I'm sure you must be in a state of shock,' said one, 'but I can help you deal with this.'

'Yes, *my* company helps business owners who have suffered from a fire.'

'*My* company will get you straightened out. You really don't need to worry.'

I stood listening to these men, realising they were battling over my business, but not hearing a word. What I wanted was a semblance of normality and that meant selecting fish to go to our customers so I had a chance to fathom out the next steps. I pushed the two men aside, and told them if they want to pitch their services, they needed to return after 8 a.m.

Three hours later, with all the fish despatched, as though a normal Saturday's delivery, and only one of the suited individuals, Nick Balcombe – trouble-shooter and all-round great guy – returned to enter my life. He offered me an outstretched hand and, without any further niceties, dived straight into his recommendations for what we were going to do.

'First things first, I assume that your property and business insurance is up to date.'

'Yes.' I was monosyllabic. It was now time for him to reveal a little more leg. If my answer had been no, I don't think the conversation would have lasted for more than another minute. Balcombe would have been racing off to find another disaster.

It turned out that Balcombe was a fellow of the Institute of Public Loss Assessors, and a Senior Professional Public Adjuster (a US qualification), as well as the senior partner in a firm of loss assessors. Over the years ahead, he would be called on to negotiate in incidents as diverse as the Christchurch earthquake, the Twin Towers attacks, various hurricanes that caused havoc on the US mainland including Andrew, Gilbert and Sandy, and crises in Dubai, Valencia, Madrid, Paris and Brussels and, currently, the Glasgow School of Art. As I would learn, he had sophisticated antennae throughout London and the south-east, enabling him to be first on the scene whenever the need arose. The Forman's fire ticked all his criteria, and he'd wasted not a moment to reach the site, his mind already fizzing with solutions. What was an epic disaster for us was a business development opportunity for Balcombe and his team. Normally, I would decry ambulance-chasers, but Balcombe was of a different ilk. He was practical, creative, assertive and focused on solutions rather than wallowing in self-pity – just my kind of advisor.

I explained to Balcombe the nature of our business. He understood immediately the dilemma. Our need was very specialist – we could only operate out of a facility with a kiln, and with hygiene standards and working conditions conducive to food production. We couldn't work in an area of excessive heat, or of temperature fluctuations. Most importantly, we couldn't survive a period of business interruption. Our clients expected continuity of service. If we let them down for a day, we probably had enough goodwill to ride through. A couple of days, and we'd be testing their loyalty. Three days, and they'd be searching for other sources of supply. And who could blame them? After all, somebody had been banging the drum about keeping sated all those hordes of discerning gastronomes at their doors.

'To summarise,' said Balcombe, 'you need a factory to cure and smoke. Your own facility is defunct for the next few months. You don't have access to a couple of kilns behind the bike sheds that you can install in an empty warehouse. So there's only one solution.'

I was intrigued.

'To work from another smokehouse. Are there any competitors you could buy out?'

He had a way of expressing a quite radical recommendation as if it were the most obvious strategy on earth. Before I could mutter, 'Why didn't I think of that!', his eyes were already darting around the other buildings in the courtyard for other solutions.

'Last night, whilst I was waiting for you, I saw a building in the opposite corner called Lewzeys. It says "Smoked Fish" above the gate. What do they do?'

'I'm not sure it's worth thinking about Lewzeys,' I said. 'The place is tiny and they smoke haddock and trout, not salmon.'

'Perfect,' said Balcombe. 'From tomorrow, they will be smoking salmon. We'll use their kilns and you can do the rest from here. When we're done, I'll make a few calls and we can get this part of the building sealed off and fitted out as good as new.'

'I don't know what you're planning, but we can't just wander up to the front door and commandeer the place.'

'Yes, we can,' said Balcombe. 'That's why you have insurance and that's why – with me on your side – we'll have all this straightened out in no time. Leave that part to me.'

'If you have a standard business interruption policy, you're entitled to take any actions necessary to salvage your business and save it from collapse. In fact, it's an obligation. That will cover the cost of any compensation we offer to Lewzeys.'

'We?'

'Yes, we. You only pay me a percentage of your claim, but I'll have all your costs covered.'

This was all happening so fast. Within six hours I'd been rudely awakened, in the midst of a blaze, packing fish, and now seemingly buying the use of a smokehouse and fitting out another new factory. But I had no alternative strategy and Balcombe came across as someone who knew what he was doing and I could trust to make the right decisions.

Balcombe spoke my kind of language. What's more, he delivered. Somehow he managed to agree an amicable deal with Lewzeys, and signed off the arrangement with the local Environmental Health Officers. For the next six months, we were allowed to prepare the fish in the one part of our factory that had somehow survived the conflagration, place the cured fillets on smoking trolleys which would then be fully wrapped in cling film so as to prevent any pollution whilst in transit as they were wheeled across the industrial yard, exposed to the elements. There, the cling film would be unravelled and the trolleys of salmon wheeled into Lewzeys steam-operated and very unreliable kilns. But unreliable was a damned sight better than twisted, burned-out metal. The following day, the trolleys, now loaded with smoked sides, would be rewrapped in plastic, wheeled back to what was left of Forman's and into our newly fitted-out space to be sliced. Usually in food factories raw fish has to be separated from cooked, and we only had one room in which to operate, so separation was achieved by time. We double-shifted the work so that, for twelve hours of the day, raw fish was flying across filleting tables and on to salting racks, and for the other twelve hours, the space was an operating-theatre-standard smoked salmon slicing and packing operation, with not a raw fish in sight. My team was incredible, changing their normal work patterns to keep Forman's in play.

I had a concern that, if the scheme was to work as a temporary measure, the Lewzey brothers mustn't feel browbeaten into it, but when I met them the following afternoon they were effervescent with charm and vibrancy. After twenty minutes discussing sprinkler systems, fire extinguishers and the combustibility of roof tiles and insulation (all of which would become lifelong obsessions; our working assumption was that our own fire had been sparked by a tiny piece of lit sawdust working its way out of the kiln through a fine wire-mesh panel and into the flue), I apologised for Balcombe marching in and barking out his game plan. Their toothy grins told me everything I needed to know. In fact, as events panned out, I suspect the deal had been a useful fillip for their bank balances, and it wasn't long afterwards that the owner took his well-deserved and (by all accounts) well-heeled retirement.

Each month, as our trolleys were clocking up the mileage, the Environmental Health Officers would contact us for an update on our search for a new premises. The cling film–wheel/cling film–wheel routine could only ever be a temporary fix.

Yet, after spending six months exploring alternative sites, I was astonished to find that almost nothing suitable was available. This was quite a revelation, because it only took a casual trip around the area to marvel at the number of abandoned plants and boarded-up warehouses. Dig deeper, and the owners willing to sell at a reasonable price were thin on the ground. They were acutely conscious of the eight-fold difference between the cost per acre of residential land compared with the industrial equivalent. And they were all patiently waiting for their 'change of use' applications to be approved by the authorities so that more of London's dazzling manufacturing heritage could be demolished in favour of identikit blocks of yuppie flats. Whenever you hear politicians talking about the decline of our manufacturing base, it's hardly surprising when a business owner facing all the daily grief of dealing with increasingly interfering bureaucracy can simply sell up to a property developer, enjoy the spoils and take up golf.

So, at the end of a fruitless half-year search, the Environmental Health Officers issued an ultimatum: 'Either refurbish what was burned or we will need to close you down.'

Rebuilding was not so much the *preferred* option as the *only* option. With the new factory, we would take the opportunity to update and upgrade and completely re-organise the production flow, which would now fully meet the new, ever-changing European food hygiene regulations. In addition to managing the operation, John oversaw the building works. Working from a single room as the building works took place was not the ideal environment to showcase to prestigious clients, so I spent most of my time travelling to clients and discussing the quality of our smoked fish (rather than the smoked factory). As new clients came on board, I realised that the fire would be but a temporary setback. We would emerge stronger and revitalised.

As our reopening approached, the casual visitor to the site would have had no clue about the devastation in our recent past. I took the opportunity to upgrade the interior layout, making the factory feel more modern and open, creating a visitors' area where guests could see sides of smoked salmon hanging up against a brick wall, conjuring up images of the old smoke holes. The final element was the installation of our new kilns, after those caught in the fire were a long way beyond salvage. With the arrival of mass smoked salmon production, another smokehouse went into receivership during the timeframe of the rebuild, and we were pleased to take the kilns from the hands of the receivers. I had kept the entire incident somewhat under the radar from our clients, so as not to provoke alarm, but with the worst days behind us it was time to adopt a more confident tone.

I decided the reopening should be an *event*. I ordered champagne by the crate load, posted invitations to almost every chef and food hall buyer on our database (yes, we now owned such a thing), and harangued everyone I knew in the media to put in an appearance. And then, my coup de théâtre. I secured the services of none other than Mr Jeffrey Archer, renowned raconteur, novelist, panellist, celebrity, wit and politician, to cut the proverbial ribbon. At the time, Archer was scarcely out of the news. He had just been selected as the Conservative Party candidate for the position of London's first-ever directly elected Mayor, and according to the polls stood an excellent chance of success. He had a cross-party appeal, floating above the day-to-day political factions due to his wide hinterland, being a 'larger-than-life character', and managing to walk the tightrope between being slightly bonkers but not threatening or dangerous. I knew his presence would be a talking point for our guests. His preparedness to spend time at our factory and lavish praise upon our product would, I believed, allow the Forman's brand to shine more brightly than ever.

Over 300 valued guests came together for our reopening, an event of perfect charm, laughter and togetherness. Archer gave a masterclass in public speaking. His voice projection wouldn't have been out of place on a Shakespearean stage. Not a word mumbled or vowel elided. His timing was spot-on; no more than five minutes of purest quality. And his content included the highest praise to our salmon (thank goodness) whilst being self-deprecating. His effervescence shone through at the start, at the conclusion, and during a number of rhetorical flourishes in between:

> Madam Mayor [referring to the Mayor of Tower Hamlets], Mr and Mrs Forman, can I begin by thanking you for that standing ovation. I had the privilege of opening a school library in the north of London recently, where there were over 1,000 children and parents. I considered it a very great honour – like today. But I'd forgotten how honest twelve-year-old children can be.

I said to one girl, 'It has been a great honour for me to have been selected to open this library,' to which the child replied, 'Well, you weren't the first choice!'

I, Sir, had the privilege of being invited by you to open this new factory some time ago, and so it's one of those weird coincidences that it's come in the middle of an election campaign, but it's an equal delight to be here. The thing that has struck me – I mean we are all aware that 90 per cent of businesses in London are ten people or less, and this is an example of twenty-five people running something of which we can be immensely proud. The one thing all of you will have seen is the professionalism. You walk in a door, whichever area you go, you go to people who are only interested in doing it properly and doing it well. That's why Forman's is number one. And that's why they are so proud. I said, 'Why haven't you got a machine to put the salmon on?' I was told, 'Because human beings do it better.' He said, 'We could cut it, we could do everything, but human beings do it better than machines. We are giving the best. We are doing quality. We are sending it all over the world.' Well, that's wonderful. It's wonderful that this firm down here in Tower Hamlets is the envy of the world. That's something you, Sir, can be immensely proud of.

Therefore, after the nine months you have waited – and all of you will have heard – that with two-thirds of the factory out of working, they worked twenty-four hours a day to pretend it doesn't happen and went on delivering, day-in and day-out. That's the sort of energy, the sort of determination and the sort of pride that makes London the greatest city on earth. Because there are thousands of little companies like this one who only like first place. Who only like the best. This is where it's smoked – down here! Not in Scotland with Gordon Brown, it's down here! This is, again, the family firm. There's nothing wrong in wanting

> to say, 'This is my firm – the others will all have to look to us.' I truly congratulate the whole family on a magnificent achievement. It's an absolute delight to declare the new factory open.

How magnificent, I felt, that the names of Forman's and Jeffrey Archer were now indelibly bonded in the minds of our customers. To cement the success, I printed a leaflet all about the event, packed with photographs of Lord Archer and me, Lord Archer and my wife, Lord Archer and my parents, Lord Archer and the other guests, and mailed copies to everyone who had either attended or sent apologies. I wanted to make some noise, and Jeffrey Archer gave me the perfect platform.

It was true that I'd been a bit bruised by the 'fire-and-rebuild' experience. But I figured that, statistically, it must be a once-in-a-lifetime occurrence, and the Law of Probability surely dictated that the next thirty or forty years would see nothing but uneventful smokehouse tranquillity. Salmon in, salmon out, then repeat the routine ad nauseam.

A few days later, the *News of the World* published allegations made by a former friend of Archer's, Ted Francis, that he had committed perjury during a 1987 libel case. Within twenty-four hours, he had withdrawn his Mayoral candidacy in disgrace. He was disowned by Conservative leader William Hague and expelled from the party for five years. The following year, he was charged with perjury and perverting the course of justice, and the case was sent to trial. He was convicted on all charges and served two years in jail, initially at the Belmarsh, a Category A Prison. Not the best time to have a leaflet in circulation in which he was shaking hands with virtually every member of my extended family. I must brush up on my clairvoyance next time I have a fire-ravaged factory to rebuild.

CHAPTER 6

FORGERY

I could scarcely believe what I was hearing.

Forman's staff are drilled that any incoming call from the Heathrow Customs and Excise Department is treated with awe and respect. It doesn't matter if Buckingham Palace and the White House are also wanting to speak with me; customs officials take precedence. If I had the chance to spend an agreeable lunchtime with any historical figure ever to have walked the planet, it would be Old Blue Eyes himself, Frank Sinatra. But even he would be left waiting in our reception area if I needed to haggle and plead with the conscientious team whose task it is to inspect and clear produce upon arrival to these shores.

So, when an early-morning caller informed our receptionist he was 'from customs and I need to talk about a serious issue', all other concerns fell by the wayside. I had been about to taste some samples of salmon fresh from the kiln, but that pleasant duty would now fall to others. I belted the thirty yards between our production line and my office at a pace that even Sebastian Coe in his prime might have envied.

Generally, my friends in the customs unit approach any paperwork issues with a reasonable and pragmatic mien, and they've helped me out of a couple of awkward scrapes over the years. They are aware that

Britain's prosperity is largely built on trade, and everyone in the country (not just smokehouse workers!) will suffer if honest commerce is inhibited and the wheels of the economy grind too slowly. But in this instance, I seemed to hit a roadblock.

'It's the rules, Mr Forman,' said the robotic voice at the other end of the line. 'The paperwork clearly states minus 18 degrees. And our readings are showing minus 15 degrees.'

'You said minus 15? Isn't that within the margin of error?'

'To be frank, I'm not a big fan of "margins of error". The rules exist for a reason, and if the tests show it's too warm, I can't let it through.'

The produce in question was 4,000 of the finest lobsters on the planet. The Western Australian rock lobsters are distinctive amongst invertebrates. Their shells change colour every year – from a reddish-brown to a creamy pale pink – just before their annual mass migration from shoreline crevices and burrows towards the deep water reefs and spawning grounds. They also lack the enormous claws with which lobsters are popularly associated, instead operating with the two huge rostral spines and hundreds of tiny forward-pointing spines that cover the carapace. As a result, their toothpaste-white meat is of exceptional quality and quantity. Food lovers don't face the frustrating experience of cracking open claws that occupy half the plate only to find a negligible amount of meat contained within. All that lobster, bound principally for Wimbledon, but also to a barbecue at Windsor Castle for Her Majesty, and also the ever so slightly more plebiscite clientele of Harrods, with only the pen of one surly border official in the way.

Since taking over the hot seat, I'd been convinced that Forman's could be an ideal partner for the All England Lawn Tennis Club. The annual Wimbledon Championship was an event with a global, star-studded profile, but was also brimming with British eccentricities. It attracted a wide spectrum of society, from the well-heeled to genuine tennis-lovers, who may have saved for months to purchase a second-week ticket. Whatever their means, throughout the tournament spectators arrive craving a memorable experience. If that includes the occasional culinary indulgence, so be it. Hence the 140,000 portions of English strawberries, 28,000 bottles of champagne, 125,000 ice creams, 60,000 portions of chargrilled meals, and 6,000 stone-baked pizzas consumed during the average fortnight. This must, I felt, be ripe territory for Forman's to proffer further temptations.

The deal had been complex to pull together, but I was confident it would be a winner. The world's finest lobster destined for its premier sporting event. It was a blessed combination, all happening because of Forman's persistence and determination to make it happen. I couldn't wait to witness, first-hand, the public response.

Except that the wretched lobsters had tested three degrees too warm for the official at the Border Inspection Post to allow through.

'But minus 15 is still solid frozen,' I pointed out. 'Are you telling me that these are dripping on your floor? Come on… When we collect them we're going to be defrosting them in the next day or two anyway as they're going to be eaten next week at Wimbledon.'

'I'm sorry, sir, but we have to go by the paperwork. The export documents state, and I have it here, that the goods need to be kept at minus 18, and this import fails to do that. They should have written minus 15 on the forms if that was acceptable to you,' said the customs official, with passive-aggressive hostility. 'My job is to tell you that your lobsters are too hot and so we can't let them through.' I grimaced at the use of the word *hot* to describe minus 15 degrees, and also how 'I' had changed to 'we', meaning the entire body of Her Majesty's officials would be in agreement with such an obviously futile decision. But I held my tongue. You don't want to upset these people as they hold the key to future imports arriving smoothly.

'Which means?' I almost dared not ask the question.

'Which means I'm going to order them to be destroyed.'

'Destr…? All of them?'

'Yes, Mr Forman. All of them.'

I was learning to keep my emotions in check in the face of adversity. I'd maintained my composure even whilst watching large parts of my factory turn to ash. I could accept that – grudgingly – as some kind of act of God. And there were incidents still in the future that would be borne with a Buddhist-like fortitude and restraint. However, the wilful destruction of 25,000 lbs of phenomenal lobster, which would have provided supreme pleasure to thousands of tennis fans as they relaxed between matches, was so senseless, so perverse, and so arbitrary. To make matters worse, I was powerless in the face of obduracy. There was no right of appeal, no court to which I could turn. I placed the phone back into its cradle and cursed audibly, not something I am prone to doing, and my office team looked away in embarrassment.

Momentary rage made me feel better, enabling me to return my attention to the awkward fact that I still had a contract to fulfil. The first rounds of play would be underway in less than a week, and my only source of Western Australian rock lobster was half a world away. If ever there was a time for action, it was now.

Full credit in onerous circumstances must go to my Australian supplier Kailis Brothers, a long-established specialist in fresh and frozen seafood sourced from the seas around that glorious continent. With the economy slowing in Japan, the usual destination for their prized lobsters, Kailis had contacted us to see whether we could introduce this southern hemisphere delicacy to our prestigious customer list, so that it might feature prominently in London's rapidly improving culinary scene. Our importation would be the first time these lobsters had arrived on British shores, by air or sea, in cartons or at the bottom of the ocean. As soon as we had communicated about the problem, they switched into solutions mode. The priority was to fulfil our delivery to the All England Club; a post-mortem into the previous shipment's unexplained temperature variance could wait for another day. Within forty-eight hours, a second consignment arrived on schedule at Heathrow, in the same insulated packaging, but with even more dry ice surrounding it, and was forwarded for customs clearance. After the previous snafu, I was micro-managing the logistics. So, rather than await the customs verdict, I had been calling for updates on a regular basis.

This time I spoke with a different official. Her voice was more soothing and her elocution more refined. But I shifted uncomfortably in my chair knowing that she, like her predecessor, held ultimate power over whether or not I'd be able to fulfil a commercial contract with a now-pressing deadline.

'I have bad news and good news,' she said after a lengthy pause.

Perhaps, for the first time in my life, I understood the symbolism of the phrase 'my heart was in my mouth'.

'I'm afraid I've tested the temperature and the boxes on the top of the pallet are minus 6 degrees and in the middle they are minus 16.'

Not just my heart but my entire body was now in my mouth as I expected her to allow only a handful of the cartons in the centre of the stack through.

'And the good news?'

'I don't consider that a material discrepancy. So I've stamped the paperwork "Approved".'

'The whole consignment?'

'Yes, they are now cleared and can be collected this morning.'

My relief at a positive outcome (there would have been no time to arrange a third shipment) was matched only by my bafflement at the vicarious nature of red tape. Weeks of careful planning and delicate negotiations could have been rendered obsolete by the capricious decisions of whoever was holding the dreaded approval stamp on a given shift. At least the Wimbledon glitterati, when they raised the first slice of succulent lobster meat to their watering mouths, were none the wiser about the palpitation-inducing ordeal behind the scenes. And, as expected, the delicacy was an overwhelming hit (minus 15 degrees notwithstanding).

The Wimbledon contract was one of a number of deals that was making for a buoyant top line, and no part of me was more relieved than my pride. If, upon taking over the business, I'd seen a string of customers defect to our competitors, I would've been mortified. If I'd been forced to slink back to Price Waterhouse, begging their gracious forgiveness for my errant ways, I would've felt humiliated. Whatever happened next, at least my early years had seen me building on my father's legacy rather than letting it fall asunder.

Which was why, when I received draft accounts for my second full year in charge, my instinct was to assume there had been a clerical error. Sales buoyant, up a healthy 25 per cent, but barely at breakeven in terms of profits.

I think it was in my second week of accountancy training that we were taught the difference between fixed and variable costs. In a high fixed cost business – such as a North Sea oil rig, or a public transport network, or a salmon smokehouse – the financial dynamics are very predictable. The first priority in any financial year is to generate the funds needed to cover the fixed costs. This can be a major hurdle, but there's also a big incentive. Once the fixed costs are paid for, much of the extra revenue falls straight to the bottom line. Or, in layman's terms, more growth equals more profits.

I still trusted the concept; I just wasn't seeing the evidence of 'more profits' in the profit-and-loss statement I was studying.

It was late October, and time for a robust heart-to-heart with my General Manager.

'John, I've seen the draft accounts, and we hardly made a penny last year. Were you aware of that?'

'I'll need to look through the detail. But I know we had a lot of one-off costs due to the fire.'

'I don't think that's the issue because the accountants treated fire-related expenditure as exceptional items, since the costs will eventually be fully covered by our insurance policy.'

'Oh, don't forget, I also recruited a few new staff into the production team. Perhaps that's the explanation? It can take a while before the new guys are properly trained up, but we still need to pay their salaries in the meantime.'

'I hope for all our sakes that's not the reason,' I said. 'We're recruiting staff all the time. If you're telling me that a couple of new hires can wipe out our annual profits, I might as well shut down the factory.'

'That wasn't what I meant.'

'What then?'

'Let me take a look and I'll get back to you.'

In business, as in other walks of life, I have always valued precision over vague generalities, so John's responses hadn't filled me with a huge degree of confidence. On the other hand, I had a pile of sales leads that needed my attention, so I metaphorically parked P&L-gate as being 'too difficult until after the Christmas season'. For the next few weeks, every spare moment in the factory or on the road had to be invested in generating a bumper festive period.

The few weeks leading up to Christmas can represent three times a typical month's sales, and in 1999 the effect was multiplied by the approaching 'dawn of a new millennium', when five-star hotels were hosting celebrations as though the world was about to end, which indeed many thought it would, and needed the finest fayre on their menus. Nothing, least of all a financial interrogation, should be allowed to distract from our underlying commercial activity, or jeopardise delighting our customers. All brain power had to be devoted to the task ahead, when sleep deprivation would be par for the course.

The extreme seasonality of large parts of our order book has flustered me throughout my time in the trade. I once vented my chagrin with my rabbi, wondering why the year had to be so lopsided. He counselled that: 'As Jews, we have a festive meal every Friday night on Shabbat. Once every week of the year. Not bad! We need to have a little forbearance with those whose families pile fifty-two celebrations into one annual family dinner.'

Or, as René put it: 'You've got too much business for a month – how can that be a problem? I'd say it's a problem if you don't have enough!'

'I blame Christmas on the Jews,' I'd mutter to myself.

I'm not sure I fully agree with the logic of either René or my rabbi, but I have learnt to accept the world as it is, not as I'd like it to be. I don't think 60 million people will change their festive habits during my lifetime, spreading their eating habits evenly through the year, just to assist the smooth running of a single salmon smokehouse in the East End.

The intensity of the workload in December – packing and despatching around the clock – means that we always defer Forman's annual staff party until January. This brings the benefit of feasting in an otherwise-deserted Italian trattoria that's obsequiously grateful to be filling a few tables during the quietest month. Once the peak has passed, most of my staff take the time off between Christmas and New Year, leaving me virtually alone in the office. I whiled away the first day bartering with the trattoria management for a few more freebies ('conforming to stereotype', I know, I just can't help it) and catching up on paperwork. On the second day, I was curious to note that, as with the first, by mid-afternoon there had been not a single scrap delivered from the Royal Mail. My Italian friend kept assuring me that the menu selection had been posted some days beforehand, and he couldn't understand its non-appearance. Impatient to get these arrangements signed off, I called the local Post Office, poised to berate them for their lethargy and incompetence – only to be told:

'We were instructed not to deliver again until 6 January 2000.'

'What? That's ridiculous. Who on earth told you that?'

'Let me check our system.'

(Pause)

'Is anyone still there?' I said.

(Lengthier pause; then, eventually:)

'Sorry about the delay, sir. I've found the note on file. The order to suspend deliveries was provided by a Mr John Cherrie.'

Now I was rattled. My forensic psyche plunged into overdrive. Why would Cherrie do that? Was he trying to hide communications from me? If so, my major concern wasn't the staff Christmas party, but our banking arrangement. In the absence of a Finance Director, or an external board, or a formal budget planning process, my only lever over the costs in our business was to insist on personally signing every cheque. If I couldn't rely upon the banking function to operate per my expectations, then my control over the company – my company – was at best neutralised and at worst subverted. Never have I been more grateful for my years of accountancy training.

Within a week, every single Forman's cheque that had, at some point in the previous twenty-four months, passed through the convoluted UK banking maze was laid out on my desk, and I was examining each one so see whether I recognised the payee's name and whether the amount seemed appropriate. It would be a massive, marathon exercise, but it would be eminently worthwhile. Because when I smell a rodent, I won't settle for one of those tame chipboard mousetraps. You can expect the most ruthless cat in the neighbourhood – ideally semi-feral and Siamese – to be requisitioned for the express purpose of hunting out said creature.

I called René to explain something had cropped up in the office, and I wouldn't be back for hours – perhaps days.

Over the hours ahead, I subjected two large boxes full of cheques to my personal verification, and failed around 3 per cent of them. During the early months of the year, the signature on the dubious cheques was – even to the naked eye – suspect. Whilst my handwriting would actually make me more suited to the occupation of a GP rather than chartered accountant, around thirty cheques bore a very different mark – a squat, flat signature that, whilst it was my name, bore as much resemblance to the signature in the bank mandate as Woody Allen does to Jean-Claude Van Damme. I couldn't believe what I was seeing, and then surprise turned to rage when I found that some of the most recent cheques were actually being signed by Cherrie in his very own name, despite his having no bank authority whatsoever. I didn't know whether to be more outraged at my trusted bank or my trusted General Manager. I felt physically sick at what appeared to be betrayal.

(In an outlandish footnote to this sorry matter, I even uncovered one cheque with a note written on the back, by some hapless bank clerk, who had semi-flagged but then dismissed a governance concern, which read precisely as follows: 'Signature looks shaky, called Forman's, spoke to John, John says it's okay.')

The next stage in my amateur sleuthing would be to follow the money trail on the questionable cheques. This was a considerable undertaking, because many of them were written to firms with whom Forman's had a business relationship, and so might have been legitimately incurred. In fact, I still hadn't reached any firm conclusions about whether malfeasance was at play when Cherrie returned from leave. I decided to confront him with part, if not all, of my discoveries, and majored on the aspect that seemed beyond dispute.

'John, we didn't get much post whilst you were away.'

Cherrie looked at his shoes, and mumbled something like, 'Och, that's good.'

'I don't think that's right, because I was expecting a package about our staff party.'

'I'm sure it'll arrive soon. I'll chase it up?'

'You don't need to, John, I called the Post Office and they told me you suspended mail deliveries whilst you were away. Why did you do that?'

Without even a pause for thought: 'Oh, I think I was speaking to them before Christmas about mailing out the sides for Pentland and whilst I was talking I told them to cancel any deliveries whilst I was away, so you didn't need to be bothered with all that.'

'Aha?'

'Yes, most of it's junk mail anyway and no one's going to be sending us in cheques that need banking that week.'

If only he knew how many cheques we did receive that week!

'Well, it seems odd to me, please don't do anything like that again. Now that Christmas is over, I really to want to find some time with you to work out what's going on with our accounts. We should be booming now.'

At the mention of the accounts, John started to fidget, scratching his ear lobe and chewing on his lip.

I'd made my point, and decided to leave the next move to him. I proposed a follow-up meeting later in the week at which we could get granular about some of the problematic cheques.

'Yes, let me get the place back in ship shape and let's look at that next week.' Cherrie stood up and half-heartedly offered his hand in a type of *let's let bygones be bygones* gesture. When I didn't immediately reciprocate, he seemed to have second thoughts and withdrew his hand as if he'd just touched hot coals, thrusting it deep, deep into the tattered pocket of his crimson corduroys.

I spent the next few days marshalling facts for our forthcoming tête-à-tête. If there was an innocent account, I was eager to hear it, and would listen to Cherrie's rationalisation with an open mind. On the other hand, if it was now time to part ways, it wouldn't be a catastrophe. The staff held him in some affection, and he kept the hours of a workaholic.

But he wasn't irreplaceable, and some of his shortcomings as a General Manager – such as his inability to differentiate between the taste of good and outstanding fish meat – had barely progressed since his first day in post. One way or another, these matters would be brought to a resounding crescendo when we met, and either he'd be reaffirmed as a man of unimpeachable integrity, or he'd be out of the door.

In the event, the grand climax of this mini-saga never took place. In the early hours – so early even Forman's hadn't yet opened for business – Cherrie's company car was deposited in front of the factory gate. The keys were left in the ignition, but there was no note of explanation. I asked our receptionist if she could track him down, but all messages left on his mobile went unheeded.

That afternoon, I sent one of my despatch drivers round to Cherrie's home address. The property was empty, although one of the neighbours mentioned that, just twenty-four hours beforehand, John and his French wife had been packing a few cases into the back of a rented van, as if they were headed across the English Channel for an extended road trip of chateaux and vineyards.

In any event, I never saw Cherrie again, and for a time I was crestfallen that somebody who had been my de facto business partner for two years would cut ties so dramatically. I didn't have the heart to continue my investigations into the bank cheque scandal – Barclays had offered fair compensation, and part of me wanted to be shielded from incontrovertible evidence of disloyalty. Rumours of Cherrie's reappearance within the industry occasionally surface (during a social event that summer, a supermarket buyer casually revealed they'd received a proposal from one of our competitors with product descriptions that were a mirror image of our own, and prices that were in every case a fraction cheaper), but these speculations have never been verified. I retain the faint (René says 'sweet') glimmer of hope that the entire episode was, at root, a colossal and tragic misunderstanding.

Whatever the facts, I was left with an unanticipated predicament. Forman's was now bereft of a General Manager, and whilst I could fulfil those duties for a time, it would be at the expense of customer service and hence would place at risk our further revenue growth. I needed a replacement GM urgently. And, this time, I was on the lookout for somebody who understood food. I couldn't fault Cherrie for his knowledge of computing, organisational skills or operational management, but his blind spot when it came to judging the product had become an increasing liability, maximising the pressure on those around him.

I discussed the role specification with a number of senior people within the trade whose opinions I respected, and became convinced that the consummate candidate should be a qualified chef. Such an individual would elevate the perception of Forman's amongst the community of chefs who form our client base. It would symbolise our timeless commitment to the highest standards of food production and would position us at a different level from the mass production operators who approach food preparation as if it were any other type of manufacture. Creating the best smoked salmon, I believe, is unlike the vast majority of factory floor activities such as assembling cars or making staplers. One is dealing with an organic product, meaning that *consistency* cannot be taken for granted. Consistency can only be ensured by professional expertise and judgement. How to embed consistency? How to continually improve standards? How to set Forman's apart? To all these questions, Lloyd Hardwick was to prove the answer *par excellence.*

Lloyd came to Forman's with an impeccable résumé. Talent-spotted at a young age by Albert Roux, Lloyd had been personally trained by the legendary restaurateur and made his reputation at some of the most prestigious restaurants in London, including Le Gavroche (the first establishment in Britain to be awarded a three-star Michelin rating) and the Connaught Hotel. He was later a Director of High Table, responsible for providing exceptional cuisine to boardrooms throughout London's Square Mile. Most recently, he'd been hired by the Tate Modern art gallery to manage one of the greatest catering challenges in the country in the latter months of the last century.

The Tate had been a few short months from opening to the public, yet its catering arrangements had been sorely overlooked. Lloyd's task was to recruit, procure, design and operationalise everyone and everything necessary for a seamless opening day, and thereafter to oversee a world-class going concern. Even with an eighteen-hour working day, there are few with the energy and knowledge to pull off such a feat. Lloyd delivered with aplomb, and the Tate Modern's early guests – all 30,000 of them in the opening week – were treated to Michelin-standard catering at affordable prices.

Unfortunately for the public (although fortunately for Forman's), new management decided its catering offer should be bog-standard rather than top-notch, and Lloyd's artistry and ingenuity fell woefully into disregard. For a man of such remarkable credentials, he was under-appreciated and under-utilised.

I had met Lloyd on only one occasion, whilst he was whisking me at high speed around the Tate Modern's kitchens, discussing smoked salmon supplies at the same time as holding half a dozen other conversations with chefs, suppliers, fitters and technicians. Fate had welded together an employee who had been mistreated by his employer and an employer who had been wronged by his employee. We put an hour in the diary for an interview at Forman's, but ended up chatting the entire morning.

'You've just walked in. What are your first impressions?' was my opening question. I awaited a couple of inoffensive generalisations. Instead, by the time Lloyd finished his answer, he had dissected every aspect of our factory – its people, its organisation, its goods handling processes, its quality assurance, its performance measurement – with the meticulous precision of an investigative journalist. I'm sure there are Oxbridge theses (including mine, no doubt) where the points are made with less cogency and clarity than Lloyd deployed for his off-the-cuff assessment.

When we'd finished our discussion, I escorted Lloyd on a tour of the factory and introduced him in turn to every member of the team. They were all blown away by his grasp of the production intricacies and by his easy charm. By the time he left, he'd made such an impression that I'd have faced a veritable mutiny if I'd failed to tempt him for the GM position. I asked for my two remaining candidate interviews to be cancelled. There was no point wasting my time and theirs. I'd found my man.

In preparation for this book, I spoke again with Lloyd about his early days at Forman's. He reaffirmed many of my own memories about the changes he'd wrought – spotting areas where retraining was necessary, modernising the factory layout to improve process flow, and above all introducing measures to embed consistency, which was to become his number-one preoccupation. 'High standards are fine,' he said, 'but if one slice in a hundred falls short, and that slice is consumed by a loyal customer, will they still trust our brand? That's why *every* mouthful must be as good as the best.'

He added one other thing that took me a little by surprise. He said: 'There was another thing high on my hit-list. Some staff were smoking a lot more than salmon. And the affairs.'

I had no idea. I guess even as the owner and boss of a small family business, it's impossible to know everything. The difference is, Lloyd sorted out the problems I didn't even know existed, and didn't even tell me he'd done it. Truly, a class act!

CHAPTER 7

FOREIGN BODIES

Twelve months passed – over half a million minutes – without calamity of any kind. Forman's was finally running like a well-oiled machine. Lloyd and I would meet at four every morning to inspect the sides of smoked salmon as they were taken from the kiln and select them for our valued clients. Once they had passed our exacting standards, a plethora of activities throughout the factory would spring into operation. One team would be responsible for the latest orders from London's restaurateurs and hoteliers, ensuring their daily supplies were ready for collection by our burgeoning team of van drivers just after dawn. Another would look after the retail trade, wrapping the fish in our eye-catching H. Forman & Son packaging so it could stand out prominently on supermarket shelves. Then we had our international shipments to be processed.

The business was not just larger than ever; it was also more complex. During my father's time, it was still just about possible for one person to control the business by 'knowing everything that was going on', but now the operation was of a scale that demanded proper organisation. Lloyd had tightened up on the process flows within the factory, and delegated accountability for the fulfilment of different categories of orders to people he trusted. He was also using his chef's flair for innovation and experimentation to launch a number of new salmon cures, such as beetroot, wasabi and ginger, and gin and tonic. The word was getting around: things were on the move at Forman's.

From my discussions with other family-owned businesses, this type of change can often be an emotional wrench. The company is transforming before your eyes from a micro- to a mid-sized enterprise. It has more documented processes, more management information, more paperwork – all the things one has previously shunned as features of slow-moving and inflexible bureaucracy. Beyond a certain scale, the alternatives are either (on the one hand) better process integrity or (on the other) pandemonium, chaos and an inability to guarantee 100 per cent customer satisfaction. If that was the choice, then in reality there was no choice.

A team was taking shape that could build the business for the long term. Unfortunately, there isn't space in this chapter to name them all – but, in addition to Lloyd, standout characters included Darren Matson who, in 2012, was to break the world record for boning and slicing a side of smoked salmon when challenged by Gordon Ramsay on the set of Channel Four's *Cookalong Live*. He famously advised Ramsay to 'concentrate, relax and go for it' before delivering forty perfect slices, each weighing between 15g and 20g in an astonishing one minute and twenty-four seconds, a record that he has now since beaten down to one minute and ten. And then there was the irrepressible, irreplaceable, unforgettable Rita Law, who fused the roles of tea lady, sage and mentor. Having grown up in the war years in the East End, Rita was as fearlessly honest as she was fiercely loyal. If she felt I'd overstepped the mark, she wouldn't hesitate to corner me in my office and give me a blunt dressing down, supplemented by a bowl of Scott's Porridge Oats. She held firmly to the view that people make poor judgments when they're functioning on an empty stomach, and took it upon herself to ensure my carb levels were forever in the stratosphere.

Almost twelve months to the day after Archer had declared the post-fire Forman's alive and kicking, there was an even more exciting birth. Annabel – our third child, but first daughter – chose to enter this world immediately following the Sabbath of Sabbaths, Yom Kippur, the Day of Atonement, the holiest day of the year in Judaism when the faithful are meant to observe a 25-hour period of prayer and abstain from anything that might distract from soulful reflections (no eating, no drinking, no bathing, no anointing with lotions, no wearing of leather shoes, no marital relations). It is quite common for pregnant Jewish mothers to give birth prematurely the day after Yom Kippur. Some believe the unborn baby, having missed its daily fix, decides to pop out to check what's gone wrong with the service.

No baby can have been hugged and kissed as much as Annabel during the first few days on the planet. René had known for some time that a daughter was en route, and had kept it secret from me at my request – it's one of the few pleasant unknowns in life and I wanted to keep it that way until our child was ready to show its face to the world – but was still overwhelmed with emotion to be holding a gorgeous, healthy baby girl, born on the tenth of the tenth, 2000. Matthew and Oliver, my two sons, could barely think of anything else for days – they were intrigued, curious, enthralled, and vigilant. Only three days old, and they were already explaining to her the workings of the household whilst she stared into the mid-distance, oblivious to their words.

One evening, after we'd put the children to bed, René noticed that I was in a reflective mood. She asked what was on my mind.

'Everything's working really well at Forman's,' I said. 'Lloyd is phenomenal and customers seem to like the new branding.'

'So what's the problem?'

'I'm just thinking about where next.'

'I knew it! You can't stand it when every day's the same as the last. I've never known anybody with such a low boredom threshold.'

'More exports maybe? Now we're supplying the top places in London, there's no reason we shouldn't be able to do the same in other cities. If they want London Cure, they can't make it themselves, so they have to buy from us. What do you think? Should I be spending the next thirty years of my life travelling the globe selling smoked salmon? That's sort of the reason I gave up on Phil. Or is there new stuff, different stuff, I could be doing?'

'You love a challenge. Something interesting will come your way and you'll know it when you see it.'

'Maybe you're right. Let's wait and see.'

* * *

You can't live in London for a few decades without learning to deal with severe showers. The following morning, it was raining so heavily that I needed an umbrella to make the dozen steps between the front door and the car. As soon as I switched on the engine, I set the windscreen wipers to maximum speed, but visibility was still impaired by the lashing waters and it took me twice as long as usual to make the early-morning drive to the factory. At one point, the rain was so intense that I couldn't see a thing, and I parked – right next to an overflowing gutter – until it was safe to continue. For my own sanity, I chose not to switch on the weather forecast.

When I arrived at Forman's, people were already comparing the drenchings they'd received during their treks into work. A couple of foolhardy souls had set off without any type of raincoat or anorak, and were now standing in the despatch bay, soaked and shivering, water dripping from every extremity to form rapidly expanding puddles on the newly resined floor below.

For the next couple of hours, I put the deluge to one side so I could concentrate on salmon selection with Lloyd. It wasn't the first time the city had been hit by a monsoon-like weather system, and it certainly wouldn't be the last. I wasn't planning on leaving the factory for another eleven hours or so, and surely it would have abated by then.

Or so I thought. In fact, eleven hours later I would be fighting for Forman's survival, and I'd be dealing with devastation that would make the previous fire incident seem like a low-key warm-up act.

The first inkling that this was more than your usual London rainstorm came when one of our packers, Brian, arrived at work, and whilst walking past Lloyd and me said, 'Christ, have you seen it out there?'

'Yes, it's horrible, but it's only rain,' I responded, unhooking a side from our rails and laying it onto the scales. With no windows to the outside world, Lloyd and I were oblivious to what was happening just the other side of our galvanised steel roller shutter, which wouldn't be opened until the vans were ready for loading in about an hour.

Another slicer arrived for work. 'The yard's completely flooded. It's coming our way.' At last, Lloyd and I decided to we should check out the cause of all this kerfuffle. The courtyard was well-lit, so despite being pre-dawn, we saw exactly what he meant. Lakes of water had formed wherever there was a slight curvature in the ground, but these were now expanding and merging together so that hardly any patches of the tarmac were discernible. And, since Queen's Yard was on a slight incline, the lakes were deepest towards our corner of the estate. I don't think I'd ever noticed that before, but nothing concentrates the mind about topography as much as the threat of rising water.

In fact, unbeknownst to us, the deluge from the heavens was far from being our major concern and was now slowing down. A couple of hundred feet away, the River Lea Navigation had burst its banks and was now allowing its toxic effluent to flow like a tributary past the front shutters of other industrial units and taking direct aim at Forman's. As we all remember from secondary-school physics, water can be obstinate stuff – always searching for the lowest level. In such circumstances, occupying a building at the far end of a slope in an enclosed area with no natural drainage or escape route for the waters ain't really a great place to be. In other words, it was time to forget about boning and slicing and packing. It was time to man the barricades!

One of the many challenges in defending yourself against flooding is that, because it's not an everyday occurrence, you have to make stuff up as you go along. We knew that, at all costs, we must prevent the onrush from entering the factory, but had no idea what that practically meant. We didn't have a huge stock of sandbags lying around, so we quickly brainstormed what might be a viable alternative. I suggested we try building a wall out of the nearest equivalent to sandbags, but all I could think of were the vacuum packs full of smoked salmon trimmings that were kept in the freezer. Nobody had a better idea, and so we each grabbed an armful of packs, loaded them into polystyrene salmon cartons, and piled each twenty-five kilo box outside the doors to form our first line of defence. 'That should do it,' I thought.

To an onlooker, it would have appeared ridiculous. The mighty waters cascading from the River Lea in our direction, and the only bulwark around our citadel was a makeshift assembly of vacuum packs from the chiller. One by one the fully laden boxes of trimmings were dislodged by the churning current; within minutes, they were bobbing harmlessly on the water's surface like flotsam. Our pathetic attempt at a defensive wall had little in common with the fight to protect the garrison at the Alamo, and rather more resemblance to how the England football team marshal their wall in the face of a German free kick in the dying moments of a World Cup fixture.

As the floodwater crossed the threshold into the factory, our focus shifted. It was no longer a matter of 'keep it out', but 'save what we can'. Everything that wasn't bolted down needed to be manoeuvred to higher ground. First, that meant boxes and crates that had been left on the floor were stacked onto any spare table surface. Files on the lower shelves of our cupboards and cabinets were moved up. As the waters continued to advance, and the tables wobbled under the onrush, anything of business-critical value was lifted higher still.

I hadn't realised that the conventional doorway was just one of many routes available to the river water as it pursued its squalid quest to annex our factory. Within an hour of the banks bursting, filthy, foul-smelling water was seeping through every crack, erupting through every drainpipe, oozing through anything that wasn't 100 per cent waterproof. One of the most unnerving sights was in our toilet cubicles, where noxious water was spewing over the rim of the pans – from the inside, out – like a scene in a horror movie. Openings that I'd assumed were watertight were shown to be anything but, as putrid liquid forced its way through the slightest gap around a window pane or an air conditioning vent. Even the walls proved porous due to the specific construction methods used in food factories to safeguard hygiene standards.

The internal walls of the factory are essentially a 'sandwich' panel. Not a smoked salmon sandwich of course, but one where the bread either side is made from a thin sheet of metal and the filling from an insulation material, such as polystyrene – although insurers don't like that nowadays because of the fire risk – or rock wool, like loft insulation, or polyurethane. Since a working food factory is essentially a very large fridge, the insulation filling is to allow the panelled room to hold its temperature. These panels stand upright in a U-shaped plastic tube which is affixed to the top of a concrete kerb, with the kerb providing protection to the walls from trolleys and other equipment on wheels. Once erected, the small gap between the plastic tube and the panel is sealed with some mastic, but this can only be done from the front not the back because it's impossible to access behind the panel once erected, unless you are a cartoon character that has been squashed by a steamroller.

As the flood water penetrated the outer brick walls, at first through weep holes and eventually through the saturated bricks themselves, it hit the back of the panels. From there, it soaked upwards into the sandwich filling, through the unsealed backs, and eventually pushed away at the mastic seal in the front, helping to fill the factory with its full force.

And still the waters kept coming, hour after hour, until the inside of the factory resembled the set of *Titanic* thirty minutes from the end of the movie. I felt physically sick and powerless.

By mid-morning, the downpour finally relented and the waters began to recede, albeit at a tortuously laboured pace. Now we could check out the extent of the devastation. The power supply had been short-circuited hours ago, so we needed torches to illuminate any parts of the factory that lacked natural light. Without the hum of machinery or buzz of activity, all was eerily calm and deathly quiet. In the worst-affected areas, the water was waist-deep. It was not how I'd been expecting to spend the working day: wading through fetid water into the bowels of my factory, with detritus lapping against my body. Fish heads, trimmings, vacuum packs, bank statements, grills, cardboard boxes, kitchen knives. Yes, it was definitely still October.

So much for griping with René about the tedium of every day 'being like the last'. I think, on that final morning of October 2000, I would've exchanged my entire collection of Cambridge Union Society memorabilia for a little bit more monotony in my life.

The experience was proving too much for a couple of younger staff members, who were sobbing uncontrollably. I was mulling over some words of comfort to use, but Rita was already on the case. She embraced them with a motherly hug and then fixed them with her steely blue eyes: 'It'll take more than a bit of water to put Forman's out of action. I know Lance and I know this business. So whatever's worrying you, it shouldn't.' Her cockney tone was defiant and feisty, and cheered everybody up.

One of the advantages of being located in the heart of London's commercial East End is that, when you're in a fix, you're never more than a block or two away from a potential solution. In the last couple of years, this had already proven invaluable when we needed an alternative place to smoke our salmon, and when I was seeking fast and brilliant graphic design work for the H. Forman & Son rebranding. Now, for a third time, the diversity and vibrancy of the Stratford business community came to my rescue. Zamo Cleaners, our salvation in adversity, was less than half a mile away – close enough to be with us in moments; sufficiently far away to have escaped the flood unscathed. They supplied us with some emergency cleaning chemicals and materials so we could make a start with the clean-up.

As with the fire, we couldn't expect our customers to support us if we failed to deliver. They would naturally gravitate to alternative suppliers. So I was soon in contact again with Nick Balcombe – the man with an answer for every crisis. He engaged a firm of industrial cleaners who had helped him out of dire scrapes before, to take charge and complete the job. He also notified both the Environmental Health Officers of the need for contingency planning, and the insurance company, the American firm ACE, of a pending claim.

Their first priority was to extract the flood water before it could stagnate, for which they deployed a fleet of industrial pumps. Alongside, they used warm fans and dehumidifiers to accelerate drying-out – this was particularly important because, as I was led to understand, the risk and extent of contamination rises exponentially if dampness is prolonged. They were especially alert to the risk of secondary damage, which could have a number of causes, not least uncontrolled evaporation playing havoc with the air's moisture content.

Initially, everyone seemed to be working towards a shared goal – the survival of Forman's. The clean-up had been so thorough that, to the untrained eye, the factory was spotless, but we knew that contamination is not necessarily visible. We started spraying floors and walls with the most lethal anti-bacterial products on the market on a round-the-clock basis, and the Environmental Health Officers supported this as a prudent interim measure, but encouraged us urgently to seek a long-term solution.

Naively, I had assumed the insurance claim process would be, if not entirely painless, at least fair-minded.

'Surely that's what we'd been paying thousands of pounds of insurance premium for over the years?' I said to Lloyd.

'And your point is?' he replied sardonically. Lloyd's experience with the Tate had made him even more cynical about the behaviour of big business than I was.

The Price Waterhouse of loss adjusters, McLarens Toplis, became near-permanent occupants of the factory. I was seeing more of them and Balcombe than my own family as we haggled over a suitable compensation payment. In particular, we were working through the financial and commercial pros and cons of rebuilding the current factory versus moving to a new site. The discussions were, I think, handled professionally on all sides. We were able to set aside emotion and concentrate on analysis and facts.

After weeks of negotiations, McLarens and Balcombe agreed a deal which we both felt was reasonable, and on which we shook hands. It involved new premises – whilst intense use of anti-bacterial spray was viable in the short-term, the damage was simply too severe for our continued functioning as a food production facility. The insulated wall panels were infiltrated with dirty flood water resulting in foreign bodies being permanently located in the fabric of our high-quality food production facility, and with the rock wool getting wet, there was a risk that the structural properties of the panels could disintegrate and eventually cave in on us. The trapped black river water was impossible to extract without stripping out the panels and replacing them, and whilst at it, allowing the perimeter bricks of the factory to dry out too, over a few months before rebuilding. If we stopped operating for a few months, we'd be lucky to retain one-tenth of our customer base. It would be commercial suicide; we might as well have shut down the business and got on with our lives elsewhere. On the other hand, finding a new site allowed continuity and, indeed, we had already started the search on Balcombe's instructions, as he knew this was the correct approach. So imagine my surprise, the next morning, to discover that ACE had fired McLarens within hours of receiving their report.

Balcombe and I were gobsmacked. 'In my thirty years in the industry, I've never known anything like this to happen,' he said.

Clearly, ACE did not like the figure McLarens placed on the relocation, and our suspicions were increased when the insurers introduced us to the replacement loss adjuster. In place of McLarens – a major and respected firm – we would now be dealing with a sole trader, Mr David Larner of Marlow MLS. Larner spent the following months commissioning a succession of experts in an attempt to demonstrate the flood had not been as damaging to our business as we had claimed. One such player was forensic accountant John Andrews.

Andrews hadn't always worked independently; he had been the UK representative of an American firm called Campos & Stratis – accounting's 'heart of darkness' according to the *New York Times*. But he had been left to fight for himself after the senior management fell victim to the Lockerbie bombing of Pan Am 103. Unlike McLarens, who quickly understood the commercial and technical issues, Andrews tended to stare blankly across the table whenever we discussed 'continuity of service to head chefs' or 'sewage damage'. He also had a frustrating tendency to request we hand over suites of documents that were tangential to the claim or had already been provided.

One afternoon, Balcombe was explaining – in painstaking detail, and not for the first time – the points of contention. 'It's a legal and regulatory requirement that the building must meet certain standards. The walls contain food safety panels, and the water has penetrated about three feet upwards behind the panels.'

'Who manufactures the panels?' asked Andrews. 'Do you have their address?'

'That was already in the dossier. The important point is: when we speak about *water*, we're not talking about Perrier. If you drank it, you'd be hospitalised for weeks. It's nasty, harmful stuff. Picture the rawest sewage you can, and you'll be getting close.'

'I'd still like to know the manufacturer.'

'The sewage won't walk away by itself. It's not polite sewage, like the audience at the opera house vacating seats after the final curtain call. This sewage is claiming squatters' rights. To get rid of it, we'd need to remove the panels, and...'

'The panels made by whom? It's a gap in my report, and I really need to know.'

'Why does it even matter? The important fact is that, to clean away all the sewage from behind the panels, we'd need to close the factory for a month. Maybe two.'

'And the problem with that is...?'

'That we wouldn't have a single customer left when we reopened!'

As the days dragged on, the Environmental Health Officers were getting impatient at the lack of progress. They had approved the use of anti-bacterial sprays as a strictly interim measure, but would never countenance it as a semi-permanent procedure. They started making dark hints that, if a sustainable solution wasn't identified and expedited, they had the power to shut Forman's down and wouldn't hesitate to use it. Our 95-year-old business would come crashing to its end-point. On my watch. All because of a stupid overflowing river.

Balcombe and I re-ran all the scenarios in case we'd missed anything. The reality was clear-cut. The only practical option was a new factory – in terms of both fulfilling our immediate obligations and securing our longer-term viability. After twenty-nine years in Queen's Yard, a relocation was now critical, and – with the EHOs breathing down our neck

– it needed to be rushed. However long it normally takes to procure and equip specialist new premises, we had around half that time. Our current building was simply too contaminated to ever again function as the site for high-end, impeccable-tasting cuisine. This didn't mean it needed to be demolished – the East End was overflowing with firms of metal bashers whose business could function with impunity regardless of whether pollutants were lurking in the wall cavity. But, for Forman's, it was time for *out*: out of the building, or out of business.

Discussions with the accountants were proving fruitless and the clock continued to tick. My time was spent attempting to disprove continuously pointless theses put forward by Andrews, rather than focusing on our customers, and for the first time since joining the business, I started to see our order book dip. Things drew to a high-noon climax when Larner decided he would now bring in a forensic scientist, Dr Andrew Moncrieff, to prove whether the claimed damage to our panels was beyond redress. One fine day in April 2001, a factory normally filled with white-suited workers was invaded by an army of suited professionals. Aside from the inevitable hangers-on, there was the loss adjuster, the forensic accountant, forensic scientist, insurance broker, Balcombe, myself, Lloyd, the building contractor, and, indeed, my own forensic accountant and forensic scientist. You can only successfully fight fire with fire, I was advised.

With a flair for the dramatic, the insurer's forensic scientist proposed he would drill a single deep hole into one panel, selected more or less at random. If the hole glistened with water, I would have a new factory built. If not, I would stay put.

Moncrieff, in what was clearly a pre-arranged tactic, turned to me and said: 'Mr Forman, before we begin, I have one question. If I drill a hole into this panel, and we find there's no flood water in it, are you going to claim that perhaps this panel isn't damaged but another one is … and then ask me to drill a further hole? And if I drill that further hole and the same thing occurs, are you going to ask me to drill yet another hole? Because I can fast-forward to what you will eventually argue, which is that your entire factory has been damaged by all the drill holes everywhere, and you need a new site. So, Mr Forman, you need to assure me that you'll accept the results of a single drill hole. If not, we can't proceed with this test.'

I pondered. My entire business' future lay on this one test and we were now six months after the flood. Truth to tell, I would've been amazed to find any water in the panels now; surely it would have evaporated? The pressure to protect my future had me thinking fast on my feet, so I said, 'In that case, let me ask you a question. What happens if you drill a hole in a panel and you find there is flood water inside. Are you going to claim that perhaps that one panel is damaged, but it doesn't mean the whole factory is? Because if that's what you're going to do, I won't let you start drilling into my factory.' For once he was speechless. He figured he'd served an ace, but I'd managed to squeeze a fiendish return just inside the baseline.

All parties agreed that one hole – and one hole only – would be drilled, and this would determine the success or failure of the £2 million claim to build a new smokehouse. The next half-hour was spent nervously wandering around the factory agreeing which panel would suffer the assault. Once the location had been identified, Moncrieff got down on his knees, removed the drill from his case and aimed it towards the panel. The dozen suited onlookers all bent their heads towards the point of incision as if they were learning from a consultant surgeon in his operating theatre.

He twisted the torque control to the maximum setting, and flipped on the power. The drill started to vibrate gently in his hand. Then he selected a spot dead centre in the circle I'd drawn, and pressed the drill bit against the food safe clad metal outer skin of the panel. He looked around at the group one final time, like a vicar scanning the congregation at a wedding lest anyone wants to reveal a cause of just impediment why the betrothed should not be wed. Then he leant inwards towards the drill, increasing the pressure of the drill bit against the wall. The test was underway.

The drill bit quickly penetrated beyond the metal skin and reached the underlying polystyrene insulation, which sprayed like confetti around the room, before settling in a fine layer on any exposed surface – the floor, our shoes. Then, with the care of a dentist extracting a tooth, he pulled the drill away, leaving behind one perfectly formed hole. Its diameter was no greater than four or five millimetres; a miniature void on which my livelihood and thirty other jobs hinged.

Nothing could be seen in the dark thin hole and so Moncrieff manoeuvred his torch to shed light on the matter. And that's when I caught it, a glimpse of light reflecting. It was shimmering after all. Yes, there was still water trapped in these panels, even after all these months. Moncrieff, conjuring up his best response, turned his head to me and said in front of all those gathered, 'Mr Forman, if the flood was as bad as you said, I would have expected a lot more water than that!'

He knew he had lost and everyone departed in glory or humiliation, like the crowds dispersing from Wembley after a cup final. Once all had departed, except Moncrieff and my man, Dr Patrick Barbour, of the esteemed forensic investigators, Burgoyne & Co., Moncrieff confided to me saying, 'I want to be very frank with you, Mr Forman, and I would not normally be so frank, since you're not my client, but I agree with the recommendations originally proposed by McLarens.'

It was time for a celebration. We cracked open a bottle of champagne and Lloyd and I raised our glasses to the end of a living nightmare. We even engaged in a bit of gallows humour: 'What a shame the flood wasn't a couple of years back. It would've helped to put out the fire!'; 'Rita mentioned the place needed a wash. I just didn't think she'd go to such extremes…'

Patrick was still hanging about in the office writing up his own report of the day's events. He enquired about some of the equipment that his foe, in this instance, Dr Moncrieff, had used for his investigation, so I offered to call Moncrieff on his behalf. As Moncrieff answered the call directly, before handing the phone across to Patrick, I thought I should be polite and thank him for his words of comfort about agreeing with the McLarens proposal. He said, drily, 'I have to emphasise, Mr Forman, that was just my personal view, not my professional view.'

'What?' My heart sank. Was he going to use the evidence he'd gathered and draw a totally different conclusion? 'How can you have two different opinions?'

'I apologise if you've misinterpreted things, Mr Forman, but my comment was simply a personal view, and not what I shall be recommending to my client.'

Later, I asked Patrick if he'd overheard Moncrieff's remarks, and of course he had.

'Do me a favour, Patrick. When you write up your report, please could you make reference to those comments? It's really important.'

'No problem, it will be done.'

I could now focus my attention on finding our new site. Just before the 'high-noon' drilling, an ideal property had just come onto the market, half a mile away in Marshgate Lane. I usually consider myself a decent negotiator, but this had become a fight for survival, so it was a matter of 'whatever it takes, whatever it costs'. It was like being asked for a tip by a twenty-stone masseur in a Turkish bath who's squatting on the small of your back and twisting your neck from side to side – sometimes, one just has to acknowledge one doesn't have a ton of negotiating leverage. If I couldn't secure a viable alternative site, all bets were off. I offered the full asking price on the site within hours of it being first advertised, knowing that my ability to exchange and complete would depend on the outcome of a single drill hole.

Until the report came through from Burgoyne, and a clear answer appeared from ACE, I had been trying to spin out our negotiations on the acquisition of Marshgate Lane. When I received the report, I flicked through it to find the reference to Moncrieff's confession, but to no avail. I read it again, more slowly, but still no sign. I called Patrick to enquire about this omission.

'I've discussed it with my partners and, as forensic scientists, we only report on factual matters, not commercial matters.'

'Surely this is fact? A statement was made, you heard it, and you confirmed to me you'd heard it. If that's not fact then what is?'

'Sorry, Mr Forman, but we cannot go further than our report.'

I was gutted. My own team, whose fees I was paying, were not prepared to confirm witnessing a devastating comment from the other side's advisor. I guess forensic scientists receive most of their instructions from insurance companies, not from salmon smokers with a one-off claim – even if, in my case, there was starting to be a string of them. Why stick their neck out for me, and go beyond what they're dutifully bound to do, if it risks upsetting their usual fee provider?

I called Nick, in despair, and we agreed the only course of action was legal. The time for negotiations was over, and indeed should have been many months ago. Nick wrote to ACE advising that we would be initiating legal proceeding, and within twenty-four sweet hours, Larner was sacked, McLarens were reinstated and we exchanged contracts on Marshgate Lane. The perfect site which, we believed, would see us through the next generation of Forman's.

Roll the clock forward a decade or two, and our Queen's Yard site is an African evangelical church – the Celestial Church of Christ Ayomide Parish. Sometimes I wonder whether they were drawn to the site by the 'Holy Smoke' or the 'Holy Water'.

CHAPTER 8

FORTIFYING

'The hills are alive with the sound of music,' sang Maria von Trapp, as she pirouetted through the undulating meadows high above Salzburg, the birch-strewn slopes of the Mehlweg mountain rolling away into the mid-distance. And, after my experience with burst river banks, I too had become an avid fan of hills.

One of the many attractions of Marshgate Lane was that – in defiance of the flat landscape of much of the East End – it followed a hilly route, bending and tilting its way through the industrial outskirts of the lower Lea Valley close to Stratford. Our new site was near the crest of a graceful incline. If there ever came a time that a trickle of flood water was seeping under our front door, it would've meant most of Newham was already submerged. Hurricanes, earthquakes, tsunamis and tornadoes were also rare in our part of town. Once we'd kitted out the premises with the most fire-resistant materials ever created, with not an ounce of polystyrene filler in our panels, we'd surely be immune to any further cataclysms.

At first, all seemed to be running smoothly. Not a single act of God befell us during the laborious process of designing, specifying, tendering and overseeing the construction work. In fact, the only unforeseen mishap during the eighteen-month period between purchase and occupation was of the human type. Lloyd was driving past the site one Friday and noticed that the main gates were flapping open, the severed chains and discarded padlock lying in the gutter. Towards the rear of the car park, a group of scruffy strangers was sitting in front of a dirty caravan. One of the men was drinking whisky neat from the bottle. Another, whose arm was heavily bandaged, was glaring at a pack of scruffy dogs, yelping non-stop like back-stage groupies. Smashed glass surrounded the main factory window – evidence that trespass had morphed into a break-in. No doubt the cause of the injury sustained by thug number two.

'Squatters!' he muttered under his breath. Within minutes Lloyd had sprung into action-man mode. He called to various heavies with whom he was casually acquainted and corralled them into joining an impromptu exercise in forcible eviction. One of his contacts, an ex-boxer called Sam, happened to own a breakdown truck, and – with a cash incentive agreed – turned up with his crew. Whilst the squatters were otherwise engaged inside the factory, Sam attached a tow bar to the caravan and began dragging the barely roadworthy vehicle, lurching and swaying from side to side, back out through the gates.

Life is a learning process. And, that night, we learnt that squatters – whilst foul-mouthed and barely coherent – can have legal expertise rivalling that of a top silk. The apparent leader of the gang forsook his Jack Daniels long enough to quote from an obscure piece of legislation that meant our efforts at vigilante justice would render us liable to punitive fines. A quick phone call to the local police station confirmed this interpretation. Our next stratagem, to hound them out by cutting off the utilities, floundered because they had already contacted the electricity and water companies to have the accounts switched into their names. I found it bizarre that, in a confrontation with people who have broken their way into my commercial property, I – the legal owner – was almost devoid of rights. I had no choice but to wait out the weekend, as their havoc wrecked whatever took their fancy, and seek a court order when the judicial system could be bothered to reopen its services.

Fortunately, the squatters were not intent on a prolonged occupation. For one interminable weekend, my factory-to-be hosted a 48-hour rave whilst the police did nothing, and then the ravers were gone, no doubt searching out the next unsuspecting victim. When we regained control of the building, their legacy was everywhere – faeces, graffiti, syringes – but at least it was once again ours.

'You could've at least got me an invite,' said Darren. I scowled. The experience had been so infuriating for me that it took a couple of moments before I realised he was joking.

For the next year and a half, I project-managed the transformation of the building – previously used by paper merchants – into a facility suitable for high-quality food preparation. The floor was re-laid with non-slip ceramic tiles, the walls were fitted with the sandwich panels that had been the subject of such forensic debate at Queen's Yard, and the factory with the requisite smokehouse equipment was installed, including two new British-made AFOS kilns. However, it wasn't simply a matter of recreating inch-by-inch what had gone before. For the first time in Forman's smokehouse history we added a production kitchen into the design. With Lloyd's culinary skills now part of our package, and with the general dumbing down of chef skills and apprenticeships in many of London's five-star hotel banqueting operations, we were increasingly being asked to extend our scope. 'We love your smoked salmon; can't you also make us pâtés/terrines/fishcakes' was a typical plea. With so much activity, I felt it was important for the staff to have a place to retire for quiet reflection, and so, adjacent to the yard, we created a garden area centred around two large teak benches. The landscaping of trees and shrubs was heavily influenced by Zen philosophy to express contrasts whilst also emphasising the ultimate harmony between humanity and nature.

It had always been part of my game plan that, eventually, Forman's would be a visitor destination – partly because I've found our customers are intrigued to understand the details of the curing and smoking process; partly because such transparency demonstrates we have nothing to hide and underlines our quality commitment; and partly because we've made it our mission to promote public education about the gulf in standards between London Cure and mass smoked salmon production. To this end, I built a viewing gallery high above the factory floor and commissioned a glass-fronted brick kiln to form a dramatic showpiece (our regular working kilns were made from stainless steel, and the sides of fish were hidden behind solid doors). When it was unveiled, the brick kiln exceeded my highest expectations. Spectacular, eye-catching, it would become a genuine talking point for any guests, and I planned to 'officially' launch it in celebration of our centenary two years after the move. Ironically, throughout our curtailed period at Marshgate Lane, it was never used for actual production. Not a single time.

Of course, back in 2002, we had no reason to suspect our residency at Marshgate Lane would be anything other than long-term, for the next generation. After almost-yearly upheavals, I was looking forward to an era of stability and calm. My focus on ensuring a seamless relocation had, inadvertently, given me a crash-course in the art of delegation. I no longer felt it necessary to inspect the fish at four o'clock each morning, or to involve myself in the minutiae of every client issue. I trusted Lloyd's judgement and ability to deliver (although I usually arrived at five, just in case!). Lloyd, too, was building a team that could function without perennial interference of micro-management. Such was my confidence in Forman's robust working practices that I even reclaimed a semblance of family life – for the best part of a half-decade, I'd only enjoyed briefly snatched moments with René and the children before another drama demanded my attention.

Unlike our post-fire reopening, there was no grand event to celebrate our move to Marshgate Lane. I was keen to get back to business, and Jeffrey Archer's implosion so soon after endorsing our company meant I was painfully aware that these things can bite back. Celebrations could be put on hold until 2005. That would be the perfect time, having properly settled in and by then with an even larger and more prestigious invitation list.

With responsibility for operational management now with Lloyd, I was able to spend more time on strategy development. One of the largest areas of growth in London was the sushi market, not so much for smoked salmon, but for fresh salmon. However, with an unrivalled reputation for the freshest produce, and (what would become known as) sushi-grade salmon in our fridges, arriving daily from Scotland, Forman's was in a great position to seize this opportunity. As well as winning the accounts of newcomers like Nobu and Zuma – not just for their salmon, but for other fish requirements such as black cod and yellowfin tuna – we also became the principal fish supplier to the intriguing 21st-century, hyper-modern, conveyor-belt self-service restaurant Yo! Sushi. Here we were, a traditional artisan food producer, working with some of the most modern concepts in food.

I was also eager to prise open the major European markets. The early 2000s witnessed rapidly rising living standards throughout the Continent, and I was happy to place a sizeable punt on the assumption that increased disposable incomes would boost the popularity of life's greatest pleasures, especially fine foods. Only ten minutes from Forman's, London City Airport became my second home. If there was a commercial or cultural centre within easy reach by short-haul flight, then it was added to my bucket list for late 2002 and early 2003. I became the master of travelling light so as to speed through check-in, breeze past security with a cool bag full of smoked salmon samples and make it from airplane to first meeting within forty-five minutes of touchdown. Before long, we were supplying the famous Italian delicatessen Peck in

Milan, Harry Cipriani's world-renowned bar in Venice, and the gourmet clubs of El Corte Ingles throughout Spain with our genuine wild smoked Scottish salmon. We also won the hearts and stomachs of the French in Paris with our farmed smoked salmon in the gastronomic food hall of Lafayette Gourmet. I even made a pit stop in the British Embassy in Paris where the ambassador's delightful wife acquired a taste for Forman's finest, and a penchant for our kippers too.

A number of retailers and hoteliers were persuaded to give us a shot, but it wasn't always straightforward. After an initial meeting in Italy with the senior buyer of one of the major distribution channels and a follow-up at our new plant, I agreed a commercial deal which would add a significant chunk to our bottom line. I was excited at the prospect of monthly containers of our smoked salmon being shipped across the channel. But just before departing my office, almost as an afterthought, the buyer asked me about our 'best before' dates.

'Well, in the UK, we put fourteen days.'

I could see he was uncomfortable with this response, and so added a qualification: 'But for export some of our clients prefer twenty-one days, and we are comfortable with that. Obviously we prefer our customers to enjoy our smoked salmon when it's freshest, but if you need twenty-one days, that's fine.'

'We need you to stamp "Eat within 100 days of purchase" on the packs.' His tone was scolding, like an army major berating a scruffy cadet.

'100 days!' I replied, thinking that this guy really doesn't understand smoked salmon and maybe had previously been a pasta buyer.

'Yes, it must say 100 days.' He wrote the number 100 on a card, and slid it across the table, as if I wouldn't otherwise have grasped the concept.

'Look, we know from laboratory tests that the salmon is still safe up to forty-eight days. It's not going to taste good, like you tasted just now, but 100 days and your customers will not return. Ever. To any shop!' I wasn't sure whether I was pleading, negotiating, reciting facts or whether this was just some kind of Italian wind-up.

'Don't worry. Nobody will leave it 100 days before eating. Of course not. Who could resist that long?'

'So why do you need 100 days?'

'Because if the Italian shopper sees two packs, and one says "Eat within 20 days" and the other says "Eat within 100 days", they will assume the 100-day pack is fresher – so that's the one they'll buy.'

With logic like that, I thought, it's hardly surprising the economies of the EU's southern states have been built on such dubious foundations. And lo, within another few years, they would start collapsing like drunken dominoes.

Anyhow, I refused to put our name to that marketing strategy and one good sales opportunity fell by the wayside. You can't win 'em all.

A chance encounter with a famous chef also took an equally unpredictable turn. I was invited to take a display booth at a promotional event organised by Relais et Chateaux for their top customers and food and travel writers to showcase their prestigious properties. It was hosted at the magnificent Merchant Taylor's Livery Hall in the City of London and I was proud to be one of the few to have been asked to take part. Amongst the well-heeled crowds sipping champagne from their flutes, there was one face I recognised across the room: Michelin-starred chef, Raymond Blanc. Le Manoir aux Quat'Saisons was not a Forman's client, but I was keen to add them to our list. I was a huge fan of Raymond Blanc, and fancying myself as a part-time amateur chef, used his recipe book for many of our dinner parties, fashionable as they were back then.

Grabbing his attention, I called him over to my display where I had two sides of smoked salmon, both farmed and wild, laid out on hardwood sapele boards which I would carve for the guests to taste the difference, an upscale version of the Pepsi challenge, I thought.

Blanc was vociferously advancing the opinion that the farmed salmon was much superior. (As an aside, I have observed that French chefs as a category can be amongst the most lukewarm about smoked salmon's allure, and I have anecdotally attributed this to tradition of fatty, pale meats of huge Norwegian salmon sides being stacked on the refrigerated shelves of village delicatessens throughout the Fifth Republic. It seemed wild Scottish salmon was too lean and dry for their taste, whereas farmed Scottish salmon can be a sound halfway house. I found that British, Italian, Austrian and German chefs all tend to prefer the wild, which was the reason we supplied Michel Bourdin with farmed smoked salmon at the Connaught and Marco Pierre White with wild at Mirabelle.)

I countered with the view that 'farmed salmon is like a light chardonnay, whereas wild is a full bodied claret'. 'However,' I added, 'I'm sure most of your customers at Le Manoir would prefer the wild.'

'Nonsense,' he exclaimed.

'Let's put it to the test,' I proposed.

For the next ten minutes, any hapless soul found loitering at my booth was invited to a tasting. Each one was offered a slice of wild and a slice of farmed, and to a person they concurred that wild offered superior taste and texture.

I turned to look at Blanc and he looked back at me.

'Harrumph,' he sniffed. 'They only chose wild because you told them it was wild and assumed that, being natural, it must be better. They wouldn't have known otherwise.'

'In that case,' I suggested, 'let's do the test again but this time we won't tell them.'

'This time it'll be different,' murmured Blanc, his arms folded. 'I know it.'

There were plenty of guests hovering around our stand and so I started: 'Madam, sir, please will you taste these two salmons and tell me which you prefer.'

'What's the difference?'

'I'll tell you after. Just want to know which you prefer.'

One by one, and I think we got to eight tasters, each and every guest said they preferred the wild smoked salmon.

Once again, I turned to look at Blanc and he stared into my eyes for about one second longer than was strictly necessary, before turning in the opposite direction and walking speedily off, exclaiming rather too loudly, 'I smoke my own salmon.'

* * *

I was becoming something of a poster child for the London Development Agency. I had struck up a professional relationship with a number of their executives, rooted in respect and a mutual determination to get the job done. Often I am first to castigate bureaucracies as remote and self-serving, but the LDA had been supportive and pragmatic throughout my relocation from Queen's Yard to Marshgate Lane. They had even seen their way to assist with some grant funding. Although a relatively modest contribution towards the top-line costs that had been incurred, perhaps 5 per cent of the total, it did go some way towards levelling the playing field (or at least making it less un-level) with Scotland's legion of corporate 'smoking' behemoths which had been universally lavished with government largesse, and consequently putting our fellow east London salmon smokers out of business by the unfair competition over three decades.

Shortly after our move was completed, the LDA produced a spiral-bound calendar, with each month featuring a supposed 'success story'. I was the case study for October 2003. Their copywriter interviewed me briefly by phone and penned these compelling words alongside my photograph: 'A key aim [of the LDA] is attracting investment from other private and public sector sources for London's economic development. H. Forman & Son is one example of a business that has benefited. Following a disastrous flood at its previous premises, our Regional Selective Assistance grant, which we administer on behalf of the DTI, was provided to help the business relocate to a new site in order to expand production and improve productivity.'

So, throughout London, from the walls of Whitehall's offices to the desks of government-backed start-ups, my face was beaming with pleasure throughout the month of October 2003. Best friends for ever – Forman's and the LDA; that was the not-so-subtle message. The irony was matchless. Because October 2003 was the date that my world, once again, fell apart. And this time, far from racing to my rescue, the LDA did everything within its power to obstruct, intimidate, bully and mislead.

Since moving to Marshgate Lane, I had become friendly with Mike Finlay, the gregarious owner of a building contracting firm called P. A. Finlay, based in the neighbouring property. Finlay's was another family-owned firm, albeit then only in the hands of the second generation. It employed around 130 staff and its niche was providing routine repairs and maintenance of central and local government buildings inside the M25. Its move to Marshgate Lane had coincided with ours, although for less dramatic reasons. They had simply outgrown their previous HQ, around a quarter of a mile away in Rowse Close.

It was, I think, a Wednesday morning when Mike invited himself into my office. I had been mulling over options for my next overseas jaunt – Berlin, perhaps, or maybe it was time to venture the other sides of the Baltics, to St Petersburg or even Moscow? As Mike sat down, he appeared flustered and uneasy. He kept running his thumb and forefinger up and down the armrest of his chair, like a child stroking a favourite toy for comfort.

'The strangest thing just happened, Lance,' he said.

I minimised my browser so I could grant Mike my full attention.

The image of Checkpoint Charlie vanished from my screen. Mike had glanced at the picture before I shut it, and – on any other day – I'm sure he would've volunteered a sarcastic remark. But today he was too preoccupied for such distractions.

'These two guys just turned up at my reception – no prior warning – strolled in and demanded to see me. I was in the middle of a staff meeting, but they were very insistent. They were wearing City suits and expensive ties, which you don't see in Marshgate Lane, and before I knew it, they'd barged right into my office.'

'Sounds like the Mafia.' I offered Mike a plate with a few slices of smoked salmon. 'On the house, by the way. The omega-3s are good for stress.'

'Even worse than the Mafia. They said they were property agents. Jones Lang. One was quite the silver fox, and from his complexion I'd say he's enjoyed rather too many late nights in Soho wine bars. He had a bone-crushing handshake, like he was about to challenge me to an arm-wrestling contest. My fingers are still throbbing. And his sidekick had a one of those – you would know, Mr Forman – posh, Eton voices. Theodore and some double-barrelled surname. I said, "Hi, I'm Mike, and I'm a builder." Anyway, I suggested a cup of builders' tea but they didn't look like they wanted to stay too long. "We'd like to get right to the point," they said. "On behalf of our client, we'd like to make an offer for your property."'

'Hmmm.' Unorthodox but intriguing.

'In hindsight, the obvious question would've been "Who's the client?" But I guess we all instinctively think about the cash, don't we? So I said: "Well, for the right price anything's for sale. But I've only just moved in," I told him, you could still smell the paint, and I made it perfectly plain that I had fitted out the building to suit us for the long term. "So it'd need to be a knockout offer." To which the bone-crusher told me their client could offer up to £1 million. I don't know if he thought he was Chris Tarrant – he made a million sound like an impressive number, as though he was doing me a huge favour. But as we'd just bought the building for £900,000, and then spent about a quarter of a million making sure it was fit for purpose, I saw things differently. Do they really think I'd want to put my staff through another twelve months of hell just to lose a huge chunk of money on the deal? I almost kicked them out on the spot. But then a light went off in the back of my head. Whilst they were guests in my office, why didn't I quiz them a bit more on what was behind this? And that's when it got really frightening.'

Mike had already chewed his way through the entire plateful of smoked salmon, so I signalled to Rita to bring some replenishments. But, when it came to ensuring we were all well fed, she was one step ahead as ever. Even as Mike's mouth was forming the word 'frightening', Rita's arm was reaching around the side of my office door, an even more generous portion of smoked salmon piled high to satisfy his craving.

'We've heard rumours', he continued, 'that various sites around the East End are being assessed for a possible Olympics bid. It suddenly occurred to me that this might be connected. So that's what I put to them. Short and sweet. "Are you working for the Olympics?" I think they were a bit taken aback by my bluntness.'

'What did they say?'

'They said they'd signed a non-disclosure agreement and so were bound by confidentiality. But the way the younger guy smirked told me everything I needed to know. After a few years in the building trade, you learn to read people. There's no doubt in my mind. They want to buy my land so they can dump a damn big stadium right in the middle of Marshgate Lane.'

'I don't think anyone's visited us yet. I'm sure I'd have been told. Anyway, I can't believe that would happen as the LDA gave us money to build our new place here. There's no way the government would have done that. It must be something else.'

'I do enough government contracting to know how these things work. They'll be picking us off one by one. You wait and see.'

That evening, René and I were meeting friends for dinner off Hanover Square. We both arrived early, and whilst cocktails were being mixed, I shared with her the hypotheses that Mike and I had developed.

I had her full, one-on-one attention.

'René, why are you laughing?'

'Because it's funny.'

'It's not funny.'

'It is.'

'No, it really isn't.'

I'm sure the cocktail waitress thought we must be a pair of bargain-basement pantomime comedians ('Oh yes it is', 'Oh no it's not') as she passed our drinks across the bar. René was still snickering as she took a first sip of her glass of Sauvignon Blanc.

'You are so dramatic. One minute you're the most laid-back person on the planet and next the world is about to end. Just because we've been through a fire and flood doesn't mean everything turns out to be a major disaster.'

'But this really could be.'

'Don't spend all night winding me up, and when Nick and Jo arrive, I wouldn't mention it. People misunderstand things all the time, and that's probably what happened with Mike.'

'Well, he's no fool. He has a bigger building than me, employs twice as many people, drives around in a Porsche, and on this occasion seems to know more than me, too.'

'Lance, you're worrying about nothing. Rumours are rumours. They're not real life.'

'I hope you're right, but I have a bad feeling about this one.'

My fears were vindicated. The following morning, the local paper printed an article about London's bid and the words 'Olympics' and

'Marshgate' found their way into the same sentence. Blair and Livingstone had decided London could make a credible bid to host the 2012 Games – either unaware or unconcerned that Forman's, and many other businesses, would be collateral damage.

Not having received any solace from René, who wouldn't have any of it, I decided to call my shrink, Nick Balcombe. At least it felt like he was my shrink by now. He had a way of putting me at ease whenever disaster reared its ugly head.

'Lance, this is not a disaster. It's just a very big IF.'

'What? Like IF we burn sawdust, we might end up with a fire, or IF our factory is 100 feet from a river, we might get flooded.'

Nick still wasn't overly concerned. Just because Blair had some wacky idea about hosting the Olympic Games in London, doesn't mean you need to fret. 'It's not going to happen.' So I took it upon myself to spend the afternoon researching the submission process and evaluation timescale for the bids. There would be less than two years – running to July 2005 – before the International Olympic Committee, meeting in session in Singapore, would vote on the Games' 2012 venue. Two years of uncertainty and contingency planning, to be followed – in the event of London's success – by, who knows what. So what I could do, what I had to do right now, was to make certain Forman's enjoyed blistering Christmas sales, and to that end, I had my secret weapon. Because our direct mail business, Forman & Field, was moving from first gear to full throttle.

The previous Christmas, having only just moved into Marshgate Lane, as well having a successful wholesale business selling our fish and now fishcakes to kitchens up and down Park Lane, we also saw the launch of our home delivery service. A beautiful catalogue had been produced at huge expense with the strapline 'Natural, Seasonal British Food Direct to Your Door', emblazoned on the front. We were pioneers – British food had not come of age, and some even smirked at our promotion of English wines. We developed a website from which we could sell food and take payment without ever having to talk to a customer – amazing at the time! And so our mail order business was born into the world of food lovers and, yes, discerning gastronomes.

Little did we realise how popular it would be. Throughout Christmas week 2002, Lloyd and I and many of our team never made it home. Many nights, we'd grab a couple of hours of sleep on the office floor, before returning to the shop floor to pack box after box after box of the most delicious handmade food, which would find its way on to the festive tables of some of the most aristocratic families in the land. A couple of years ago one of our packing team decided to place a pedometer on his shoes to measure just how committed our packers are. In the space of six days and confined to a walk-in fridge the size of a squash court, he managed to pace three marathons whilst hand-picking award-winning cheeses, handmade cakes, smoked fish, charcuterie and a diverse range of Michelin-standard food products, like potted lobster, now made in our own kitchens.

Having survived this 'sink-or-swim' introduction to the logistics of peak season mail order, we invested heavily to ensure Forman & Field was an even bigger success for Christmas 2003. This was helped somewhat by the friendly personnel at the House of Lords, who kindly invited me – and it became an annual tradition – to hand-carve sides of our smoked salmon for the Lords and Ladies at the banquet immediately following the State Opening of Parliament on Westminster's riverside terrace. As well as being there in person, together with my salmon, knife in hand, the staff kindly allowed me to display a stack of our Forman & Field catalogues, which were enthusiastically hand-bagged, especially by the lady peers of the realm.

So, for our second Christmas, in 2003, I decided to make a statement, and publish the most fabulous and comprehensive catalogue that has ever celebrated the best in gourmet British foods. Vivid photographs by Martin Brigdale, mouth-watering descriptions, printed on the highest-quality paper, and within a cover wrap packed with morsels so appetising that people would be tempted to rip them off the page to digest directly. It was more akin to a coffee-table book than a promotional catalogue, and I'd be mailing a copy – accompanied by a personalised letter from me – to every single individual on the Forman & Field database, plus another 60,000 from a list of high-net-worth individuals that we'd purchased. It would be the biggest one-off investment I'd ever committed to a marketing initiative.

My excitement levels surged when I saw the calibre of the work turned in by the designers and the printers. This was a publication without peer. It would solidify our reputation as champions and connoisseurs of the best of British. I couldn't wait to get all 100,000 mailed out, then sit back and await the euphoria. The timing of the mail-out – October half-term week – was strategic. This was the time – not too early, not too late – that families start planning their annual festive menus, and our catalogue needed to be on their kitchen counter tops for that critical moment.

Which was when the Royal Mail decided to go on strike.

Was the entire course of life in Britain being geared towards making my world miserable? As the old saying goes, it's not paranoia if they're genuinely out to get you.

I looked at the pallets piled high with undelivered catalogues and resolved that I couldn't let matters rest. Why should I face a huge business write-off because the workforce of an organisation with a quasi-monopoly on residential deliveries was grotesquely abusing its privileges? I fired off a letter to the Royal Mail's Chief Executive (which had to be hand-delivered, of course) expressing my outrage, and demanding to know what he intended to offer by way of compensation for both my wasted production costs and my loss of revenue.

I knew that massive organisations are adept at brushing off legitimate grievances, and there was no point engaging lawyers to fight my corner against the Royal Mail's almost unlimited resources, so I had no real expectation of receiving a constructive reaction.

Yet, blow me down, what should arrive on my desk barely a week later but a personal response to my 'compensation' letter from the Royal Mail CEO himself, Adam Crozier, in which, after an obligatory few paragraphs laden with saccharine clichés expressing deepest sympathy yadda yadda (no doubt scribed for him by his PR team), he did indeed make an offer of a financial settlement. It was regrettably not possible, he said, to individually compensate affected businesses, because that would set an irresponsible precedent. However, as a gesture of goodwill to all those affected, the Royal Mail would be donating £1 million to a cause which, he was certain, all Londoners would support. The £1 million would be given to the London Olympic Bid Team (whose plans for Marshgate Lane had now been confirmed), boosting their resources as they prepared the most compelling proposals for consideration in Singapore.

I was livid. The knife had not only been slid into my chest, now it was being twisted. The Royal Mail's so-called gesture of apology was to increase the likelihood that Forman's would be forced to vacate our new state-of-the-art factory.

I dashed out a press release, entitled 'The Royal Mail strikes again', in which I lambasted them for their cack-handed publicity stunt. I was to become adept at such PR zingers in the years ahead.

CHAPTER 9

FORFEITED

The Marshgate Lane Business Group was east London's equivalent of Marvel's *Avengers*. There comes a time when the threats to planet Earth are so dire that a single superhero, battling alone, cannot prevail. Facing the gravest danger, resources need to be pooled, and our heroes must swallow their pride, bury their differences and team-up to fight back against the merciless alien perils. The *Avengers* comic book was created by a couple of Jewish New Yorkers, Stan Lee and Jack Kirby, hunched over their art boards in the mid-1960s. Forty years later, the doctrine they'd crafted was adopted with relish by another good Jewish boy, myself, facing an existential menace which was almost on par with a mutant robot invasion from planet Zogg.

It was not an entirely new body. The Marshgate Lane Business Group had been meeting, on and off, for a number of months to discuss matters that were as parochial as they were dull. I'd attended one or two sessions, but left quickly when I realised the raciest items on the agenda were the desirability (or not) of speed humps and the adequacy (or not) of drainage. Keeping the area free from travellers was one area in which I was able to offer some expertise. Yet, these were hardly topics to set the heart pounding or the pulse into overdrive.

But, now that our corner of London had been confirmed as the Olympic bid team's chosen site, we needed a vehicle to coordinate our concerns and, if need be, to raise our protests. For the next eighteen months, the words 'speed humps' were banned from Marshgate Lane Business Group meetings. We were in a campaign for survival, and the group rose gloriously to the challenge.

Five firms were particularly active in those early days: ourselves, P. A. Finlay, Edwin Shirley Trucking (who provided logistical support for major rock bands on their world tours), Laurier's (who made protective netting for scaffolding on building sites) and Sortex (who manufactured the world's most sophisticated sorting machines, able to spot and extract a single black grain of rice from a container full of wholegrain). At our inaugural meeting, we agreed on the need for professional advisors. We knew about running our businesses, but were far from being expert in navigating the perilous byways of compulsory purchase procedures, where a single misstep could cost us our livelihoods.

Nick Balcombe had been a reliable guide, so I introduced him to the group, and they were unanimously impressed by his combative nature and clarity of thought. We had our numbers man!

Next, we needed to appoint a legal representative. Mike recommended Mark Stephens of the law firm Finers Stephens Innocent, who – as well as being his neighbour – could have been tailor-made for our needs. Firstly, he was not conflicted. The LDA, with a Machiavellian streak, had been engaging a large pool of London solicitors so as to render them all unable to act on the opposing side, but had clumsily overlooked FSI. Secondly, he was a media lawyer, not a planning lawyer, which would prove invaluable when our disputes would be played out in the press and over the airwaves, as much as in front of magistrates. He has been nicknamed the 'patron saint of previously lost causes' for his ground-breaking advocacy on behalf of anyone being hounded by the establishment – over the years, this has included the likes of James

Hewitt, the Brent Spar oil platform victims, Julian Assange and the McLibel Two. I later learnt that Ken Livingstone and his LDA were aghast we had appointed a specialist in media matters, which made me more certain than ever that our choice was exemplary.

My first meetings with the LDA since the Olympic site announcement gave no inkling of the troubles ahead. The Authority had recently appointed Gareth Blacker as their Director of Development, and he agreed to an early discussion of the options for Forman's. I'd made some enquiries about his background and learnt he was primarily a property man, which I took as a plus (the civil service has an irksome tendency to parachute so-called A-listers into technical roles for which they have no competence), and despite being known as 'dour' and 'surly', had a reputation for getting stuff done. I figured (as Thatcher once said of Gorbachev) that this was a man with whom I'd be able to do business.

'I'm sure you know our recent history,' I explained. 'We renovated after a fire. We moved after a flood. In the food industry, it's critical to provide continuity of service to our customers, since they have many other choices. The LDA helped me survive the last crisis, and you even featured me in your calendar.'

This first meeting was held in my black-stained-wood-clad boardroom at Marshgate Lane, with its secret James Bond-style door to the viewing gallery. I was keen to show Blacker the complexity of building a new smokehouse and the attention to detail in the design that any new property would need to replicate. Having twice struggled to find suitable property in the area, there was only one question on my mind: 'If London does win the bid, how long will you give us to relocate?' Anything less than two years, and the Olympics would be putting out our fourth generation torch. It was quickly clear that Blacker's side of the table was as much in the dark as mine.

Four months later, I attended a follow-up meeting in a conference room at the LDA's offices in St Katherine Dock. From the first-floor windows, there was a magnificent 270-degree view that took in long stretches of the Thames and numerous high-class developments around Tower Bridge. I thought, 'Let's hope they're this conscientious when sorting out locations for displaced manufacturers!'

'You know that our mission is to support London industry,' said Blacker. 'Firms exactly like yours, that employ local tradespeople and export around the world. We've helped you before, and we'll help you again.'

'So how long will you give us to sort ourselves out?' I asked, having already waited four and a half months too long for an answer.

'We can give you up to two years, Mr Forman.'

'But...'

'Yes, I understand your concerns about timing, so here's what we'll do. You identify a new building or site that works for you. Then, we'll buy it. We'll pay for all your planning and designs, but we won't start building until we know if London wins the bid. This should save a considerable amount of time. If London does win, we'll swap it for your current site, and pay for the entire conversion. If, on the other hand, London loses, you can stay put and we will simply own another piece of land, which is fine. We are a development agency and we do own land. You will not be out of pocket.'

I felt this was a fair solution, and we shook on the deal. Moments later, I was calling Lloyd from the car. 'This could be more straightforward than I'd feared,' I said. 'If he's true to his word, we'll be rehoused within a year or two, and not a penny out of pocket. All we need to do is find another site.'

'I have my doubts,' said Lloyd. 'But let's give him the benefit of the doubt.'

* * *

For the next few weeks, I barely set foot in Marshgate Lane as I was whisked from site to site by different firms of eager-to-please commercial agents. On a couple of occasions, I felt pangs of guilt about heaping too much onto Lloyd's shoulders, but I knew they were broad, and also that I'd be unable to concentrate on day-to-day matters until I was confident about the small matter of our future existence. Many of the possibilities about which the agents gushed were non-starters – in some cases, I didn't even bother getting out of the car. Then, just as I was wondering whether Marshgate Lane was the only land in the capital that ticked all our criteria, I was shown an ideal site in New North Road, in the neighbouring borough of Hackney. I was tingling with excitement. Within moments, I was on the phone to Blacker, imploring him to lock down the option before any other purchasers appeared on the scene.

At which point, his 'generous' undertakings started to tumble, one by one, like eggs from a bird's nest that has been ripped asunder by storms.

I had been prepared for a bit of haggling about the build costs, but Blacker's focus was more fundamental. Returning to his conference room with a portfolio bulging with information about the New North Road site, I noticed from the opening exchanges that his demeanour was light years away from his previous bonhomie. Five minutes into the meeting, and he still wasn't looking me in the eye. At his paperwork, at the wall, out of the window – anywhere but in the eye.

'£4.2 million. That's more expensive than I was expecting,' he muttered into a sheaf of documents. 'How do I know you're not overpaying?'

'Apparently that's the range for similar transactions in the last few months. But that's not really my issue,' I said. 'It's not like I'm looking to relocate. I'm quite happy where we are. You're the one telling me I must move!'

'Let me suggest a different solution. Why don't you purchase the site yourself? Then, if the London bid succeeds, we'll buy Marshgate Lane off you, and contribute to the fitting out on the New North Road.'

'And if London loses?'

'You decide which one to sell.'

I was crestfallen. 'We're not property speculators,' I said. 'I can take a risk on a bad batch of salmon, but not on when the London property cycle will peak. Whatever happened to your mission to support London industry?'

'There's no need for sarcasm,' he replied. He had strolled over to the window and was gazing out below, as if fixated on the yachts in the harbour. Not only was there no direct eye contact; I now found myself staring at the back of his head. 'We have no legal obligation to guarantee your business' survival and if you want our help, that's what you're going to have to do,' he added for good measure.

I couldn't leave the building without the outlines of a deal with which to move forward. Eventually, Blacker agreed that – if Forman's obtained a commercial mortgage to complete the purchase – the LDA would provide a back-to-back guarantee to make good any shortfall if New North Road was subsequently sold at a loss. It wasn't quite the gold-plated solution I'd anticipated, but it provided downside protection, which had been my priority concern. Over the coming weeks, a Heads of Agreement was drawn up between my lawyers and the LDA's. I submitted my offer to the New North Road vendor, which was duly accepted, but to line up the funding I needed a full legal agreement with the LDA, 'i's dotted and 't's crossed. With the Heads agreed, this should have been a legal formality.

Apparently, I was told, there was a minor clause in the agreement that needed to be reworded and they would come back to us with a suggested revision. When we saw the redrafting, however, it was far from 'minor'; in fact, it opened up a new dimension, never previously discussed, which would worsen our position. However, for fear of losing the site, I compromised quickly and the agreement was once again ready for signing. Each time I had my pen to the ready, the LDA would find another reason to wiggle and procrastinate. As a result, we had no basis on which to secure our loan and proceed with the purchase. It dawned on me this was not a matter of legal wranglings, but of wilful obfuscation. Despite their public claims to provide tailored support and to respect the unique needs of each business, the LDA's actual strategy was to provide a single, overarching solution rather than entertain endless back-to-back guarantees and contingency arrangements. In this light, there was considerable benefit in dragging out the deal, until it provoked the vendor to return the property to the open market. I cursed my naiveté. A few months later a £5.1 million offer was submitted on behalf of a property developer, and I grudgingly accepted reality. It was like an expensive watch had slid from the wrist of a Golden Gate Bridge climber and tumbled into the San Francisco Bay below. I felt nauseous with the realisation that something so suited to our business had just slipped through my fingers.

Throughout the 'bid assessment' period, a number of delegations were sent by the International Olympics Committee to conduct technical evaluations of the potential host cities. The other members of the Marshgate Lane Business Group had experienced equally unsatisfactory meetings with the LDA, or had received absurdly low-ball offers, so we agreed this would be the perfect excuse to raise the profile of our plight. If the IOC representatives reported to their superiors that firms of good standing were being sacrificed on the altar of official intransigence, the possible outcomes would all be in our favour. Either IOC voters would be tempted to back other candidate cities, or the LDA would be pressurised to up their game. We had two weeks to ferment a groundswell of opinion so blatant and vociferous that it couldn't be ignored.

We debated how to make the greatest impact. The first step was for each firm to select a three- to five-word message that contained a groan-inducing pun. Hence:

H. Forman & Son: 'When will salmon help us?'

P. A. Finlay: 'Rebuild your bridges with us.'

Bedrock Crushing: 'Awaiting concrete proposals.'

Bywaters Waste Management: 'Don't waste our time.'

These slogans were to be printed onto huge, gaudy banners, arranged by Laurier's, to be hung across the front exterior of each building. It would, we figured, make for a devastating broadcast image. TV crews would be accompanying the delegates at every step of their journey, and the producers wouldn't be able to resist a cutaway to these statements of defiance. With luck, close-up footage of our banners would become one of the defining images of the visit. I patted Mike on the back. 'The fight back has begun,' I said. 'I predict round one to us!'

In the end we settled on the phrase '2012: Killing Local Businesses', which was blunt and relevant to all, although some also went for a second banner to appeal to the tabloids, stating simply: '2012: Don't blow our jobs.'

What we didn't expect was Newham Council's cavalier disregard for our private property rights. Around midnight, just a few hours before the inspectors touched down, council officials sent a fleet of workmen to sever the cable ties that were holding our banners aloft and requisition the entire collection for disposal. It was an outrageous attack both on free speech and property rights (the banners were, after all, displayed from buildings in private ownership). Yet there was no time to organise a reprinting. We convened an emergency meeting of the Marshgate Lane Business Group and consoled one another on a bitter lesson learnt. We vowed never again to assume the other side would act ethically or with honour. The initial skirmishes had descended into full-scale war, and wars are rarely won by the faint-hearted. The Olympics are supposed to be about fair play and originated from the home of democracy. There was certainly nothing *fair* or *democratic* around us now.

In a panic measure, the LDA claimed that fifty businesses changed allegiance and supported the London bid. This followed a £12 million offer by the London government to one landlord owning a two-acre site, six times what had been offered to other businesses. The landlord's site, in fact, only represented twenty-two business tenants and no more than 100 employees. The claim by Livingstone that the businesses of Marshgate Lane now support the Games was a blatant misrepresentation, but one which the IOC inspectors were happy to hear, and they were delighted to see a banner on this particular building in support of the Olympic ideals and welcoming the circus to town. Ironically, this loyalty was never followed through as it would have set a precedent for the rest of us and so the landlord's flirtation with the devil ended in hell.

Whilst all this was occurring, the LDA was seeking the simplest, cheapest solution to eject a handful of troublemakers from its in-tray. They invited a number of us to inspect some derelict land, a little further north and east, which they had acquired in both Leyton and Beckton. They were adamant it could quickly be transformed into a vibrant business community. The area was not without merit, but the show-stopper for me was transportation. Our vans, laden with supplies, were making continual deliveries to the hotels and restaurants of central London and now, with our production kitchen, we had almost become an extension of some of London's best-known hotel kitchens. If the Savoy called us because they needed another terrine within forty-five minutes, and we let them down, this could jeopardise the entire working relationship. The route from Leyton to Zone 1 was notorious for bottlenecks, even before five years of Olympic Park construction got underway. Unless the LDA was proposing to equip us with a fleet of refrigerated helicopters so we could soar above the carnage, we needed other options. My newfound chums were also irritated by the cack-handed attempts of our guides to oversell the benefits of the Beckton proposal:

'The location is good, being close to central London.'

'The transport infrastructure and connections are excellent.'

'There is enough land to relocate all the businesses.'

'The site is brownfield, so we can design new properties appropriate for your needs.'

Glossing over genuine concerns, and foisting impractical solutions, was not – in my opinion – a legitimate way for a publicly funded body to behave. I brought the conversation to a shuddering halt when I raised my hand, and cattily observed: 'I have just one question. If it's all so wonderful, why don't you hold the Olympics in Beckton, and leave the rest of us to carry on unaffected?'

With the passage of time, we felt increasingly friendless at the LDA, and I reached out for support in other directions. The Sunday supplements had been strong allies over the years – editors would warm to the strong visual image of fresh salmon being loaded into a kiln, and journalists loved to tell the story of a plucky East End family business prospering against the odds. But, this time, strange things were happening. The interview would go well – I'd maintain a good rapport with the journo and slip in a few pre-crafted sound bites. We'd speak again once the copy had been filed, and I'd be assured it would be the lead feature on, say, page 8 the following day. But, when the papers hit the stands, and I rifled through the pages in search of the Forman's story, there was *nada*.

'I can't understand it,' I said to Mark Stephens, after a third or fourth interview in succession had ended up on the cutting-room floor.

'I can,' he replied, mournfully. 'When the establishment closes ranks, freedom of the press be damned. And no one in Fleet Street wants to be held responsible for the failure of our Olympics bid.'

'Is it really that easy to push around a proprietor? John Major would've loved to have had that power.'

'Major never had the aura of invulnerability that Blair's got. Two elections won and – according to the polls – number three will be a no-brainer. Plus, he's got Alastair Campbell, who knows exactly where the bodies are buried. If Campbell wants to kill a story, he's got all the top people on speed dial.'

'He'd do that?'

'Downing Street thinks Blair's biggest legacy will be bringing back the Olympics. That, rather than the Iraq War. Anything that is a risk to success must to be trampled underfoot.'

'I'm not sure I like the metaphor.'

'It'll get worse before it gets better, darling.'

Ignored by the media, I explored political connections. I wrote to Mike Chattey, at Conservative HQ, asking him to use his influence to arrange a meeting with Sports Minister Lord Moynihan, and I offered to host visits from Culture Secretary Tessa Jowell and Ken Livingstone. All I received were not entirely unexpected brush-offs. Everyone was afraid to talk to us in case this was taken as an acknowledgement that 'issues existed with the bid'; it was so much easier to brush awkward facts under the carpet and hope they would go away. Even when we explained that we are not anti the Olympics coming to town, but simply needed to be able to relocate without being out of pocket, we were stonewalled.

I was especially disappointed in the wall of silence surrounding Sebastian Coe. Coe had been an ambassador for the London bid from near the beginning, after the early resignation of Barbara Cassani, and in early 2004 he was appointed the bid Chairman. On paper he was uniquely suited to the role, having been a medal-winning Olympic athlete as well as an elected politician. It was an important part of his duties to engage with the businesses that would be affected by the Park; in any event, surely I had banked some goodwill from the times I'd briefed him as an aspiring MP ten years beforehand? I looked forward to the chance to present our case.

My first half-dozen attempts to reach out to Coe – emails to his offices, a letter, even a fax (the machine hadn't quite yet been retired) – went unacknowledged. I didn't take it personally at that stage; I assumed he had a team of advisors screening his correspondence, and was confident that, with a bit of perseverance, we'd be face-to-face. So it was like a punch to the solar plexus when I finally received a reply that was both dismissive and curt. 'I recently received letters from organisations that have independently reviewed the LDA's general approach and found it to be robust and fair. I am satisfied that this is the case,' he wrote, without deigning to name the organisations, provide their terms of reference, or explain why their independent review hadn't included engagement with the 350 firms affected. 'I hope you will understand that I am unable to comment on your specific circumstances.' How I wished in retrospect I'd said 'I can't comment on your specific circumstances' when he'd been begging me for advice about dealing with hostile questioning during his run for Parliament in 1992.

Conveniently for Coe, the three independent reviews just happened to land the week the IOC were on one of their inspection visits. The first was from a quango called Gateway to London, who received huge grant funding from the LDA, and so were hardly going to be critical. The second was from the Royal Institution of Chartered Surveyors, who wrote that they had set up a helpline to advise affected businesses, yet when we called it, the people answering had no idea of its existence. The third was from an organisation called ELBA. Nothing to do with Napoleon's place of exile, an IOC inspector could easily be forgiven for thinking the East London Business Alliance was an alliance of local businesses. Instead, it was a collection of social workers and ex-teachers with hardly a day's business experience between them. Their website claimed: 'The area has long been in serious need of regeneration and is currently full of derelict buildings and land that can only be described as a disgrace to a *world class city*'. Thanks a lot, ELBA. Their CEO,

Liam Kane, was formerly Chair of that sensational business success, the Millennium Dome… Oh, and they also received grant funding from the LDA. Coe really knew how to pick his allies.

With neither New North Road nor Leyton proceeding, albeit for different reasons, my search for a permanent alternative site was growing more desperate by the day. Shortly before the Singapore bid result was announced, I spent a few hours, at the LDA's suggestion, with their local agent, Colin Cottage of Glenny's. We toured the area looking for any piece of land that held out promise. The only site that was remotely viable was known as Bow Lock, less than a mile away, and which had been derelict for years, and on further investigation I was encouraged to discover was owned by the London Borough of Tower Hamlets. Excellent, I thought, since it's state-owned and with the state needing my site, surely it can't be too difficult to arrange a simple exchange – the actual cash values would be irrelevant. I figured, a deal would suit all parties. I'd have a new factory; Tower Hamlets would have found use for an abandoned plot; local residents would see jobs brought to an area of high unemployment from a 100-year-old heritage business founded in that very borough; and the LDA would have another 'redevelopment' success story involving Forman's to parade on its calendars. For all these reasons, I found it odd when almost nobody else shared my enthusiasm. The LDA overtly shunned any involvement; Blacker told me that it was up to me if I wished to negotiate directly with Tower Hamlets, but the LDA couldn't assist. Bow Locks, when said quickly, was just how I was feeling about all of this.

During the darkest days, the main glimmers of encouragement came from within the trade. Michel Roux wrote to say: 'The government should be making every effort to ensure that Forman's continues to flourish instead of putting it under financial strain. This would never happen in Paris! The French are very protective of their traditional industries.' Rick Stein said: 'Losing Forman's would be a tragedy. The artisan skills of salmon smoking as carried out by your company are unique to our country.' And David Michels, Chief Executive of the Hilton Group, which had sponsored London's bid, wrote to promise 'whatever little influence I have' to push for a fair settlement. If London's hoteliers and restaurateurs had been in charge of the Olympic redevelopment, I'm sure I'd have been spared the coming ordeals. In any event, their moral support was of great comfort, and helped keep me grounded and sane.

One night, René and I spread property information around our living-room table and listed all the options that hadn't yet been discounted. With New North Road and Bow Lock seemingly beyond reach, just three options remained viable. We then spent three hours (and an equivalent number of bottles of Merlot) considering the risks of each one. I wrote out our conclusions, which made depressing reading, and circulated it to Stephens, Balcombe and a small group of friends in case there was something blindingly obvious that I'd overlooked. This was what I wrote:

Option One: Extinguishment
Risk factors –
1. *Courts argue that I was unreasonable not to take Leyton*
2. *Extinguishment compensation might be poor*
3. *Whilst fighting for fair compensation I will have no business/source of income*

Option Two: New appropriate site
Risk factors –
1. *This could be paid for through loss of profit claim on disturbance or successful legal challenge, but if these fail, would be heavily burdensome for business in finance costs*
2. *Short term high capital cost may never be recouped*

Option Three: LDA's Leyton site
Risk factors –
1. *Would be operationally hard for business, stunting growth and causing losses and not allowing us to get back on growth trend prior to the Games bid being announced. Continuous ongoing battles required to prove this to the LDA*
2. *Business would be forever swimming against the tide*

The bottom line was that I was petrified of every single option. Each one exposed me financially and commercially, and left me in a far more vulnerable position than the status quo. Publicly, the government and the LDA were claiming that nobody should be worse off as a result of the Olympic bid. It certainly didn't feel like that from where I was standing.

I shortly found out the LDA had fallen woefully short of its stated commitment to have a contingency plan in place for every business affected by the time of the 2012 award, which was the line Livingstone had been parroting to the press. In actuality, just six deals were done, of which four were for public sector bodies in the affected area and one was a site owned by the pension fund of one of the board Directors of the LDA. If the LDA had signed perhaps 100 conditional agreements out of the 350, one could claim that this was a huge task and they did their best. But six was a woeful result. The grim reality was that they had no incentive to resolve every issue before Singapore. If London won the bid, the LDA would have the armoury of CPO powers at its disposal, massively increasing its leverage and ability to trample over contrary opinion.

Faced with prevarication and double-dealings from Blacker, I had nothing left to lose and appealed to his boss, Tony Winterbottom. My correspondence left no room for ambiguity. I wrote that his team had been 'petty, uncommercial, unfair, and willing to renege on agreed heads of terms'. I suggested that 'any outsider would think they are deliberately attempting to wreck our deal'. I accused him of 'burying your head in the sand, a very cowardly way for someone in your position to behave'. And I appealed to his better nature: 'This may be a political game for your colleagues. But it's people's livelihoods you're playing with. Please be open minded, human and leader-like, and meet me – now.' I felt better for putting my anger down into an email, but my finger was still hovering over the 'send' button as I played out the possible retaliation. I read the text to Rene, asking whether she thought it was harsh, or could be counter-productive. 'Playing their game hasn't worked,' she said. 'Don't worry about offending Blacker. It's not your responsibility to protect him from the consequences of his arrogance.' I read it through once more and pressed *send*. Then I switched off my laptop and retired for the night.

In fairness, my robust language finally woke Winterbottom and his cronies from their stupor. The LDA agreed to a public meeting with the Marshgate Lane Business Group at Newham Town Hall, and I volunteered to lead on behalf of the local businesses. It was time to rekindle my skills in audience engagement, strident advocacy, polemics and wit, honed all those years ago at the Cambridge Union Society. Then, I'd been debating trivial matters such as whether the government should stand or fall, or whether nuclear weapons protected or imperilled us. This time, my words would have weightier consequences. I was allotted five minutes on the agenda, as were the other businesses, but they were happy to assign their time to me, on the basis that I not only speak for Forman's, but represented all the businesses of Marshgate Lane. I felt like a trade union leader – heaven forbid! Never have I prepared so assiduously for a single occasion. Night after night, I honed my script until I was satisfied that it appealed to both the head and the heart, and rehearsed my delivery until I was commanding and authoritative. I imagined every possible intervention, and practised how I would respond. By the night of the Town Hall meeting, I was as pumped up as a heavyweight boxer entering the ring for the final round of a world championship title fight in Las Vegas. This would be my moment, and nobody could stop me from milking it.

But first I was forced to sit through interminable opening remarks from the Chair. Is this what it's like every day working in the Town Hall? I mused. How do people stand it? I started to fidget. Mike was sitting next to me egging me on and I had not planned on holding back. Finally, it was time. I walked to the podium and looked around the room for dramatic effect. Then, I began:

> Colleagues, putting aside the personal issues relating to our factory and business, I am a supporter of the Olympic Games. Sport builds national pride and unity and creates a healthier community, and at a local level it encourages team spirit and provides challenges, recreation and stimulation for young and old. If we win the bid to host the 2012 Olympics, it will be wonderful for east London, in fact for all of London and the entire nation. I whole-heartedly support it.
>
> So why are we being screwed by the LDA?
>
> The short answer is – I don't know, but I have my ideas.
>
> Who is the LDA? The LDA is the Mayor's Agency for Business and Jobs – it says so on their stationery. What these people don't know about business and jobs isn't worth knowing. They are experts in this field. Unlike you and me, who have businesses and create jobs in this run-down, derelict, dirty part of east London, these people sit in gleaming offices over a beautiful marina watching the tourists meander by – and they know about business and creating jobs – they know what's best for us. They've been there, they've read the book, produced the manual and can now tell us how it's all done. They know whether it's

better for us to be in Leyton, or in Dagenham or whether your business would be better off if it didn't exist at all – because in your place, there may be another business, a cleaner business, selling popcorn or T-shirts. Yes – these people have the solutions.

So I called them to ask them when they would need my land in the event that London won.

It only took the LDA five months to give me an answer. Five months, to tell me that we would have two years to relocate. But that's not long enough, I told Gareth Blacker when he came to visit – we've just been through the process. Not to worry, assured Gareth. With solution to hand, he told me to go seek out a relocation site, and when we found one the LDA would buy it for us, hold it for us, pay for a new factory to be designed and planned, and if London won the Games, they would build us our perfect replacement. And if London lost, we could pretend it had all been a dream.

Of course, this was not our idea of a dream. Did we really want to spend the best part of a year and a half looking for a new site, securing it, designing a factory, submitting planning applications and preparing for a hypothetical future only for the entire exercise to be a waste of time and money due to a vote taking place on the other side of the planet.

Since that first misunderstanding, there have been numerous more, month after month. We decided that we'd rather be destitute than dead, and so played Gareth's game. But every step of the way the goalposts would shift. Our business remains in a state of limbo and I personally have spent over 800 hours trying to solve this conundrum. The LDA assured us that if we signed an agreement in principle to relocate, they would deal with our claim for the disturbance we were suffering. What they didn't explain was that dealing with our claim meant calculating how much we've lost but not actually reimbursing us. How stupid of me! How could I have been so easily misled? I must have thought these people were British civil servants, not second-hand car salesmen.

So I told Mr Winterbottom that the businesses in Marshgate Lane had three main concerns – the affordability gap, the value of the land, and the fact that it's a year on and no deals have been done.

Mr Winterbottom said that the LDA does not want to do deals. I will say that again. The LDA does not want to do deals. Well, if that's the case, why did they write to all the businesses last summer offering them deals? Why have they been wasting your time and mine – as well as the time of the mills producing the paper, the printers making the stamps, and the postmen delivering the letters?

This is the heart of the problem. Why can't they just be straight with us? Why do they have to mislead us, and string us along? Either they are not competent enough to do deals and are afraid of making wrong decisions, or they haven't got any money – although they keep telling us they have – or they have no intention of assisting us now, because if London wins the bid, we will all be washed away in the tide of euphoria. What confidence can we have, given the despicable way they have behaved in the last year and a half, that things will be any better after the vote in Singapore?

At Forman's, we have almost no runway left. If we haven't secured a site in the next few weeks, we won't have enough time to relocate and our 100-year-old business will be destroyed. Who will be responsible for this? Gareth Blacker? Tony Winterbottom? Gordon Brown? Tony Blair? We have survived two world wars, a fire and a flood, but two weeks of sport looks like it could destroy us. I beg the powers that be at 2012 or government – look at this again and look quickly.

> And if we do get washed away, what a waste it would be. If we go bust, two years of lost tax revenues would have paid for the extra support we need to protect our future. So is our destruction the way to squander tax payers' money? And what about the hundreds of thousands of pounds that have been spent on professional fees on our negotiations to date? Again, further wasted tax payers' money. If the LDA has no intention of doing deals, it's all been a scandalous waste.
>
> My simple contention is the businesses should not be put in a worse financial situation as a result of the 2012 bid. It is unethical, immoral and simply unequitable – not just for me as a business owner, but for the hard-working and loyal staff I employ. The businesses are stakeholders in this bid, and we should not be dismissed and disregarded. The LDA is gambling with our land, land they don't own, and whilst they are gambling with our land, they have left us all in a position of uncertainty.
>
> I say – be fair with us and we will work with you. Let us build our trust in you and demonstrate your real commitment to help us, not mealy mouthed waffle that you have no intention of sticking to.
>
> The Games could be a beautiful opportunity for this part of east London, but part of that beauty should be reflected in the spirit and manner with which the local community is treated. London 2012 – make us proud of you, too.

I slammed my fist against the podium to signal that I'd reached my peroration, at which point both Mike Finlay and others yelled 'hear, hear' and started their applause. Within moments, half the Town Hall audience was on its feet, cheering, clapping and stomping. Even when the Cambridge Union Society had been at its most drunkenly boisterous, I'd never received an ovation quite like it.

Retaking my seat, I folded my arms and glared at Blacker who sat at the table alongside the lectern, with his head buried in his hands. I could see his relief as my assault ended, a brief ceasefire whilst he had a chance to survey the wounded and reload.

CHAPTER 10

FORAYS

Sir Samuel Pepys, in addition to being an acclaimed diarist, was a famed letter writer. Whilst serving as the Member of Parliament for Harwich, he was appointed Chief Secretary to the Admiralty under King Charles II, and oversaw far-reaching reforms which laid the foundations for a professional naval service. In this capacity, he corresponded with parliamentarians, naval officers, friends and dignitaries about his charges, and his letters were inevitably eloquent, vibrant and erudite. He wholeheartedly merits his stature as a first-rank Man of Letters.

It's probably fair to suggest that, in all likelihood, the letters of the Marshgate Lane Business Group won't be acclaimed throughout the centuries, à la Pepys. Nevertheless, there were two of which I was particularly proud. We had obtained (through means that need not detain us) the personal contact details of every voting member of the International Olympics Committee. The most gung-ho members of our group argued that we should immediately go nuclear with our concerns. But the majority favoured a warning shot, which – if ignored – would be followed by a rapidly escalating arms race. In April 2005, the warning shot was despatched – two tightly written pages in which we summarised the 'threat of extinction' to businesses in the area, and implored the IOC to use its 'unique [position] to influence the outcome of this sad situation'. We said we would correspond again if there were no positive developments during our forthcoming meetings with the LDA and Newham Council. We were keen to strike a tone of pragmatic realism. That way, any subsequent denunciation would be all the more hard-hitting.

When those meetings proved fruitless, representatives of five of the affected businesses and an energetic PR consultant, David Russell, met with our solicitor, Mark Stephens, at his offices to craft the second and final letter. An intern, on his first day of work experience, took note of our coffee requests, but had clearly never been trained on what to do next, and was unaware that a 50/50 ratio of boiling water to Nescafé granules doesn't make for a palatable result. After our first sips, we were spluttering and grimacing, but as it happened our collective caffeine overdose gave an extra frisson to the words we were drafting.

Every sentence brimmed with bile as we castigated the woeful manner in which the London 2012 team and the LDA were dismissing any legitimate concerns of the business community. Like a beautifully structured three-act play, our letter built remorselessly, inevitably, towards its devastating crescendo. Our masterpiece. For Michelangelo, it was the ceiling of the Sistine Chapel. For Rachmaninoff, it was his second symphony. For Shakespeare, it was a little tale about the vacillating Prince of Denmark. And, for us, it was sixty words, written more in sorrow than anger, in which for the first time we called upon IOC members to vote for other candidate cities:

> We write with a heavy heart because since the bid was announced we have supported the principle of London winning. However, its legacy should not involve the destruction of thousands of jobs. Therefore, it is with great regret that we are compelled to

> withdraw our support for the bid. We urge you to take this into your most serious consideration.

This was not a conclusion we had reached lightly. We were also slightly wary of the repercussions (none of us had ever gone into battle with a national Olympic bid team before!). But our options were diminishing before our eyes. Mike summed it up perfectly: 'It's already a disaster for us, so we haven't got much to lose. They could hardly make the situation worse.'

'I agree,' I said. 'It's a risk, but a risk worth taking. Let's do it.' I swigged the dregs of my coffee in a show of defiance. Mike flinched as I slammed an empty mug back on the table. I was the only one amongst us that had successfully imbibed the entire brew.

'Leave it with me,' said Mark. 'I'll arrange for the text to be translated into all the languages spoken by IOC members, and it'll be on their fax machines overnight and with emails too. Belt and braces.'

'Thanks for all you help,' said Mike. 'But I do have one suggestion.'

'What's that?' asked Mark.

Mike pushed his cup towards the conference phone in the middle of the table. 'I really wouldn't recommend that you open up a Starbucks franchise.'

As the date of the IOC vote grew closer, and the media's appetite for Olympics-related stories grew more insatiable, Mark and I were speaking three or four times a week about how to ramp up the noise. When it came to getting messages out via the press, he was unashamedly in the 'take-no-prisoners' camp. One morning, as I'd been preparing for an interview with the *Evening Standard*'s Ross Lydall, Mark summarised his philosophy in two pithy sentences:

'No editor wants to run an article full of nuanced legal prose with lots of caveats and footnotes. What they're looking for is pure, raw, unvarnished emotion, backed up with numbers – lots of numbers.'

'Can I get personal about Blacker and the LDA?'

'Nothing vitriolic. That makes you look bitter. Keep the focus on how it's affecting you, and the people who work for you. Puns help too – journalists adore puns. Saves their sub-editors the effort of having to think of any headlines themselves.'

'Something like "Olympics not sporting"? Or "A fishy situation"?' I volunteered.

'Or "Salmon Business: Smoked Out by 2012"?' Mark responded.

In the event, I must after all doff my cap to the ancient guild of sub-editors, because they devised a headline that was wittier and more accurate than anything we supplied. In the 2005 London Marathon, British runner Paula Radcliffe had taken an unscheduled toilet break part-way through the race, even though there were no toilet facilities nearby. So, in reporting on our latest altercations with the LDA, a full-page feature in *The Times* was blessed with the headline: 'What Paula Radcliffe paused to do in the streets of London, bid organisers are doing to the locals.' It should have won the Pulitzer.

This wasn't Mark's first rodeo, and from his experience he shared numerous snippets on how to orchestrate the most potent media campaign. The Marshgate Lane Business Group didn't impetuously rush into the decision to *go public*. On the contrary, it was taken reluctantly, once it became clear that following the strict rules of the LDA's processes was getting us nowhere. Having reached our resolution, I called Mark for his comments on an email I'd drafted to Blacker. 'Dear Gareth,' it began. 'If you continue to prevaricate and deliberately delay, we'll be going to the press to talk about your and the LDA's handling of our affairs…'

'Lance.'

'Yes.'

'Tipping them off is the last thing you should be doing.'

'Oh.'

'It means they can get their retaliation in first – phone up the editor, call in some favours, these things happen. Plus, we want them to be a little afraid of you. They won't be frightened if they know they'll get a tip-off before you do anything controversial. If they can't predict what you'll do next, let alone control it, well ... that's a good place to be. If they don't have time to prepare a response, you might get them to agree something in a panic.'

Mark was right. Ultimately these civil servants didn't care what the Olympics was costing. It wasn't their money. But seeing their competence and behaviour trashed in the media would be another matter entirely – something that, in the age of Google searches, could even affect future employability. That would hit a raw nerve. In a meeting at the LDA, on Friday 13 May 2005, Blacker entered the room with his colleagues as I waited for their arrival. As we sat down, he said: 'There are two schools of thought here at the LDA about how to deal with you, Mr Forman.'

'How strange,' I thought. 'You are a civil servant, and my taxes pay your wages. Surely there should only be one school of thought, and that is to deal with me fairly, not shafting me, as you've been doing so far.' This meeting was held in the aftermath of a good-news story about our campaign, and it had the desired positive effect – temporarily. The LDA promised to progress our case if we toned down the rhetoric. But for every one step forward, there were two steps back. A few weeks later, we had no choice but to go back to the journos.

The other reason for the media strategy was that, by this stage, I had researched every aspect of compulsory purchase law in such great detail, far more so than for my university thesis, and realised that even winning a CPO battle in the courts was a bad result, as the law itself was unfair. Far better to win in the court of public opinion, which could lead to the other side treating you fairly, rather than as the outdated law provides. And there was one further benefit. By this time, it was clear that either the Olympics would destroy us, or we would survive.

Not only could the media hopefully assist us in that survival, but if we did come through it all, our small family business' brand, H. Forman & Son, would be known far and wide.

For years, irrespective of the Olympics, Forman's has enjoyed a decent share of national media coverage. There are enough technical and commercial aspects to salmon smoking to make for a lively article that a lay reader with passing curiosity can enjoy – especially when coupled with a well-lit photograph of two dozen sides of cured fish hanging on a rack in a kiln. But, with Stephen's and the PR office's support throughout 2005, coverage went into hyper-drive. In fact, we were receiving so much publicity that one day I received an unexpected call from a Mr John Fisher from New York City, one of other cities bidding to host the 2012 Games. The coincidentally named Fisher had seen plenty of media coverage about our campaign and was leading an equivalent group of New York businesses facing potential eviction, or 'eminent domain' issues, as he called them. He congratulated me on our success and asked whether I could fly out to New York to share my experience and offer advice to the New York businesses under threat.

'Why would I do that, John?' I responded. 'I'd be delighted if New York won the bid!'

I too was a hero in Paris for a day, when TF1, the French equivalent of the BBC, filmed me suggesting that Paris had a far stronger bid on the grounds that, since the stadia already existed, it didn't threaten the existence of 12,000 jobs.

* * *

I didn't have time, despite numerous offers, to undertake formal media training. But I was a quick student. I soon realised the need to stay on-message, focusing on a maximum of three key points. In a typical interview, I'd start by referencing our 100-year heritage – it positioned us as a long-term investor and employer; not a fly-by-night operator. Next, I'd namecheck a couple of the other businesses in the area (as they would me) – stressing that my situation wasn't exceptional, and the same story of uncertainty and fear was being played out in hundreds of other factories across the Lower Lea Valley. Finally, I'd mention how reasonable our expectations were; our priority wasn't to derail the Games, but to protect our livelihoods. 'Is the Olympics about destroying 100-year-old businesses? Should the greatest concentration of manufacturing land in London be destroyed for two and a half weeks of sport?' were phrases I repeated until even I was bored of them.

In the month leading up to the IOC vote, the Marshgate Lane saga featured in almost all the mainstream press, and – given the pressure on the fourth estate not to jeopardise London's bid chances – the coverage was generally balanced and fair. Martin Samuels of *The Times* wrote a number of trenchant pieces (not just the one with the Paula Radcliffe reference) that highlighted the impact of the uncertainty upon our trade. Even though no compulsory purchase notices would be issued until after Singapore, the demands on my time – as with all the other owner-managers – had grown more onerous. It had reached the point where the distractions were no longer a Byzantine nuisance, but were actually affecting our ability to win and service our clients.

The Independent was also impeccable in its reporting, taking the trouble to interview and photograph an eclectic range of those at risk – not just commercial operators, but a family of travellers, Europe's largest independent church, and an art deco theatre that since the 1820s had housed a circus, a nightclub, a cinema and a car auction house. Paul Curran and others at BBC TV London were also regular visitors to our factory, sniffing around for the latest update, although I suspect my parting gift of a packet of smoked salmon to the news presenters and journalists may have contributed to their continued interest. 'Enjoy it whilst you still can,' I would say as the thank-you gift changed hands.

In fact, during those times, there was only one press hatchet job that was genuinely malevolent. *The Observer*, misrepresenting me as a 'caviar trader', said their 'investigations' had 'revealed' I was once an advisor to Peter Lilley and a consultant at Price Waterhouse, as though either were things I'd tried to hide or should undermine my entitlement to fair treatment. By contrast, they reported as fact the LDA's 'firm assurance that no business would be financially worse off', as if making spurious and palpably unfounded claims put the matter to rest. I started to pen a demand for a retraction, but Mark advised me to resist the temptation. 'There's no point prolonging the story,' he counselled. 'Readers will just remember the substance of the argument; they won't recall who won on points.' Sound advice which was followed verbatim. Regrettably, after *The Observer*'s diatribe, I didn't even enjoy any spin-off benefits from being smeared as a 'caviar trader'; my reception staff recorded not a single enquiry about 'Forman's caviar' the day after it hit the stands. So much for any publicity being good publicity!

Playing out our battles through fax machine and the dead tree media was necessary, but not sufficient. We also needed face time with decision makers. I had received a number of polite 'declines' from 10 Downing Street, but one day remembered that Lord Levy, an acquaintance of my parents, regularly played tennis with the Prime Minister. Finally, I had an 'in'. Levy was kind enough to schedule a call and I found myself virtually counting down the minutes to a conversation which, I felt, might turn my life around. Then, when the moment arrived, it was over within seconds:

'There's nothing I can do,' said Lord Levy, as I explained about the imminent threat we faced. 'I can't be seen to be helping out friends.'

'In that case, let's now terminate any friendship! So *now* can you help us?' I thought, but stayed shtum out of respect for my parents.

I wrote to Tessa Jowell in May 2005, shortly before the Singapore vote, almost begging for a meeting. After all, as the Secretary of State for

Culture, Media and Sport, she had direct responsibility for our awful situation. I eventually received a response in October, months after London's victory, stating, 'It is not appropriate for the government to comment on specific cases' (although she was perfectly happy to refer to us on air as a group) and apologising for the delay. She certainly wouldn't have won any Olympic medals that required a burst of high speed.

We were rushing out letters in all directions, and wrote again to Tony Winterbottom asking him to deny claims I had heard made by government ministers about our situation. From Tessa Jowell we were described as a 'bunch of greedy businessmen down Marshgate Lane; nothing to get concerned about'. The Chief Whip went further, telling a colleague that 'all there is down there is a heap of derelict land' and, when pressed about the business' concerns, her response was 'you need to crack eggs to make omelettes'. Winterbottom offered no denial.

So much for Whitehall. I'd also been attempting for months to meet with Mayor Ken Livingstone, to whom the LDA reported, either in his offices in County Hall or during a tour of the site, but he was proving as slippery as the great-crested newts for which he's nurtured a lifelong passion (he's written about the hours he spent, as a child, 'mesmerised by the exquisite detail of the colours and patterns in the tail, crest and spotted belly'). Every attempt to schedule a meeting was rebuffed on the grounds of conflicting commitments and pressing matters requiring Mayoral consideration. In desperation, we realised that our best – indeed only – chance of a hearing would be to join the audience at the London Development Agency's annual general meeting, which had the added benefit of being a televised event. I arrived early with the principal protagonists of the Marshgate Lane Business Group and we claimed occupancy of seats within easy visibility of the main stage.

The phrase 'Dodgy Dossier' had just entered the lexicon as a result of Tony Blair's manipulation of intelligence reports about Saddam Hussein's chemical weapon stockpile in the run-up to the Iraq War.

So we borrowed the phrase to lampoon the government's case that the Olympics were integral to the regeneration of east London. We created a short leaflet entitled 'Marsh-Gate – London 2012 Olympic Scandal – A dodgy dossier sexed up by £30m Government Olympic spend', in which we seized upon Tessa Jowell's description (as reported in Hansard) of a confidential report by consultants Arup, which had formed the basis for much of the bid plans, as being full of 'impenetrable, estimated, aggregated costs … of limited use for the purposes of accountability and none with regard to public debate'. Yet, with impenetrable dossier to hand, she decided to recommend that London throws its hat into the ring, or 'rings' in this case.

Our leaflet included a section entitled 'The Facts', in which we itemised sixteen occasions where the Games' advocates had played fast and loose with the truth in an effort to win over the IOC.

I was especially proud of the hard-hitting parallels, which, unable to sleep, I drafted two days before the meeting:

> This is a major scandal, reminiscent of Iraq. A dodgy dossier with facts being hidden from the public. On the back of this, the London government has spent £30 million of taxpayers' money sexing it up in efforts to persuade Londoners to back the bid. In this case, we have found the weapon of mass destruction – CPOs or compulsory purchase orders, which will destroy 11,000 jobs and 300 businesses on the proposed Olympic Park. This is the real threat that hangs over east London.

It continued:

> The Chair of the London 2012 Forum, an organisation which promotes London's bid to the public, Richard Sumray, said at a London Government Assembly meeting of the Arup Report

> – which to this day, has never been released to the public – it is a 'warts and all report' – 'The danger of making it public is that it could be used by competitive cities to rubbish London and I think that it is a very good reason not to have it public.' The British taxpayer and London rate payer need to know, warts and all, what the problems are before they can give support to the bid. This is not an issue of national security for the country. It is a sports competition.

Surely, if other cities could rubbish our bid because of our own independent findings, British taxpayers ought to know what they are letting themselves in for too and not have these findings buried.

We left copies of our leaflet on every chair in the auditorium, and watched with grim satisfaction as most of the audience devoured our polemic exposé whilst they waited for proceedings to commence. As soon as the meeting reached the Q&A slot, my hand shot up faster and further than any other.

'Mayor Livingstone,' I said, standing for added impact. 'Let me tell you about Forman's. We are a fourth-generation family business based in Stratford. We have survived fire and flood. Yet we now face a far more dangerous threat to our continued existence. And it doesn't come from an act of God. It comes from the decision of London to bid for the 2012…'

'Oh, it's the fish man,' interrupted Livingstone. 'Get to the point. This sounds to me more like a speech than a question.'

I was fuming with indignation, but kept my cool. I've been to plenty of events where the politicians at the podium are heckled by the public, but I'd never seen the heckling take place vice versa. I looked him directly in the eyes, and said: 'A hundred years of trading on the verge of extinction. And you're trying to limit me to ten seconds. That's low, even by your standards.' Livingstone was temporarily deflated. The Chairman allowed me a little more time to develop my points, but then Livingstone swatted them away with bland, and wholly false, generalities:

'The LDA is empowered to reach fair settlements with affected businesses. You will be dealt with fairly.' And that was that.

Or, at least, that was that until the *next* AGM, twelve months thereafter, when we sought to repeat the campaign, whilst ramping up the sizzle.

Once the meeting was called to order, it was quickly clear that this time the LDA was better prepared to resist our ambush. Crucially, they had taken the decision to bar the TV cameras from the venue, depriving us of the oxygen of publicity beyond the immediate confines of the meeting hall. And a professional moderator had been engaged, a BBC presenter no less, who called upon the owner of every raised arm but mine to put their question to the Mayor. She had clearly been briefed to avoid eye contact with the 'fish man', which became increasingly embarrassing when she ran out of other questioners before the end of the allotted time. When my arm was the only one left, she announced: 'Ladies and gentlemen, we shall now move on to the next item on the agenda.'

It was obvious to the hundreds of others in the audience that I was being ignored, so I leapt to my feet and blurted out, 'Madam Chairman, your programme, which I have here, states that the Q&A part of this meeting is not scheduled to end until half-past, and the time is only twenty-past. Therefore I hope you don't mind if I ask my question.' She looked across to Livingstone, seated behind her on the stage alongside other officials and had little option but to give way.

'Twelve months later, no progress whatsoever. How can that be justified?'

Livingstone repeated, almost verbatim, the words he'd used one year beforehand: 'The LDA will reach fair settlements. You will all be dealt with fairly.'

'But…' I began.

'I'm sorry, sir, that's all for today,' said the Chair, cutting off the power to the roving microphone. Now I understood how opposition politicians must feel when they are finally called upon to put a question to the Prime Minister during PMQs and are batted aside with vapid, pre-packaged platitudes.

Outside the AGM, concrete-crusher Seamus and I were proving to be quite the tag team. Think of an episode of *The Bill* where the 'good-cop/bad-cop' routine works to exhilarating effect, and that's how we were operating. I would turn on my urbane, university-educated charm. Then I'd hand over to Seamus, who, although I've never seen him hurt a proverbial fly, exuded an air of menace worthy of either of the Kray twins. In fact, that made the Krays seem like Princess Anne. He was a towering man, who would lean towards you as if the concept of 'personal space' had never been invented, and who struggled to complete a sentence without a rash of expletives, usually piled atop one another like pheasants after a shoot.

As decision day approached, I had abandoned hope of ever being face-to-face with Culture Secretary Tessa Jowell, but Seamus was not so easily deterred. He had obtained a copy of the schedule for her constituency surgeries, and spent a wet and windy Friday afternoon loafing around outside the building until her final consultation was complete and she was legging it to a waiting car. At which point, Seamus pounced and unleashed a torrent of nouns and adjectives the likes of which do not, I suspect, feature prominently in the typical Red Box briefs prepared by her civil servants. Jowell, caught off guard, promised that someone from her office would call him the next day. When he told me that story, I snorted dismissively, 'They fobbed you off.' Yet Seamus's tactics paid dividends. The call came through, as promised. On the next day, as promised. At four minutes past nine. Not just a promise kept, but a promise smashed.

Meanwhile, Livingstone had become more fastidious about his

public appearances, lest he find himself being held to account by the Stratford business community. We were invited by ITV to be part of a live TV 'Mayor's Question Time' audience, chaired by straight-talking LBC presenter Nick Ferrari, with a pre-arranged question, but when Livingstone noticed we were amongst the audience, only five minutes before the show was ready to broadcast, he threatened to bail on the event unless we were side-lined. ITV had no option – Mayor's Question Time without the Mayor might be a little lame, and so once again we were sacrificed on the altar of free speech. Instead of calling on us to pose our question, Ferrari asked a watered-down version on our behalf. The Mayor exuded bonhomie as he glossed over the seriousness of the matter. I was irritated by the way he smirked as he waffled, as if the question had been to name his favourite brand of cheesecake. As he left the studio and the audience exited their seats, he looked over, muttering 'fish man' under his breath.

More than once, I was staggered at the level of ignorance amongst senior public body personnel about the processes and activities for which they were notionally responsible. Tony Winterbottom, Blacker's boss at the LDA, agreed to meet with the Marshgate Lane Business Group early on. That willingness was much to his credit, but little else was. Thirty of us assembled in Sortex's boardroom to hear his remarks, and for the first ten minutes listened respectfully to his enunciation of the LDA's position. But then, in a glib aside, he commented to the MD of Sortex: 'That man who is sitting on eight acres doesn't realise that Christmas has come. A housebuilder will pay good money for that. Once EDAW's (the Olympic master planners) plan opens the area up for housing, people will be throwing money at him.'

At which point, pandemonium erupted. Not only was his condescension unbearable – how dare he suggest the LDA was doing us all a favour by uprooting businesses we'd spent years building? – but he was displaying a complete lack of knowledge about the rules surrounding compulsory purchase, let alone the gulf between the budget allocated for land acquisition and the combined valuation of the area within the Olympic Park boundaries. Comparing the situation we faced with the season of yuletide gifts could only have occurred to somebody who enjoys secure employment and a gold-plated pension. Somebody who had never had to fret about meeting a payroll or retaining customers who may defect at any moment.

It is worth paying tribute to a few brave souls who offered fulsome, and often public, support during our darkest hours. Researchers had found that most of the population was warming to the prospects of hosting the Olympics, so anyone who had the temerity to raise a cautionary flag risked being painted as 'anti-UK' or 'anti-sports'. Damian Hockney, UKIP member of the GLA, took to our cause like a ferret and refused to let go. He quizzed Livingstone in a public forum about the Marshgate Lane CPO process, interrogating him about everything from the methodologies used to calculate land values to the LDA's lackadaisical manner. He even once took Livingstone to task when the latter had implied my motivations might be political not commercial.

Livingstone said: 'I have a four-page brief on the personal dealings of Lance Forman and the offers he was made and the assistance he was offered. I think he has played his hand very badly. He got diverted into a political campaign.'

Hockney: 'I cannot accept it is a political campaign.'

Livingstone: 'It is the case that we said to the firms that we will pay your costs, some of them then started lobbying the IOC not to award the Games to London. I think that was a mistake and some people with their own political agenda I think wasted a lot of time and effort.'

Hockney: 'What do you mean by "politically motivated"? What party does he belong to? Does he belong to a party?'

Livingstone: 'As a political advisor to a former Tory Cabinet minister and Chair of the Conservative Friends of Israel … Basically, Lance

Forman primarily led a political campaign, that is not party political, to oppose London winning the Games.'

Hockney: 'To keep his business!'

This was a bizarre outburst by Livingstone, and why would he bring Israel into it? I am not and have never been Chair of Conservative Friends of Israel, although I do sit on its board. Was this a signal to his chums that the Jews were out to get him, once again, following claims of anti-Semitism on his part? Months later, he attacked the successful Reuben brothers of Indian Jewish descent as obstacles to progress in developing the Olympic site. He said, 'If they're not happy they can always go back and see if they can do better under the ayatollahs.' He was asked to clarify his meaning. Back where? 'To Iran,' he said, 'if they don't like the planning regime or my approach.'

This racist faux pas was picked up by the Deputy Chair of the GLA, Brian Coleman, at the Mayor's Question Time.

COLEMAN: 'Do you regret the remarks yesterday morning that the Reuben brothers should go back to Iran and do business with the ayatollahs?'

LIVINGSTONE: 'I want to make it absolutely clear I do offer a complete apology to the people of Iran for any suggestion that they be linked in any way to the Reuben brothers. It was not meant to be offensive to the people of Iran.'

COLEMAN: 'Can you not see how it could be perceived to be offensive to the Jewish community? You knew the Reubens were members of the Jewish community, did you not?'

LIVINGSTONE: 'Only by a malignant and distorted mind perhaps worthy of a Goebbels award.'

COLEMAN: 'Did you know the Reuben brothers were Jewish?'

LIVINGSTONE: 'Of course not. I do not wander round asking people's religions.'

COLEMAN: 'It never occurred to you that they were Jewish? You thought they were Iranians?'

LIVINGSTONE: 'Someone had obviously said to me they were from Iran. If you had asked me, I most probably would have said that was most probably likely to make them Shia Muslims. As I do not have a religion myself, it is not at the forefront of my thought about what someone's religion is when I am dealing with them.'

COLEMAN: 'You are either very naive or very ignorant. Which is it?'

LIVINGSTONE: 'How am I to be certain about someone's religion? How do you know they are Jewish?'

COLEMAN: 'Simon and David Reuben? You live in Cricklewood in north-west London, Mr Mayor. You have many Jewish neighbours.'

LIVINGSTONE: 'Are you telling me that only Jews are allowed to be called Reuben? What a ridiculous presumption. I am sure there are many Reubens in the world who are not Jewish.'

COLEMAN: 'In other words, you are gratuitously rude and insulting without finding out your facts first.'

LIVINGSTONE: 'No, I was being absolutely clear that I think these two people have been bad news for London, as they were bad news for Russia. They are now threatening the orderly progress of the Olympics and I was going to be critical of them. I do not care where they come from, what their religion is, or what their names are. If they are threatening the progress of the Olympics and threatening the taxpayer with another potential bill of £700 million, I am going to be critical.'

COLEMAN: 'Even to the extent of anti-Semitism?'

LIVINGSTONE: 'How is it anti-Semitic to be critical of sharp business practice?'

COLEMAN: 'Sorry, if you are rude and offensive about Jews, if you condemn the state of Israel, and if you have the track record that you have, what are Londoners to draw in conclusion?'

LIVINGSTONE: 'No one discussed Judaism yesterday; no one discussed

Israel. We were discussing the Olympics. Only you seem to have some secret list of everybody's religion where you can pontificate about what people's religions are. I do not.'

COLEMAN: 'Perhaps I have more understanding of the Jewish community than you do.'

LIVINGSTONE: 'No, you try to milk it for every vote you can get out of it. You have been prepared to dance on the memory of the Holocaust to get votes out of it, frankly.'

COLEMAN: 'That is just outrageous. That is disgraceful.'

Whether or not he'd done his homework on Reuben, Livingstone was certainly fully aware of my background from our encounter a few months earlier. He knew I was Jewish, and made a point of twisting this information into his argument however irrelevant it might be to the matters under discussion. It jarred at the time; even more so when, during the writing of this book, he was forcibly suspended from the Labour Party for remarks made with an allegedly anti-Semitic hue.

Broadcaster Jon Gaunt was also intrepid in his drive to skewer anyone in a position of power who sought to dissemble and hide the truth behind bluff and bluster. There was a wonderful moment when he exposed the lies of the Olympic Bid Team on live radio. He was interviewing Mike Lee, London 2012's Director of Communications and Public Affairs, and asked him whether his organisation had ever written to the International Olympics Committee to give supposed 'explanation' about the situation with the affected businesses. Lee refuted the charge without hesitation. 'Are you sure about that?' Gaunt checked. Because, unbeknownst to Lee, we had been inadvertently on copy to a fax from the IOC to the London 2012 bid team in which they thanked them for the very correspondence whose existence was now being denied. A document that had been personally signed by Lee when he asked for it to be forwarded internally to two colleagues.

But, even after this humiliating exposure, London 2012 persisted with its uncompromising refusal to release copies of any proprietorial documents about the affected businesses. Despite being the subject of the note exposed by Gaunt, our request to view a copy had been refused on the outrageous grounds that the Freedom of Information Act didn't extend to so-called private companies. So whilst London 2012 benefited from all the advantages of governmental power and state funding, when it was under threat, it resorted to being just a private company in need of protection and secrecy. Its every word could have been designed to misrepresent our position or mislead the IOC, or could simply have been wrong, because it was written before any of the Olympic protagonists had deigned to meet with the businesses to understand their concerns, so we had no chance to correct points of detail or provide a differing perspective. London 2012 Commercial Director Charles Wijeratna told us bluntly, 'It is not our intention to make public our documentation and correspondence (about land acquisition) as it is private and confidential.' The IOC also refused to share the correspondence regarding what was written about us. So much for transparency and fair play. And when the meeting happened between the Marshgate Lane businesses and the IOC, London 2012 insisted on participating – refusing us the privacy from which they themselves benefited. After our early successes, it felt as if we were now trapped in a nightmarish Kafkaesque world, with bureaucrats closing ranks to deny us legitimate information that might support our cause.

I'll never forget the support from Hockney and Gaunt, and others who heroically stood shoulder-to-shoulder with us during our plight. Steve Norris, who had run against Livingstone for Mayor in 2004, used characteristically earthy and colourful invective about our treatment when he addressed a meeting of the Marshgate Lane Business Group. The eternally gutsy Edwina Currie and I exchanged a number of hysterical emails, after I had seen her as a panellist on Dimbleby's *Question Time*, located in east London, fully supportive of the bid, and with no knowledge of the sacrifices that would have to be made. After a brief education from our side, she reciprocated offering practical words of advice – including the suggestion to 'turn up at 10 Downing Street with a load of rotting salmon!' – and regretted she no longer had the power to do more.

The support from these gallant souls was hugely appreciated. But I was conscious that the mid-2000s were the high watermark of Labour power. Those who sympathised with our predicament lacked any authority to order or even influence the LDA to act with a proper duty of care. In fact, even those with influence and sympathy were sometimes unable to assist for other reasons – such as Newham Mayor Sir Robin Wales. There has been a decade of mutual respect between myself and Sir Robin; he is my 'favourite socialist', and I think I am reasonably high on his list of 'favourite capitalists'. But when I sought his support, he recused himself from taking sides during the land acquisition discussions due to his 'being conflicted' (he was also responsible for promoting the general economic development of the borough). Wherever I turned, bright avenues turned into cul-de-sacs. By the summer of 2005, I thought I'd experienced the full gamut of emotions known to man.

By June 2005, we were accustomed to being insulted, ignored and patronised. But nothing prepared me for my treatment at the hands of Mike Lee in the lobbies of the London Assembly, even after the bid had been won and we were chasing decisions and solutions.

The Marshgate Lane Business Group would continuously inspect the agenda of the monthly Mayoral Question Time at the GLA and if Olympics discussions were to take place, we would make the journey to the South Bank to the public gallery to listen to proceedings. On this particular occasion, the only effective intervention during the entire morning was made by Seamus, who shouted from a sedentary position 'They're worse than Mugabe' when Livingstone mentioned in passing the work of the LDA.

At the end of the session, we headed to the lobbies to discuss whether anything new had been gleaned from proceedings. I spotted Mike Lee across the room and decided this was the perfect opportunity for an impromptu meeting.

With Mike Finlay by my side, I made the opening move, with courtesy and grace. I congratulated Mike on winning the Olympic bid for London, and he responded to Mike Finlay, rather than me, saying that now London had won he had no further responsibilities.

'Mike,' I continued, 'given the fact that the Olympics will be taking place on our land, don't you feel any responsibility to ensure the businesses are fairly treated by the LDA?'

He was in my face so fast.

'You want our help?' he said, raising his voice.

'Isn't that what you're here for?' I stuttered.

'You really want our help, do you?'

'Is that a problem?'

At which point, he jabbed two fingers against my chest and bellowed, 'You wrote to the IOC! Why should we help you? You wrote to the IOC! Why should we help you?' Every time he mentioned the IOC, he thumped me again.

Mike Finlay worked his way in-between the two of us so that he could prise us apart, but Lee's fury would not easily subside. The blood vessels on his neck were bulging and his cheeks had turned puce with rage. 'Let's calm down, shall we?' said Mike, as if addressing a toddler in the midst of a sugar-induced temper tantrum. 'We don't want anyone getting hurt, do we?'

'Too late for that,' I thought, rubbing my chest to alleviate the soreness from Lee's finger-jabbing and wondering how on earth I'd explain to René the presence of a juicy purple bruise a couple of inches from my heart. Why was he being so vindictive even after London had won the bid? It did not bode at all well for our future.

At the end of that year, Mike Lee was honoured by the Queen with an OBE for his services to sport – it wasn't boxing. He later went on to assist Qatar win the bid to host the World Cup. He was, of course, not the only one to receive a gong for his masterful Olympic endeavours. Richard Sumray, the wart-spotter, received an MBE, Coe and Jowell were elevated to the Lords, Keith Mills and Paul Deighton, both Chairman and CEO of the London Organising Committee of the Olympic Games, received their knighthoods, too. Celebrations all round, your Majesty.

Except in Marshgate Lane.

CHAPTER 11

FORLORN

The week-long 117th International Olympic Committee session took place at the Raffles City Convention Centre in Singapore, during which board members considered a number of arcane matters such as a request from the Chinese authorities for the 2008 equestrian events to be held in Hong Kong. But, of course, there was only one decision for which the world held its collective breath: the award, on the fourth day of the session, of the 2012 Olympic Games to its host city.

Five venues had made it through to the final selection: London, Madrid, Moscow, New York and Paris, and from 3–6 July, the most popular people on the planet were undecided IOC board members, who were barely able to visit the hotel bar without being accosted by hordes of politicians and celebrities representing the various bidders. Tony Blair, who just two months beforehand had seduced the British electorate for a third and final time, was joined by Princess Anne and David Beckham, to cajole, twist arms and call in favours. Although since exposed as a wily charlatan, Blair then still possessed a personal magnetism and silk tongue that could enthral the most cynical of souls. He certainly oozed more charm than French President Jacques Chirac, who – just before voting began – casually derided the London bid on the grounds of Britain's culinary shortcomings. He would no doubt have got away with this undiplomatic aside, but for the fact that he phrased his comments as follows: 'The only worse food than British food is Finnish.' Unfortunately for Paris (and also for the Marshgate Lane Business Group), two of the IOC voters represented Finland. If the flap of a butterfly's wings in Chile can cause a tornado in Texas, how much more damaging was Chirac's five-second utterance to the prospects of the Paris bid?

And, in the 2005 IOC session, small margins – such as the choice of the delegation from Finland – would make all the difference. Four of the five bidding cities had received glowing reports from the technical inspection teams – the exception being Moscow, although the New York campaign had also received a late setback when, with one month remaining, the state of New York declared it would not be funding the bid's centrepiece West Side Stadium. Any IOC members who had previously expressed warm words towards New York were now being hounded by Blair and co. to switch allegiance forthwith.

When the day of the vote arrived, I sat with the owners of many other local businesses to watch the unfolding drama on the big screen in Mike Finlay's boardroom (he provided the venue, I laid on the catering). The wait was interminable. The leaders of each bid team delivered a one-hour presentation, in which they boasted of their vision, their passion and their commitment to deliver the greatest Games in Olympics history. The talks were interspersed with money-no-object videos in which the bid proposals were brought to life in stunningly rendered graphics, complete with CGI athletes breaking records and CGI spectators awe-struck at the wonder. My stomach turned as I watched the London slot. The word 'legacy' was sprinkled like stardust in almost every sentence, but references to the 'fair treatment of local businesses' came there none. Did Coe's scriptwriters really believe all the hogwash about 'legacy'? If they did, they were fools. If not, they were liars. I wasn't sure which was worse. The only legacy I envisaged was a devastated community, a crowding-out of the urban regeneration that was already underway, and – years after the Games had completed – parkland with a stadium that would probably be used for nothing other than premier league football. As if the world of football was so starved of cash that a pressing social policy priority should be providing it with yet another stadium.

After both Paris and London had presented, I turned to Mike. 'Paris made a huge error in their pitch.'

'I thought it was quite good,' he said. 'Especially showing the facilities already exist. It will cost them less. The IOC has come in for a lot of stick in recent years for bankrupting cities. It'll be close but Paris will clinch it.'

'No way,' I said. 'The people deciding are all ex-sportsmen. They're not politicians. Do you really think they give a toss about bankrupting their host city? They just want to have a great Games and a good time. Why would they want to spend a few weeks in buildings that have been around since the sixties when they can have two weeks of luxury in brand spanking-new facilities? New arenas, new hotels, new beds, new toilets, shopping in Bond Street. It's a no-brainer.'

'Maybe you're right, Lance. We'll be put out of our misery soon.'

When the time for voting finally arrived, it lasted nearly an hour and a half. There were four rounds; after each vote, the city with the lowest total was eliminated, and IOC members were asked to reconsider their preferences for the subsequent round. As anticipated, Moscow was the first to drop out, with just fifteen votes from the ninety-seven available. Almost every Moscow supporter then switched to Spain, which emerged as the surprise leader in the second round – Mike and I were fist-pumping the air as the news came through. However, Spain was unable to maintain its momentum, and, by the fourth round of voting, only

London and Paris were still standing. Widely rumoured as the strongest contenders, it was now a bare-knuckle, winner-takes-all contest between Europe's two world-class cities. For an eternity, or so it seemed, the screen was filled with news and sports presenters and former Olympians speculating and hypothesising about the eventual outcome. Occasionally, the broadcasts would cut away to show the crowds gathered in Trafalgar Square and on the Champs-Élysées, where giant screens had been erected to relay the decisive moment. Five minutes before the vote, one station was running an interview with two teenagers from Harrogate who were so overcome with emotion that tears were rolling down their cheeks. 'Whatever happens today,' I said to Mike, 'let's try not to cry.'

The Marshgate Lane Business Group spent the prior day with Shimon Cohen, David Russell's boss at the PR office, drafting two press releases, a winner and a loser option. Whilst discussing these, Shimon made the point that 'it's not the Games coming to London that we object to, we have been consistent in that. We object to the high-handed and bad treatment we received. I am convinced that in typical perverse UK media fashion, if London wins, we will be able to get even more media attention than we have already achieved.' He added, perhaps for comfort, 'Seb's honeymoon won't last – remember PY Gerbeau?'

Mark Stephens agreed. 'My concern is the persistence of the suggestion that a few rapacious businesses are screwing the bid. Nothing could be further from the truth. The LDA's position has moved from land swaps to sales of land merely because they will make a profit. It is they who are profiteering out of the Games.'

In the end a decision was made, not to issue releases, but simply to speak directly with the media, and we agreed that the BBC could send a crew to Mike's offices and film our reaction in real time as the result was announced. This was an additional reason not to blub at the news – my street cred would never recover if I broke down on live television like a jilted sixth-former after a bad date. The showrunners had already arranged for a number of us to be interviewed about our expectations ('What are you feeling right now?' was the question du jour), but their main task was to secure a great money shot – at the moment the winner was announced. Our reaction – despair, elation, violence, cursing or dance-moves – would be immortalised for the generations.

It was around midday when IOC President Jacques Rogge took to the stage to declare the result of the final round. A billion people around the globe were tuned in, but few with a greater sense of trepidation than the forty assembled in Mike's boardroom with seats laid out theatre-style, Mike and I sitting together in the front row, eyes fixed to the large screen he had hired. Rogge was handed the envelope by a Singaporean sailor. He extracted the card, gazed around the auditorium to eke out every last moment of dramatic tension, and then voiced the words I'd been dreading for nearly two years:

'The Games of the 30th Olympiad in 2012 ... are awarded to the city of ... Lond ... on.'

In those fleeting seconds, the next few years of my life were defined. Visiting salmon producers, exploring international markets, spending days with chefs and hoteliers, building up Forman & Field, expanding the supermarket channel – any and all growth initiatives would perforce be consigned to suspended animation, like a cryogenically frozen body, until normal service could be resumed. My every waking hour would be devoted to handling the fallout from Rogge's words. I placed my head in my hands, oblivious to all around me as I contemplated the future. That image, my hands covering my face as it shook from side to side, was chosen by the news editors to symbolise the mood in the Lea Valley. There was, I'm told by friends glued to the coverage, a moment where the screen was split. On the right-hand side, Lance Forman of H. Forman & Son in the slough of despair; on the left, the euphoric crowds in central London, chanting, shrieking and jumping into the Trafalgar Square fountain with joy. As Mike said later, it was hard enough trying to make sense of the catastrophe that had just befallen us; knowing that 90 per cent of our fellow countrymen were bubbling with glee made it even tougher.

The news was still sinking in when a BBC journalist thrust a microphone in my direction. 'Mr Forman, your reaction please?'

In my heart I wanted to ask, 'Why can't you leave me alone?', but that would have been disingenuous; after all, it had been our choice to invite them. Plus, we still had a media war to win.

I knew, and had confirmed with Mark Stephens, that nothing would be gained if I came across as a killjoy, consumed by bitterness and muttering nasty thoughts in the corner like Scrooge on Christmas Day. 'No one loves a curmudgeon,' he said.

So I struck a positive, but still defiant, tone. 'This is wonderful news for the country,' I said. 'Congratulations to the bid team and best wishes for a hugely successful Games. For the businesses of the Lea Valley, it is a bittersweet moment. We know we'll need to move, and we simply ask to be treated fairly and respectfully. Thank you.'

Since the turn of the year, my willingness to engage with the media had established me as a kind of torch-bearer (though not an Olympic torch) for the displaced businesses, and for the next few hours my phone barely stopped ringing. Every news channel and print journalist wanted a sound bite they could broadcast. By late afternoon, I was fed up with the word *bittersweet.* It became my mantra, like Gordon Brown's 'no more boom and bust' (in 2005, Brown's vainglorious grandstanding had not yet unravelled). And in between every interview I'd check my phone and read another dozen messages left by friends and relatives. I spoke briefly with my father, who understandably asked a series of questions about how I'd now save the firm that bore the family name; I was unable to give a cogent answer to any of them.

René called to say she had every confidence I'd pull through. 'You'll work it out,' she insisted.

ABOVE LEFT Harry Forman, founder of H. Forman & Son, with wife Passy.

ABOVE RIGHT Louis Forman (the 'Son') in the Homburg hat, with the largest salmon caught in the twentieth century, in 1935.

LEFT Marcel Forman (*far right*), my father, taken in our Ridley Road smokehouse in the 1960s.

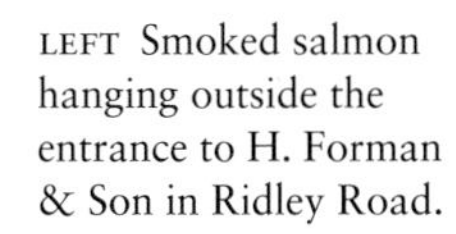

LEFT Smoked salmon hanging outside the entrance to H. Forman & Son in Ridley Road.

H. FORMAN & SON
SALMON CURERS
CLISSOLD 2010 - 5978
OFFICES

TOP LEFT H. Forman & Son in Queen's Yard, Hackney Wick in 1971.

TOP RIGHT Me speaking at the Cambridge Union in 1983 in my infamous yellow silk dinner jacket.

ABOVE Flying up the greasy pole at Cambridge University, becoming President of the Union in 1985.

LEFT Fire destroys Forman's smokehouse, October 1998.

Flood destroys Forman's smokehouse, October 2000. Rita Law stands outside with the salmon box barricade.

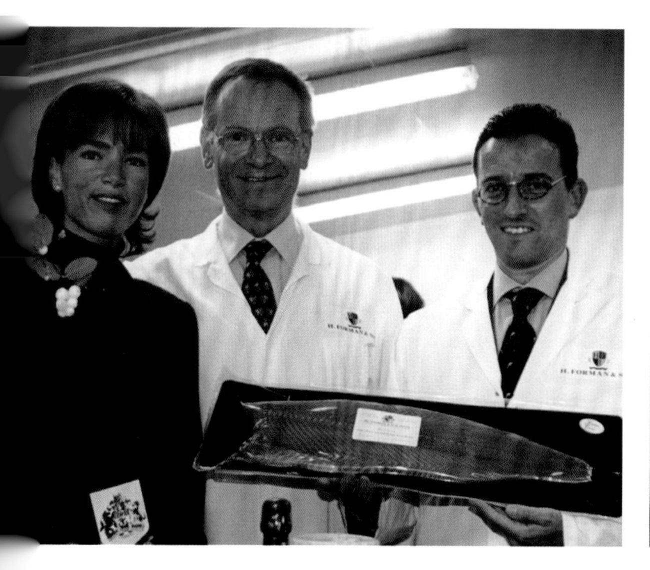

Jeffrey Archer with René Forman and me, officially opening our plant following the fire.

New branding for H. Forman & Son's smoked salmon in 1995.

Banner affixed to our Marshgate Lane smokehouse for the attention of the IOC inspection team. © Alamy

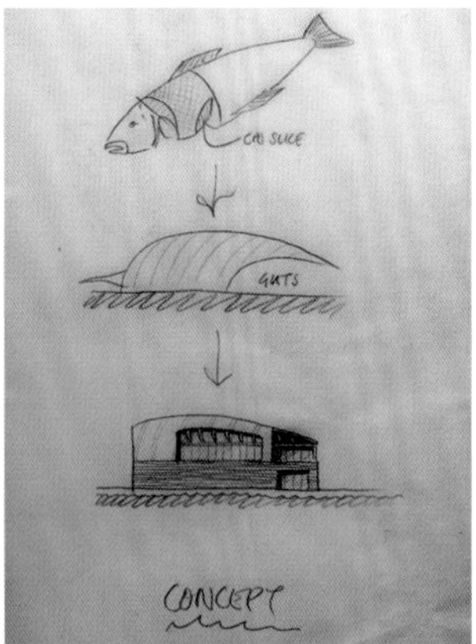

ABOVE LEFT Our Marshgate Lane smokehouse stands alone, after all other factories had been demolished to make way for the Olympic Park.

ABOVE RIGHT Architect Phil Hudson's design concept for our new smokehouse in Fish Island.

LEFT Forman's smokehouse, venue and restaurant as it stands today.

A peek at our Airmaster kilns from Reich.

ABOVE LEFT Forman's from the air – only 100 metres from the Olympic Stadium.

ABOVE RIGHT Boris Johnson officially declares Forman's smokehouse 'even more open than it was before'.

LEFT Ken Livingstone enjoys a gourmet walnut whip as my guest at Forman's restaurant for a three-year Olympic countdown.

Phil Hudson's design concept for our hospitality site, which was rejected by the Olympic planners.

LEFT Olympic opening night at Forman's Fish Island Riviera.

Daley Thompson, who, along with other celebrities, came to visit Fish Island Riviera.

Rahman Ali (Muhammad's brother) and me on our roof terrace for the opening of our Ali exhibition. Note my gauntlet-style cuffs.

LEFT Internationally renowned photographer David Bailey allows me to take a photo of him with our mischievous 2012 calendar.

BELOW H. Forman & Son's Darren Matson is challenged by Gordon Ramsay to bone and slice a side of smoked salmon for the Guinness World Records.

BELOW LEFT René Forman on the evening of Oliver's bar mitzvah celebrations, April 2007.

BELOW RIGHT The fifth generation: (*l–r*) Matthew, Annabel and Oliver, summer 2003.

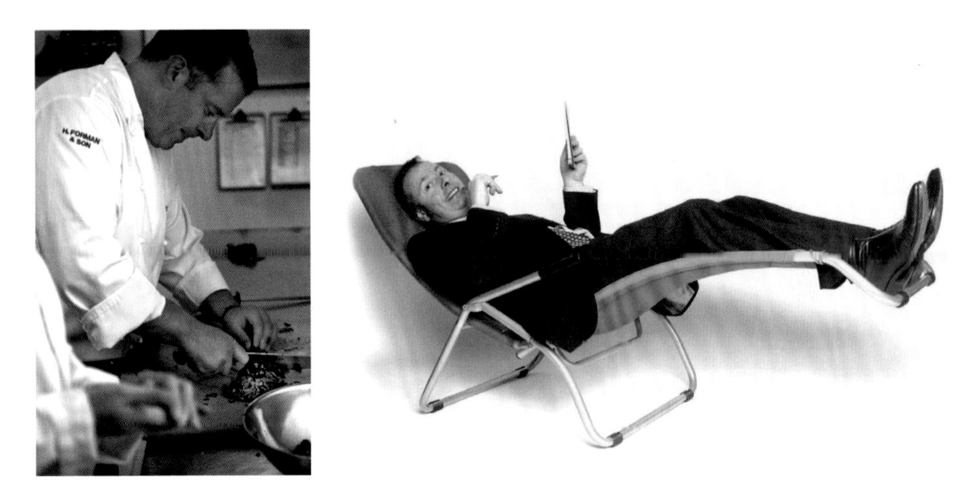

ABOVE LEFT Lloyd Hardwick, Executive Chef of Forman's, Director of Operations, my right-hand man and rock.

ABOVE RIGHT Hon. Arthur Somerset, managing our laid-back Forman's Fish Island hospitality operation.

The Forman's team, summer 2016. I salute you.

I felt emboldened by her support, but the effect was somewhat ruined when I arrived home later in the day to my two boys who ran up to give me a hug and greeted me with words I shall never forget: 'Daddy, will you still have a job tomorrow?'

One of my American relatives sent me an inspirational message first used by Pierre de Coubertin, the founder of modern Olympics: 'The important thing in life is not the triumph but the struggle; the essential thing is not to have conquered but to have fought well.'

I replied: 'That's a worthy principle for an athlete. But when you're battling the LDA, for your very survival, the *only* things that matter are triumph and conquering. There's nothing to gain from being a gallant loser.'

Kate Baumber, who runs a boutique food promotions agency, wrote to commiserate with our distress, and made a broader point about the fact the UK's 'food heritage was being (steadily) lost'. An acquaintance, the food writer Marlene Spieler, emailed to say simply: 'SOS – Save Our Salmon'. Darren Wightman, Executive Chef of Yo! Sushi, sent me a photograph of a flaccid piece of cod resting on a pile of greasy chips, with the hysterical strapline: 'We've got crap food, now we've got the Olympics.' And Jackie Lawson emailed me a photo of an elderly market trader in some backstreet Parisian market with stacks of Paris 2012 T-shirts and a large sign written on the back of some corrugated packaging which read 'half price!' It was accompanied by a personal message: 'I am not sure if you will find this funny. Love, Jackie.' I read and kept each one of those supportive messages; they brightened up an otherwise desolate day. Laughing or crying were the only two options available.

By mid-afternoon, when there was enough footage of shell-shocked and numb business owners to last a lifetime, the TV crews packed up their equipment and left us to grieve alone. For a time, we sat in silence. The big screen had long ago been killed – there were only so many times we could watch Trafalgar Square erupt in ecstasy without wanting to throw up. But it was an eerie silence; we had so much to discuss, but everyone was too emotionally exhausted to start the conversation. Eventually, Mike said blandly: 'Thanks for coming, everyone.'

'Don't take it personally, Mike,' said one of the other business owners. 'I'm sure the result would've been the same wherever we met.'

'I wasn't offering to take the blame,' said Mike, tracing his forefinger around the rim of his beer glass.

'What's next for the Marshgate Lane Business Group?' I pondered aloud.

Then I thought: 'Nine o'clock tomorrow. I'll be first on the phone to the LDA. Can't be any harm making sure I'm at the front of the queue.'

'Another beer?' said Mike, and we all nodded without enthusiasm. By the time I left, we had filled up three dustbin-liners with empties.

That evening, I wasn't in the mood for conversation, and couldn't bear another moment contemplating the Olympics' vampiric ways. I thought I had blanked out what happened that evening, but in researching this book I found out that I'd still been dealing with emails at around 10 p.m., including one from an old college friend, Laurence Smith.

> Great to see you and René and the children at the weekend. We all had a ball, and many thanks for making the journey out to Brimpton. Anyway, good luck over the next couple of years now the Olympic decision has been announced. I saw the article about Forman's in the Times yesterday, so at least the high-profile publicity is continuing. I guess the priority now is to ensure the government makes life as easy as possible for you and the other businesses affected. Hopefully now the decision is known, HMG's purse-strings will loosen a bit…! Looking forward to seeing you and René again soon…

On that friendly note, I must have checked in for the night with René, both mentally drained and in fear for our future.

My call to the LDA office the next morning, 7 July, didn't quite go as planned. Firstly, nobody was available at nine – unlike the Marshgate Lane business owners, I suspect they'd been indulging in lavish celebrations at the news from Singapore. I left a message with the receptionist, and promised I'd try again in half an hour.

For the rest of the morning, I wouldn't be able to concentrate on business. There were soon reports of explosions across the capital. In 2005, just four years had passed since the collapse of New York's Twin Towers at the hands of a coordinated terrorist attack, and London had long been considered next in line, on account of the UK's being the White House's most willing sidekick whenever it dived head-first into its latest Middle East conflagration.

Suddenly, my morning's resolution to re-engage with the LDA was overtaken by events. I was reminded that, however troubling my situation, it paled into insignificance against being the hapless victim of a terrorist attack – killed or maimed for no better reason than trying to travel to work during the peak commuter hour. Over the next few hours, the storm of rumour and counter-rumour gave way to some disconcerting truths. The UK had suffered its first ever Islamist suicide attack, and also the worst terrorist incident on British soil since the 1988 Lockerbie bombing. Fifty-two people had been killed as a series of bombs had detonated at locations across London's Underground and bus network, with hundreds more maimed or injured – many with life-changing severity. I quickly established that none of my workforce had been affected, which was a blessing, and reflected on the astonishing, roller-coaster twenty-four hours in the capital's history. One moment, asked by the IOC to host the planet's most high-profile sporting event; the next, in the terrorists' crosshairs. No wonder that my emotions that day were such a mess. With images of the atrocities seared into people's minds, tension remained palpable throughout the capital. It wasn't until the following week that Londoners were once again able to go about their business with a spirit approaching normalcy (even then, it took a brave soul to carry a backpack and run the gauntlet of worried glances from one's fellow travellers).

Soon after hearing of the attacks, I pinged a short email over to Blacker. 'Gareth, truly sorry about the tragic problems that we're all facing today in London. I trust your people are safe and secure. Perhaps we can speak tomorrow.'

We never did speak the following day, but I did confirm that the New North Road site was still available. However, the asking price had doubled to £8 million since the previous summer. If the LDA thought the price had previously been steep, they were unlikely to leap at the opportunity now.

It was months before my next substantive conversation with the LDA. Not expecting to win the bid, they were under-resourced to deal with success. Everything else would be placed in limbo whilst they were recruiting the recruiters who would recruit the team of agents who would handle the land programme.

So, whilst it was impossible to speak with the LDA, there remained plenty I could do. It was time for another round of letters and emails to anybody who might be able to offer solace or succour. Over the past two years, I'd perfected a letter-writing style of which I remain proud. A smidgen of defiance, a dash of outrage, a mite of flattery and a clear statement of my desired outcome – all mixed together like a witch's brew to create a result of potency and power. However, proud though I was of my riveting prose, the outcome was as dispiriting as ever. 'It's not my responsibility, sir', 'I'd like to help out, but…' or, 'Accept my very best wishes for the future, sir.' These were the much-repeated refrains. So, if judged by results rather than effort, my letters were still not up to scratch.

From Geoffrey Norris of No. 10: 'I hope you will understand, it is not appropriate for the government...'

From Peter Wright of the Olympic Games unit at the Department for Culture, Media and Sport: 'It is not appropriate for the government to comment...'

From Sir Robin Wales, Mayor of Newham: 'It would be inappropriate for me to interfere...'

Me (thinking): 'What's the point of having you all on the public payroll if everything is inappropriate? You might as well go and get productive jobs and at least save us small businesses from bearing the burden of your costs!'

As time passed without resolution, the situation grew more dire and the media coverage took on an increasingly sombre hue. A few months prior, Forman's had been fêted for its feisty and gutsy spirit, but now the focus was on our potential extinction. BBC One ran a feature on *Inside Out* that was headlined: 'Can London's oldest salmon smokers survive the Olympic Games?', in which the narrator intoned: 'The clock is ticking for the salmon smokers. If something isn't sorted out soon, the fire could really go out for ever in their kilns long before the Olympic flame arrives. A feeling that leaves a very bad taste in the mouths of the long-serving workforce.' The *Inside Out* piece was just one measure of the seriousness of our predicament, and my helplessness in turning things around. I felt like I was in charge of a truck that had just careened off the top of a cliff and was hurtling towards the rocks below, musing over the best options, before realising that the only conceivable strategy was: 'Don't get yourself into the situation in the first place.'

Lloyd had never before seen me feeling so powerless, and by now knew me well enough to speak openly about the future.

'There must be something I can do to help, Lance,' he said. 'You don't need to take the burden entirely on your own shoulders.'

'The best you can do is make sure we keep providing great product to our customers,' I said. 'The last thing we need, with the Olympics hanging over us, is to have any hiccoughs in our quality or service or for our customers to think we'll soon be out of business. They may start hunting around for other suppliers even before the nails are in the coffin, so let's not give them any reason to assume we won't sort this. We made it through fire and flood. The bastards aren't going to get us without a fight. Just keep the operation ship-shape, as you always do. Then I can focus on what I need to do.'

'You got it,' said Lloyd.

In the moments following the announcement, all my workforce were champions, their dedication and commitment as deserving of a gold medal as anything that would be taking place on the 100m track in 2012. I'd always had huge regard for Rita, but in those uncertain months she was a trouper's trouper. She had an almost telepathic ability to sense my stress levels, and – if I'd been having a rough day – would hang about long after she was supposed to clock off, always checking, double-checking and triple-checking I was okay. She always had the perfect phrase to lighten the mood and bolster my spirits. She became the emotional heart of the business. 'I'll chain myself to the fence,' she would say. 'Like the suffragettes.'

I couldn't get my head round how unlucky I had been; not one, not two, not three, but four disasters in the space of five years – in each situation a serious existential threat to our business. What had I done to deserve this? There are so many colourful adjectives I could employ to describe my state of mind during those seismic months – weird, out-of-body, psychedelic, erratic, surreal. But whichever one is chosen, just when I figured things couldn't get any more extreme, my life took on a whole new dimension of strangeness.

It all began in an innocuous fashion. Gavin Riding, whom I knew through the Lea Rivers Trust and the Fish Island Business Club, a networking group for businesses in the neighbouring area, and who was aware of my plight, said he felt it would be useful if I met an estate agent named Richard Fieldsend, who might be able to assist. We met briefly in my office, with not much more than a hello, some loose talk that Fieldsend may be able to help me, and a goodbye. Fieldsend left first whilst Riding hung around a few moments longer, assuring me that this chap could really help. 'What's in it for you?' I asked and he responded that if this introduction led to successful resolution of our problems, he would want 1 per cent of the spoils. Reasonable, I thought – even Balcombe usually went for more than that! A couple of days later, Fieldsend called me directly. He said that he was aware of the issues I was facing and suggested I should meet a gentleman with whom he was working on a number of deals and who, he believed, might have a solution to my problem. I was given no further details, not even a name, but, I figured, what harm could there be in a meeting? As the sinner said on his deathbed when asked to renounce Satan: 'But this is no time to be making enemies.' Quite frankly, I'd meet anybody, anywhere, if it held out even a remote prospect that my ordeal might come to an easy and early resolution. No date was arranged for the follow-up, but Fieldsend said it would be 'in the next few weeks'.

I heard nothing further for a week, and Fieldsend's phone call was fading from my mind. I was receiving calls and flyers in the post from estate agents on a daily basis offering to support my relocation – and attaching details of either unsuitable premises in fantastic locations, or wonderful new facilities in ridiculous locations (one tried to persuade me that Peterborough, sixty miles away, was my future). Then, unexpectedly, Fieldsend called me one Friday morning in my office to explain that his principal was in town and would like to meet if I was available. I invited them to meet at Forman's, but Fieldsend murmured something about this out-of-towner 'not wanting to be seen in the area' and asked if instead we could meet in the lobby of the Holiday Inn in Stratford High Street. He said they should be there around noon and he would call when they had arrived so I could make my way over. It was only a five-minute ride. My curiosity had been piqued. It all seemed a bit shady and hush-hush, meeting discreetly in hotel lobbies – but, what the hell? I thought. I had nothing to lose and so, like salmon being reeled in by an angler, I couldn't ignore the draw. The call came at 11.45 a.m. and by noon I was there.

I had left my car on a side street outside the Holiday Inn, and without even bothering to check about the parking restrictions, was walking through the hotel's automatic sliding doors. There at the entrance was Fieldsend, accompanied by two other men. We shook hands and introduced ourselves. One of the men went by the name Child or Childs and the other, an older man, had a very strange name which I didn't quite catch, especially with his brusque Scottish accent, but I registered it as 'Lafanee'. He was wearing a trilby and trench coat and his arm was held in a contraption, like a sling, that he later advised me was a blood-monitoring device. No business cards were exchanged.

We all headed over to a table in an alcove on the far side of the reception area and Fieldsend arranged for some coffee to be brought over. My mind was still whirring, and in addition to my failure to catch their names, I only vaguely caught the name of their company – Courtland, or Clevedon, or something like that. Our conversation lasted over an hour, and – except during the introductions and final remarks – Fieldsend and Childs barely said a word, their contributions limited to the occasional supportive nods. It was as if 'Lafanee' and I were the Presidents of the United States and the USSR during a 1970s peace summit, thrashing out weapons policies, and accompanied by courtiers who were terrified of opening their mouths in case a misspoken word inadvertently precipitated a nuclear holocaust.

For the first quarter of an hour or so, whilst Childs served the beverages, 'Lafanee' chose to discuss the current political scene, and it crossed my mind that perhaps this was a clandestine ploy by Conservative

Central Office to tease out any interest I might have in standing in the local elections. I wasn't in the mood for a deep political debate, so gave largely noncommittal responses about the state of the economy and foreign affairs. I was also wondering why someone who had taken the time to call me out of my office to discuss a solution to the rest of my life would be pressing his Conservative credentials rather than focusing on the issue at hand. I also found myself staring at the contraption around his chest which forced him to rest one arm on the table in front of me throughout our time together, thinking it looked like some kind of recording device. Then, like a motor car on a hairpin bend, the conversation switched direction, and in a voice so hushed that I leant forward to make out his words, 'Lafanee' said:

'Let me tell you a bit about myself. I'm very close to the military and have recently spent time in Bosnia, where I've been acting as an advisor for the Ministry of Defence. John Reid is a good friend of mine.'

Reid was, from 2005 to 2006, Secretary of State for Defence in Tony Blair's Cabinet. This was even stranger now. He'd just told me he was a Conservative, yet was also a friend of Reid. Where was this leading?

'And I own a smoked salmon factory,' I said.

'You don't need to tell me any more. I know all about your business. Now, you're probably wondering why we've made contact with you. Well, it won't surprise you to know that there's a serious problem with the planned siting of the Olympic Games in the area.'

'Tell me about it,' I said. 'That's what I've been saying for the last two years.'

'Then it also won't come as a surprise if I told you that the government has seriously under-budgeted for the land purchases. The numbers included in the bid were ludicrously broad-brush, and frankly invented to make it all look affordable. They bore no relationship to reality.'

I nodded but said nothing. I was keen for 'Lafanee' to reveal as many of his cards as possible before I committed myself through a comment.

'So, here's where I fit in,' he continued. 'My company already controls around sixty acres in Stratford, and we're buying more, either land that's inside the proposed Park boundaries, or that's within shooting distance. I'm taking a long-term view and acquiring as much as I can. If we're a major landowner, we'll have a helluva bargaining chip.'

'I'm not following. Won't a lot of it be subject to Compulsory Purchase?'

'I have an agreement with the government that I will gift them the use of my land for the Olympics, so they won't need to find the cash to buy it. In exchange, I will get the planning for residential when it's all over.'

My mind very quickly worked out that even with his sixty acres at industrial prices, which is what the LDA was offering at around £1 million per acre, this would be worth eight times that, in other words, almost half a billion pounds once the Games were over. Over £400 million profit for just a few years. Not a bad deal!

He paused for breath, but I was keen to encourage him to divulge more aspects of his thinking. 'It sounds risky,' I prompted.

'I can't tell you too much more, at this stage,' he said. 'This is only our first meeting, after all. And I'm keen to stay out of the limelight, so I'm trusting your discretion. But I can tell you that, because of my wider plans, I'm able to offer you significantly more than the LDA ever will.'

Fieldsend and Child nodded vigorously at the mention of 'significantly more'.

One of the hotel waiting staff was approaching our alcove, presumably to take an order for further refreshments. But 'Lafanee' and crew were building towards their great reveal, and, with a glare at the intruder, the waiter cowered back towards the bar.

'Mr Fieldsend here advises me that you occupy 0.6 acres on Marshgate Lane. Is that broadly correct?'

'Two-thirds of an acre,' I said.

Fieldsend then came forward with what he described as 'an exceptionally generous offer' for my site, which, at £2.5 million, was 25 per cent higher than what the LDA had been offering me. (He knew what I'd been offered even though I hadn't told him.)

My head was spinning. An hour ago, I'd been sitting in my office trying to figure out an exit strategy that made commercial sense. Now I was being offered cash on the table. How could I possibly form a judgement on the best course of action when matters were moving so quickly?

'It's very kind of you,' I said. 'But, to be honest, it's not money that I need. What I actually need is a new site. So it doesn't matter to me whether you offer £25, £25,000, £2.5 million, or even £25 million – what matters is that we find another site to move to nearby and when we build a similar factory we are not out of pocket. The value of my site now is irrelevant as far as I am concerned, kind of you though it is to make the offer.'

'Yes, we understand,' said Fieldsend. 'We are buying a lot of land in the area, some of which may turn out to be outside the boundaries of the Olympic Park, and so most probably will be able to help you find something.'

'Well, great, you know where to get hold of me.'

'Leave it to us. Don't worry, we will find something for you.'

We all rose from the table and as we shook hands, 'Lafanee' added, 'And, Mr Forman?'

'Yes?'

'I suggest we keep this discussion ... between ourselves. We'll contact you.'

'Sure.'

I left the hotel with the three of them still standing in the lobby.

My car did not have a parking ticket; small mercies. As I drove back to the office, I reflected on this strange meeting. The politics, the military, and the reasons behind their offer to assist me – chief troublemaker for the LDA. Was 'Lafanee' acting on his own initiative, removing the troublemaker from the landscape to curry favour with the LDA and make their land development strategy run more smoothly? Or was the LDA behind the entire operation, using a third party to sort me out with a preferential deal that would neither set a precedent nor be open to public or media scrutiny.

'Being bought off by the state!' I thought. 'That doesn't happen every day. Time for discretion – at least until I publish my memoirs...'

CHAPTER 12

FOREBODING

If life had worked out differently, I might have been an Ad Man, not the Fish Man.

I've always had a veiled fascination for the work of the 'Hidden Persuaders' – the term used by social critic Vance Packard when he blew the lid on how Madison Avenue influences the psychology of the general public in order to peddle its clients' wares. Research suggests that, in the Western world, the typical adult is exposed to more than 1,000 brands every day. Breaking through that wall of noise with a memorable message is no easy task, and full credit goes to anyone able to use words, visuals and storylines to make an impact in a thirty-second commercial or on a billboard poster. The giants of the advertising world – such as David Ogilvy, or Leo Burnett, or Charles Saatchi – all had the knack of making *their* message the one people would be discussing around the water cooler the following morning. Plus, in my case, it was always the ad agencies that delivered the most compelling graduate recruitment presentations – 'Join us', they beamed 'and you'll be mixing with Hollywood starlets and attending the hottest parties.' How I ended up in accountancy is, looking back, one of life's unanswered mysteries.

By comparison, my friend Nick Young couldn't resist the lure.

He was tempted by the promise of a lifetime's glamour and glitz, and by 2005 had spent two decades as one of the biggest beasts in adworld's creative zoo. FirstDirect and Egg were both clients that bore his company's imprint. Clients metaphorically queued to pay his far-from-paltry fees because they were confident it would deliver a huge revenue return – ten-fold or even a hundred-fold his costs. Often, when I catch up with Nick, I find myself wondering whether that's a world in which I'd have excelled – or from which I'd have been rapidly expelled.

Nick shunned partisan politics – the nature of his trade meant it was expedient to have a foot in all camps, and he often suggested that some of my current travails stemmed from the fact that, in the Labour election landslide in May 1997, a large chunk of my contacts database had become irrelevant overnight. He had offered to help me with access into Labour circles, on the understanding that I avoid any monologues about the evils of the European Union or the virtue of laissez-faire economics. As a result, just a few hours after my Holiday Inn encounter, Nick and I were in the boardroom of lobbyists Four Gritti (now rebranded as Four Communications), being fêted by one of their founding Directors, Jeremy Fraser. The offices overlooked Leicester Square, where a red carpet was being rolled out in preparation for the arrival of various celebrity guests for the evening's movie premiere. 'My life is starting to resemble a bad film script,' I remarked to Nick.

'Horror, comedy or farce?' he replied.

I wasn't quite sure what to expect from the meeting, but I was expecting Fraser to pitch that an active media programme could cajole the authorities to treat Forman's fairly and, most urgently, help us find a site. The LDA had borne the brunt of my media onslaught until now; maybe it was the time for sweet-talking. Nick agreed, and indeed that was his purpose in helping arrange a meeting in the first place. However, Fraser had his own agenda, which took both of us by surprise. In brisk manner, he set out his credentials for working on my behalf, including his close connections with both Tessa Jowell herself (his son, apparently, was currently interning in Jowell's private office) and Gareth Blacker, the man at the LDA who had made my life, and the lives of others, a misery, yet was responsible for assembling the land required to develop the Olympic Park. Fraser mentioned that he was formerly leader of Southwark Council, and had been involved in the leadership campaign for Blair's choice of London Mayor, Frank Dobson. However, he was more specific about Blacker.

He explained that, in his previous role at Southwark, he had employed Gareth Blacker, whom he described as 'a Rottweiler', being brought in to 'savage deals'. He said he remained very close to Blacker and could call him on his mobile, day or night. He confirmed the LDA had no money, and that the reason they'd been lackadaisical about contingent deals was because they'd assumed Paris would be awarded the Games.

Five minutes into the meeting, I would've signed any engagement letter he'd put in front of me, however draconian the small print. Finally, somebody was offering me a credible lifeline – a somebody who could help me say the right things to the right people at the right time. A definite step up from my existing strategy of flailing about like a drowning man unable to distinguish between lily leaves and lifeboats.

But Fraser's repertoire had not yet reached its climax. Without recourse to any notes, his next trick was to recite intimate details of almost every meeting relating to the Olympics relocation that I'd attended during the last six months – not merely the dates and the locations and the attendees, but also the items discussed and the decisions reached. I was certain he hadn't been present at any of them, and none of this information was in the public domain. Somebody had apparently been tipping him off about my activities, in extensive (and uncannily accurate) minutiae. I'm not often lost for words, but on this occasion my jaw hung open and sound came there none. It was as if the top GCHQ master spy was briefing me about a 24-hour surveillance on a suspected mole – except that, in this instance, the subject of the surveillance was me!

Fraser concluded by leaning forward and, arms crossed, telling me: 'Lance, you will soon be contacted by a property developer. He will offer to help you. You should heed his guidance. He will get stuff sorted for you. Please don't ignore his words. His company, Cleveland, aren't concerned about the money as they are looking at a long-term, all-in deal. The LDA cannot do this, they can't show a short-term loss, but Cleveland can, and will recoup later.'

I was speechless. My meeting with Cleveland had taken place under clandestine circumstances that very morning. Other than Nick, I hadn't told a soul about the conversation, and yet a lobbyist I was meeting for the first time, in a venue I was visiting for the first time, was up to speed. These were murky waters. I wondered if I was being tested for my discretion – 'Lafanee' had, after all, urged me to keep our discussions confidential. It made no sense to jeopardise a potentially viable solution for my business through wanton indiscretions, so I stayed motionless. At least, motionless above the table. Underneath, I had just kicked Nick's anklebone. My way of signalling to him, in guarded manner, that 'Wow, this has just got seriously creepy!'

As Nick and I were leaving, Fraser lightened the conversation by saying he thought I was doing a 'great job' on the publicity front, but that it was unlikely to help. 'Jowell is smart enough not to soil her hands with this. Caborn [who was the Minister for the Olympics] is irrelevant as no one knows him. Livingstone doesn't care what people think of him, and Coe is too stupid to understand or care.' Finally, he added, 'Many of the businesses will be wiped out.'

Nick and I left Fraser's office totally shell-shocked. This was not what either of us were expecting. And how was it that the meeting with 'Lafanee' just happened to be the same morning as a meeting my close friend had set up, in which the morning's meeting was referred to?

We both concluded that this was definitely the government's way of 'taking care of me', and once Nick had alerted his friends and the fuse had been lit, Fieldsend must have contacted me at that point to set up the first meeting. I just had to hope this fuse did not cause an explosion. Nick calmed me, saying, if this is what you need to do to save your business, you just need to play along. 'It's the government, it will be fine.'

The Four Gritti conversation was still playing on my mind that weekend. As I often do when I'm trying to zone out, I settled into the leather chair in my home office, closed my eyes, and listened to some music. 'Rocket Man' by Elton John is one of my favourite tracks (salmon and rocket being a fine culinary combination), but a few weeks beforehand, in a wistful mood, I'd rewritten the lyrics as 'Salmon Man'. Alone in my study on the Sunday evening, neat Islay whisky in hand, I sang the new and improved version, without inhibition or restraint:

He took my land last night – my site
Zero hour 2012.
And I'm gonna be high as a kite by then
I miss the fish I smoke, I miss my life
It's lonely with no space
On such a wasted flight

And it's really been a long, long time
Olympic ruin brings me round again to find
I am the man, they made me lose my home
Oh no no no I'm a salmon man
Salmon man smoking out his oak up here alone

Ours is the kind of place they'll put new grids
The fact we're old as well
And there'll be no one there to smoke fish like we did

And all this science I don't understand
It was my job five days a week
A salmon man, a salmon man

And I think it's really been a long, long time...

Unlike Elton, I haven't the vocal chords, temperament or perseverance to carry a three-hour set, so after two more bouts of 'Salmon Man', my fingers were hovering uneasily above my keyboard. What to do with all the information I'd been assimilating? I started to compose an email to my key advisors – Nick Balcombe, Mark Stephens and Shimon Cohen – but realised all I had were snippets and conjecture. I couldn't even properly recall the names of the people I'd met – 'Lafanee'? – or the company he represented. Did Fraser say Cleveland, or was it Cavendish? My mind had been focused on the verbs, not the pronouns: 'contacted', 'heed', 'sorted', 'don't ignore'.

If I was to follow the course that 'Lafanee' and Fraser were pressurising me to take, I needed more information about my potential bedfellows before getting under the covers. So maybe now was time to check in for the night and I could figure it all out with a fresh head, on Monday morning at my office desk.

I'm not sure if it was the whisky or the weekend's fretting, but I found it hard to sleep, so, rather than lie in bed speculating, I got dressed and drove to the office, where I turned to everybody's most indispensable source of data validation: the Google search bar.

Thirty minutes later, I'd established at least one fact: that my memory was far from perfect. Throughout the realms of cyberspace, there wasn't a single reference to anybody by the name of Lafanee (or indeed Lefanee, Lafenee, or Lafeney) whose profile remotely matched the individual I'd met. I searched Cavendish, Clifton, Cleveland, Clevedon in the hope that something might show. If this company had spent and was intending to spend even more hundreds of millions of pounds acquiring sites, you'd expect to find something – but no, it seemed I'd reached a dead end. I needed a clearer head if I was to figure out where to go from here. There are various techniques I've used over the years to overcome a mental block, such as meditation or sorting out the piles of paperwork on my desk. In 2005, I liked to walk around the office sipping a strong coffee in the hope it might stimulate a breakthrough moment. I was midway back from the canteen, when the way forward hit me. If 'Lafanee's' company had indeed been buying development land in the general area earmarked for the Olympics, that would presumably show up on the public record. Thank goodness for the restorative powers of an intensely concentrated caffeine blast upon my mental faculties.

I clicked through to the planning websites of each of the boroughs with land in or close to the Stratford area – Newham, Tower Hamlets, Hackney. Sifting through all the notifications was a mind-numbing and laborious task; in that single day, I'd seen enough architects' drawings about conservatories and loft conversions to last a lifetime. Then, as I waded through about the hundredth bundle of virtual documents, a company name jumped from the page like a migrating salmon leaping the Falls of Braan. The application to redevelop a near-derelict warehouse had been submitted by none other than Cleveland Development Company Ltd! That was the name, I was certain of it! I felt like Peter Falk's Columbo when one of his lines of investigation produce a 'gotcha' moment.

Armed with the company name, there was now a slew of related public data I could access. I began with Companies House, where official documents for all UK limited companies are available for download, including the articles of association, the registered address and the names of the Directors. From this, I was at last able to confirm the identity – and spelling – of the person I'd met at the Holiday Inn. He was Daniel Lafayeedney (no wonder my 'Lafanee' enquiries had yielded so little), a former major in the British Army, and registered since 1978 as a practising solicitor with the Law Society of Scotland. The society described his work as 'legal advisor to a number of large US companies active in the UK', but without giving any specifics about these contracts.

Two things merited further investigation. Firstly, there was a string of Cleveland companies registered at the same address, some of which were limited liability partnerships as opposed to companies, nearly all registered offshore in Jersey, and hence faced less onerous filing requirements. The second was the name of the other parties involved. James Edward Child – whom I'd also met at the Holiday Inn – was listed in connection with Cleveland Development. But in different parts of the Cleveland web, other names cropped up, including a business called Pluscarden Investments, which appeared to be a partner in many of the businesses and had been recently incorporated and registered in Glasgow at the address of a law firm. I figured this was also worth a follow-up.

Whereas the name 'Cleveland' is relatively bland – as the second city of Ohio, it's nicknamed 'The Mistake on the Lake', and for many years was noteworthy for nothing more upscale than being the scene of social and racial unrest in the 1960s and its inability to produce a decent sports team – 'Pluscarden' was more distinctive, and so it became the focus of my next phase of research. Two references caught my eye. According to anonymous sources, Pluscarden was the codename given to an undercover programme to identify any counter-terrorist threats against the West emerging from the former Soviet Union. It was run by an organisation called the Keston Institute. This was eerie given that Lafayeedney, in the little he had divulged about his background, mentioned both his defence interests and his friendship with John Reid. It was also the name of an 800-year-old Benedictine monastery in the glen of Black Burn, some six miles south of Elgin, in Moray, Scotland. And Lafayeedney had been Scottish to his core. These did not seem like coincidences any more than the 'coincidence' of Jeremy Fraser knowing all about my recent endeavours.

My research had uncovered a few answers. I could now be certain about names and places. But they had also thrown up a host of other questions – mainly ones beginning with the word 'why'. Why was a developer so keen to construct a deal for property the LDA would be soon be acquiring, in ways that were sheltered from public view? Why had secret discussions filtered to a lobbying company in Leicester Square? Why did that lobbyist know enough about the turning of the wheels of power that he could implore me with confidence to take up a particular development proposal? And why did any of these connect with counter-terrorist programmes and Scottish monasteries? All these issues created additional lines of enquiry. But my head was already exploding with conspiracy theories.

The problem with an inquiring mind is that it doesn't like rest, and so the research continued. I had focused on the people and organisations, but not much had come to light. Where next? I decided to focus on the addresses. Whilst not much could be ascertained from a Google search of Cleveland Development, perhaps now that I had their registered address, it was possible that Lafayeedney controlled other companies registered at the same address that would shed some more light on my dangerous new business partner.

But first things first. I researched Lafayeedney's personal address, from his officially lodged 'Change of Director's Details' forms. This address also threw up some curious connections. He was based at St Antony's College, Oxford and his home was, in fact, the former address of the Keston Institute, established in 1969 to advance the study of religions and religious expression in Communist and formerly Communist countries – the Institute had been regarded by the KGB as dangerous and subversive during the darkest days of the Cold War. Again, my mind was swirling at some of the recurrent themes – religion, geopolitics, the ex-Soviet states of central Europe.

I decided to draw a line under my research, the thought of being sucked into a world involving warzones and monasteries was too much. I had read Dan Brown's *Da Vinci Code* that summer and already it was becoming my life. I kept reassuring myself this must be coincidence. Health officials advise against self-diagnosis using Wikipedia since it's a recipe for paranoia – mistaking a virus for a terminal illness. Perhaps I was experiencing something similar. Whether searching online sites, or searching for physical sites – both were causing unbearable stress.

Whilst the LDA needed to obtain CPO powers before it could forcibly evict businesses on the Olympic site, this did not mean the entire land reclamation programme was in abeyance. Some of the area was wasteland, or already in public ownership, or was occupied by tenants who had pre-existing reasons to relocate. This meant that, in some parts of the Lower Lea Valley, the bulldozers were already moving in. Over the next eighteen months, 'business-as-usual' would become progressively less 'usual' for Forman's, as one building after another was erased from the landscape, and our vans were forced to navigate the debris and roadblocks caused by such a mammoth clearance operation. It was like being a chess novice up against Garry Kasparov, forced to watch your rooks and knights and bishops being swept from the board until just one or two forlorn pieces – a king, and perhaps a pawn or two – remain standing.

In their rush for a simple solution, the LDA had overlooked a number of technical matters relating to the area. As a hub of manufacturing, many of the businesses involved 'dirty' by-products, meaning they held specialist waste licences. These often carried restrictions on the firm's practices and obligations upon the firm's conduct. Waste of any type involves numerous regulations, but some of the waste in Marshgate Lane was not your common-and-garden waste, such as nasty chemicals or plastics that won't biodegrade. Some of it was nuclear waste. About 200 yards from our factory gate was the building which, for thirty years, had processed nuclear waste on behalf of Queen Mary

College's Engineering Department. At some point it had been deemed politic to move the processes further away from a densely populated area, but the site had never been formally decommissioned, and for this reason demolition was – in theory – a complex matter, involving arcane procedures, biohazard notifications and specialist handling. These were procedures that, if folklore is true, should have involved years, if not decades, of consultation and risk assessment. The existence of background readings was kept hidden from the IOC throughout the bidding period.

Fortunately for the LDA (if not for local residents hoping to live out their years without acquiring luminous green skin or a third eye), they were able to forsake anything resembling good practice, propriety or corporate responsibility in the rush to build a stadium. This isn't simply my parochial hyperbole – many aspects of domestic law were over-ridden by clauses within the Olympic Act that the British government was obligated to include as a condition of being awarded the Games. A cavalier approach to nuclear waste was the latest in a long line of official behaviour that would never be tolerated under any other circumstances. However, suddenly 'it's for the Games' could be used as the all-encompassing justification, to brush aside anyone urging caution or care. Within a week, visible evidence of the nuclear waste processor was gone, but who knows what after-effects linger? Most local businesses were aghast at what had happened, but were too preoccupied with their own survival, so the matter largely passed without comment – except for a few off-colour jokes about the toxic effect on athletes from countries that were notorious for drugging competitors to their eyeballs.

Another week passed and still nothing. The Marshgate Lane Business Group was meeting less regularly. Whilst being supportive of one another's plight, we were all competing for sites. We would even have to keep some secrets of our own. Things were tense and I had developed a strong burning sensation down my left arm which came and went with thoughts of Pluscarden.

'Maybe you should take the site in Leyton,' said René, as we discussed my situation over dinner with Spencer and Nicole, our neighbourly friends.

I had not gone into detail about all my Pluscarden revelations, even to René, as I didn't want to worry her.

'I've come so far. I'll never forgive myself for taking something I know isn't right.' The words of my old economics teacher John Smullen came flooding back into my mind – 'You make progress by the brave choices.'

I knew that continuing the fight would be brave, but would it be reckless?

Having spent an initial few hours googling Lafayeedney's back story, I found myself returning to the search engine with increasing frequency, in case any more details could be unearthed, and quickly learnt that whilst Google can be as addictive as smoked salmon, it is far less conducive to one's psychological well-being. The more deeply one delves into the hidden corners of the internet, the more one becomes immersed in a cesspit of conspiracy theories, unsubstantiated accusations and libellous, ribald comment. As I came across bodies such as Pluscarden and the Keston Institute, I worked my way through the series of links that would be presented alongside. Usually, the first dozen would take me to credible webpages with fascinating material on their worthy activities. By the time I reached the second or third page of links, I was being directed towards the dark side of the internet, where allegations – plentiful, colourful, outrageous, anonymous – flowed without structure, context or evidence. I found myself reading of whistle-blowers, vigilante-style police forces, the Medellin drug cartel and sex trafficking. At any normal time, I would have dismissed all this as so much cyber-noise, the scribblings of over-imaginative, middle-aged geeks tapping away on their keyboards in the dark of their mothers' basements at three in the morning. But after the unnerving meeting with Jeremy Fraser, as well as the clear and present threat to my livelihood, I found that the internet's myriad of half-truths and innuendo was playing remorselessly on my mind. On one occasion, I noticed the stress was causing my heart to pound against the inside of my chest like a prisoner slamming his fists against a cell wall in the hope it might collapse and set him free. I closed my eyes and sank back into my chair and hummed 'Salmon Man' until I was finally able to recover my composure.

At Four Gritti, Nick Young had jokingly asked me whether my life as a movie would be horror, comedy, or farce. It now felt like none of those genres. It felt like I was a character in the 1998 spy thriller *Enemy of the State*, starring Will Smith and Gene Hackman, in which Robert Clayton Dean (played by Smith) comes into possession of incendiary information about the assassination of civilians at the behest of the National Security Agency. Although (being Hollywood) all eventually works out well for Dean and his wife, I knew that, in real-life, there was no such guarantee.

I confided my research with a few close friends, who recommended that I should 'leave no stone unturned'. I started to prepare contemporaneous notes of the events, which I kept on a USB stick in a bank safe-deposit box. This was not a time for half measures, after all.

CHAPTER 13

FORAGING

Phileas Fogg had it easy. On the face of it, the challenge set by his friends at the Reform Club (now an esteemed Forman's client) was onerous: to circumnavigate the globe in just eighty days if he hoped to win their £20,000 wager. But at least he could zip through each new country without the burden of seeking out a suitable factory site! I wasn't exploring quite such exotic locales – Fogg shot out of London by train and barely paused for breath until he reached Suez. By contrast, my increasingly desperate foraging deep into London's East End would be unacknowledged and unrewarded unless I found somewhere to build a smokehouse.

As the days turned to weeks, and the weeks turned to months, I was exploring ever more remote and outlandish locations, hoping some undiscovered nirvana would abruptly present itself. It would have been the perfect way to spend eighty days and more – *if* my goal that year had been, in the spirit of Phileas Fogg, to befriend vibrant characters from an array of cultural heritages. Or if, like William Hogarth, my mission was to bring the world's attention to London's unseen underbelly – its bawdiness, its crime, its despair. Unfortunately, I had a more pragmatic and personal obligation. I needed to identify a patch of land that would be suited to a large, clean, functioning, well-connected, state-of-the-art production factory. And time was running out.

I learnt never to take property particulars at face value. Lafayeedney had become my occasional guide, and one day, together with Fraser, he escorted me to a site which, on paper, seemed tailor-made. I felt uncomfortable walking along dark East End alleyways in his company, so asked Lloyd to join me. Later, I also declined his invitation to stay overnight with him in Oxford.

Channelsea House was a bleak office block next to Abbey Creek, a watery cul-de-sac off the complicated network of waterways known as the Bow Back Rivers. He persuaded me that, despite its inauspicious appearance, it was ripe for an overhaul, and – once I'd got my creative juices lubricated and flowing – I saw his point. The grounds were ample, allowing plenty of space for all my production stages; there was a side building that could be converted into the management offices; and the structure was effectively derelict, meaning that demolition could proceed apace without the complications of evicting one last pesky tenant. I even managed to overcome the proximity of the Northern Outfall sewer, running close to the premises from Bow through Stratford. Dared I believe that Lafayeedney had rescued an unlikely victory – like a flamboyant poker player revealing a straight flush during a showdown, when the game had seemed all but lost.

'Didn't I promise that I'd sort you out?' Fraser said with a flourish. 'All that unnecessary worrying.'

Lloyd nodded to me to indicate that he felt it could work. 'It has potential,' I replied. To be sure, I felt it was now important to re-engage Phil Hudson, my business partner and architect during my Ukraine and Eastern Europe exploits. I was confident he'd always provide me with an honest and informed assessment. However, before he had the chance to comment, the deal was killed due to unrelated reasons.

Halfway through the Channelsea House inspection, I'd noticed the faint sound of the Muslim call to prayer (the adhan) issuing from a mid-sized mosque a little further along Canning Street, but thought little of it. It turned out the venue was called the Masjid-e-Ilyas mosque, also known as the Abbey Mills mosque, with the capacity to accommodate around 2,500 worshippers. So far, so inconsequential. Except that a little further digging by my advisors revealed that the mosque had rather more grandiose ambitions. Plans had been formulated, and were under consideration by Newham Council, to expand the mosque into a 70,000-square-metre Islamic Centre, making it the largest religious building in the country, around three times bigger than St Paul's Cathedral. The concept had been nicknamed the 'mega mosque' in the local press to reflect its proposed 12,000-person capacity. Some rumours suggested the eventual aspirations soared yet higher, and, indeed, in 2008, designs would be presented by architects Mangera Yvars for a complex fit to accommodate 40,000 visitors, with the potential to expand to 70,000. Unsurprisingly, there had been some resistance to the proposals, but Mayor Livingstone was an unapologetic supporter, and around a year later would go on record to castigate 'the particularly vicious nature of the campaign against a possible Muslim place of worship'. I couldn't help but contrast the enthusiasm with which he supported the Masjid-e-Ilyas vision with his uncompromising and obstinate refusal to lift a finger in our aid.

'I'm not sure how easily my vans will get to the end of the street when tens of thousands of worshippers are lining up during Ramadan. It's a good site, but this kills it. I know they don't have planning yet, but it's a risk we can't take,' I said a few days later, when Lafayeedney called for my verdict.

'I do see the issue,' he responded.

So we let one further opportunity slip quietly away. The LDA was continuing to push the wasteland in Leyton, to which most of the affected businesses had already blown a proverbial raspberry. They were acting like an obsessive teenager who won't take the hint that you have zilch interest in a date. On a more positive note, I had maintained a continuing interest in the Bow Lock site, which had first attracted my eye in the lead-up to Singapore, when Blacker had washed his hands of the option and insisted that, if I wished to pursue negotiations with the Borough of Tower Hamlets, I was on my own. Despite having written to Tower Hamlets Council, I was getting nowhere. They kept telling me that the site was inappropriate for a smoked salmon factory, despite the fact that it had sat derelict for over eight years, since this would be incompatible with their Area Action Plan. If I understood correctly, a few theoretical bullet points in a council document were being given priority over a real-life opportunity to bring employment and a heritage food business, founded in that very borough over 100 years prior, to one of the most deprived parts of the country. Without the LDA's support, I turned to the London Thames Gateway Development Corporation, which had been established to promote urban development and regeneration, and found them supportive. Their Development Director, Jim Sneddon, a former architect, took a close interest in our salvation.

I still couldn't understand why the LDA was being so obstructive, and speculated about possible behind-the-scenes pressure from Livingstone, Mike Lee or even Blacker, so I called a meeting with their Head of Planning Emma Peters to see if I could uncover the truth. Sneddon, Hudson, Tony Winterbottom from the LDA and a lawyer who worked for Mark Stephens were also around the table. I hoped that, with all parties present, a deal could be thrashed out.

I was quite fired up for the meeting, because en route I had been interviewed by an aggressive reporter from the *Sunday Politics* programme who had charged me with mounting an attempted seizure of a publicly owned asset. I pointed out the irony of this accusation given that I was only in this predicament because my own property was being seized by the state.

I barely even sat down across the table from Emma Peters when I dived straight to the crux of the issue.

'We have explored every possibility and Bow Lock is the ideal solution for us. What's more, it's perfect for the LDA, because it's state-owned land. You can agree a value between you, it doesn't matter to me,' was my opening gambit.

'But this site is not appropriate for a smoked salmon factory,' she replied.

'Why not?'

'It doesn't fit with our Area Action Plan.'

'Well, yes, it does actually. Look, I have the plan here. If you read the objectives, it ticks literally every box. It calls for commercial sites along with residential. What is your problem here?'

'It doesn't.'

'Yes it does, let's turn to page...'

After twenty minutes of tedious back and forth, Peters halted the discussions with a statement that arrived from thin air, like an asteroid crashing through the window and into the meeting room.

'Okay, Mr Forman, if you really want me to tell you the truth, I will.'

My ears pricked up. 'That would be nice. After all, we're trying to find solutions. This is not a game.'

'This site was awarded to a developer some years ago in a development competition, but when London won the Olympics, our plans changed, and we're trying to extricate ourselves from the deal. We're involved in a legal dispute with the developer, and can't simply hand over the site to you, otherwise you'll end up embroiled in it too.'

As the realisation hit me that there was a genuine reason, which was only now being revealed, I felt like Tom Hanks in *Cast Away* as he watches another ship, which may have provided a lifeline, vanish over the horizon. 'Who is the developer?' I enquired.

'I can't say. These discussions are strictly confidential.'

Winterbottom had been silent to this point, but now a huge grin spread across his face. 'I told you, Mr Forman, you shouldn't have been wasting everyone's time for the last six months.'

I drove back to my smokehouse from Tower Hamlets' palatial new offices devastated and mentally exhausted. Where next? I called Sneddon to see if he could shed any further light.

'I can't believe what's just happened. We've spent months drawing up plans for Bow Lock, showing it would be a great asset for the borough. Why didn't you saying anything to me?'

'I didn't know. I think it's a great site for Forman's.'

'So who's the developer they're in dispute with?'

'They've asked me to keep it confidential and I know you respect that. If you told me something in confidence it would go no further.'

Another dead end. Or maybe not. Being told the developer's name was a secret was like being set a challenge. For the second time in a month, I turned to the gems that can be found hidden in the pages of planning applications. The application led me to the architect who, in turn, led me to property developer Bellway Homes. Five minutes later, I was on the phone to Jason Honeyman, their Director for east London.

'Ah, hello, Jason, you won't know me, my name is Lance Forman, and I'm in the smoked…'

'I've heard of you. You've been in the news with the Olympics.'

'That's right. I won't take up too much of your time, but I wanted to ask you about a site called Bow Lock, where we've been looking to relocate.'

'Yes, I know, on the A12.'

'I understand you're in a legal dispute about it with Tower Hamlets?'

'Definitely not the case!'

'Really?'

'We don't have a contract on the site and in fact have no claim on it at all.'

'So why would Emma Peters tell me otherwise?'

'I don't know. She's quite sensible so I suspect she's being led by the LDA.'

'This is astonishing. So, you really wouldn't have a problem if I built a new smoked salmon factory there?'

'Not at all. In fact I am familiar with your existing factory and I'd be interested in talking to you about building the new one for you.'

'Would you mind putting that in an email?'

'With pleasure.'

Jason was true to his word. Within moments of hanging up, my inbox received this welcome message:

> Subject: Bow Lock.
>
> Lance. Further to our conversation today, I would confirm that we are no longer pursuing this site. Should you be successful in securing a position, I would be only too happy to become involved. Good luck in your negotiations. I will keep in touch.
>
> Jason Honeyman,
> Managing Director,
> Bellway Thames Gateway North.

* * *

My time was being consumed not only by the labyrinthine world of local politics, but also with the side effects from my raised media profile, not all of which were beneficial. As news of my plight became widespread, I started receiving unsolicited calls from property agents almost on a daily basis. I could've written the script myself: 'We sympathise with your situation ... but we're here to offer solutions ... we have more great sites on our books than anyone else ... we know Stratford better than anyone else ... we'll work harder than anyone else ... we're not cheap but we deliver better value than anyone else ... sign with us on an exclusive basis and you'll never regret it.'

But one of these cold calls seemed more authentic than the rest. The voice belonged to one Ian Rose, of M&A Associates, who claimed to know not only Blacker, but also one of my sisters. He argued persuasively that he worked closely with, and was trusted by, the LDA. Given that any residual levels of trust between me and Blacker's team had dissipated into the ether in the months since the award announcement, I realised I'd need assistance if bridges were to be rebuilt. Rose suggested that, working in conjunction with a firm called Caradon Consulting, he had the resources to scour the area for up to twenty sites that could meet our requirements, and was not averse to knocking on doors of properties that weren't even on the marketplace, to test whether a deal could be done within our timeframe.

It seemed a no-regrets action, especially since the LDA was amenable to paying his fees, so I instructed Rose to get his team mobilised and crack on with the job. I should have learnt by now that, with the LDA, everything comes with a catch, and their consent to fund M&A's work was contingent upon my agreement to avoid any media comment for a two-month period. In the circumstances, this was not a fatal wound, especially since the two months ran over the Christmas break when media comment would've been largely futile, but it still left a slightly nasty taste, like I was subject to a one-sided gagging order (the LDA, of course, was under no such constraints). I've been my own boss for so long that I shudder when somebody gives me orders. However, the commitment was duly formalised in a legally binding agreement, and I scrupulously observed the sixty days of self-restraint and speechlessness as demanded.

It wasn't easy – I had built a strong rapport with a number of journalists, and a few were perplexed by my unexpected and sudden reticence.

I couldn't allow the period of purdah to extend a moment beyond the expiration of the agreement, so I dropped a note to the LDA requesting a meeting towards the end of January. My plan was, with M&A's support, to present them with three suitable properties, each one of which had held up to M&A's rigorous and objective scrutiny. I proposed a half-day afternoon meeting so that each of the shortlisted options could be explored at leisure; no one would be able to levy the excuse that discussions were prematurely curtailed. If, at the end of that meeting, no contender had emerged as front-runner, worthy of LDA support, I would need to turn to the extinguishment option. But at least I'd have visibly explored every conceivable avenue that might deliver survival. It would be the LDA that, once again, had thumbed its collective nose at a workable, viable, affordable solution.

M&A recruited teams to go walking around the streets of east London, knocking on doors of any vaguely suitable site and asking if it was for sale. 'Everything has a price,' said Ian. They prepared a report for me with around a dozen properties listed, which were quickly whittled down to one, in Ratcliffe Cross Street. Not only did it meet our operational criteria, but the owner was able and motivated to sell. Added to Bow Lock and New North Road, I now had three viable contenders, each of which, in M&A's professional opinion, could save our business. The report was compiled and sent to the LDA in advance of a meeting scheduled for 31 January 2006. This, I was assured, would be when the LDA would make its choice and our fate would be sealed.

A few days before the LDA meeting, I called Lafayeedney. Aside from the Channelsea site, he had shown me another, the Walker Hebborn site a little further north of Bow Lock, but – despite Fraser's rapturous assurances – was yet to present me with any practical solution. It simply wasn't happening.

'Dan, I'm meeting with Gareth in a few days and will be presenting him with three options. Do you have anything for me or not?'

'Yes, I have a good solution. Let's meet at the Savoy on Monday at eleven, and I'll explain.'

'I don't think that's a great place. The annual lunch of Conservative Friends of Israel is happening there that day and I'll know a lot of attendees. If they see me with you, they'll ask who my new friend is. How about the Howard Hotel instead, next door in Temple Place? Same time.'

Matters had become so delicate that I couldn't run the risk of either having my words misrepresented, or being told that's I'd misunderstood an offer he was making. I had been advised to make avid notes, but how do you do that when it's a government agent telling you to keep everything hush hush? One comment twisted or taken out of context, and I might see my relocation options fall apart. As the saying goes, desperate times call for desperate measures. In such circumstances, I've seen enough episodes of *24* to know the value of the hidden recording device. There's no other way to put it: this was my Jack Bauer moment.

Just north of Selfridges, at the bottom of Baker Street, is a store I'd walked passed many times but had never previously ventured inside. Called Spymaster, it describes itself as the country's 'leading spy shop, supplying surveillance and counter-surveillance and personal protection equipment'. Some might call it paranoia, but given my state of mind at the time, taking a few precautions to have an unimpeachable record of my discussions with Lafayeedney seemed nothing other than common sense. When I arrived at the store, I was wearing a long overcoat and a scarf wrapped around much of my face – after all, if anyone from the LDA chanced to spot me diving into somewhere with the name *Spymaster* above the door, my future attempts at subterfuge would be undermined at a stroke. One final look around Portman Square; I didn't think I was being tailed, but having never been trained by the security services, how would I really know? In any event, I crossed over the threshold and into the store.

There were no other shoppers present, so I had a few moments to cast my eyes around. To my right was a mannequin adorned with body armour and night-vision goggles – hopefully neither would be necessary for my rendezvous with Lafayeedney. And on the far wall, the specifications for a panic room, the size of a large wardrobe albeit with its own dedicated air and electricity supply and phone line. If I needed to take refuge from my nemeses behind an unbreakable, camouflaged door, things really would have gone nastily wrong. And, on the shelves, there were rows of shiny devices whose purpose I could barely fathom. If I hadn't had a specific purpose in mind, this would've been a browser's paradise.

My entrance had presumably triggered some type of hidden alert within the store, and after just a few moments the store manager – a petite brunette – appeared to usher me into a separate room where we could converse discreetly. I explained my requirements, and she didn't so much as raise an eyebrow or puff out her cheeks. I could've been explaining my need for a new pair of shoes; I guess her week comprised the gamut of cuckolded husbands, jealous relatives, suspicious business partners and members of criminal gangs who have fallen out with the ringleader. My need – to record a meeting – was probably on the duller end of the spectrum she encountered.

'You could try this pen,' was her first suggestion. 'It's popular with clients who are engaged in last-minute business deals with millions or tens of millions at stake. Let's say you've made your final offer. Then, you offer to leave the other side alone in the room to consider their response. But are they really alone? You leave your 'pen' and pad casually on the desk, and little do they realise, as they're debating the attractiveness of your terms, that you're monitoring their every comment from the restroom! By the time you walk back in, you know exactly how to clinch the deal.'

'I'll never trust anyone with a pen again,' I said. 'I love the idea, but it won't work for my meeting. There are only two of us – if I walk away, he'll be on his own, so unless he has a nervous tic that makes him talk to himself, I'll be monitoring ten minutes of pure silence.'

'OK, let's rule out the pen.'

Eventually I selected a small recording device, about the size of a Twix bar. It was connected by a thin cable to a very powerful microphone that could pick up sounds from five metres away. The microphone was about the size of the head of a matchstick, and also black. The brunette advised me to place the device in my pocket, running the cable inside my shirt, and the microphone could be neatly woven into a knotted tie. 'It's very small, no one will ever see it.' I was petrified that something would happen to alert Lafayeedney to its presence and insisted on a number of trial runs before concluding this was the solution for me. In many digital recorders, there's a light in the corner that signals when recording is underway; that was obviously a non-starter, as was any type of beep or click when the device was switched on or off, or when the battery started to run down.

The morning of my meeting, I tried on every tie in my wardrobe, and I have quite a collection. Even with the busiest patterns in paisley, or Liberty print, the little matchhead stood out to me more like a Belisha beacon. All it might take would be a cough or sneeze and the mic could pop free from the knot, and I could be dead meat. Thank goodness we weren't in hay fever season.

I arrived early, so I could check my tie in the men's room mirror. I don't think I've ever been so scared. There was no hiding place if things went wrong that day; no opportunity to blame the boss or blag for a second chance. I hadn't even checked whether surreptitious recordings were legit in the eyes of the Old Bill (I later confirmed that they were). I had this nightmarish vision of Lafayeedney sensing something wasn't right, and asking the porters to call the Metropolitan Police. Was that my immediate future? Being hauled from the Howard into a waiting police van, and abandoned overnight in a sleazy Holborn cell for interrogation the following morning. A cursory phone call from the inspector on duty to René, Mark Stephens, Lloyd, Nick Balcombe and a couple of others to explain, 'Lance has been a naughty boy. He may be away some time.' Would my life story have more in common with Jeffrey Archer's than I'd assumed when, after his appearance at our post-fire launch, I'd despaired at how easily he'd let the cavalier become the criminal?

I sunk into a sofa in the far corner of the Howard's lobby area to wait for Lafayeedney. We were assured of privacy – the lobby was spacious and deserted but for some elderly Asian travellers enjoying tea and cake. Yet, in my anxiety, I have never felt so claustrophobic, as if I was trapped in a cocoon. In my mind, the walnut panels and seventeenth-century tapestries were barriers, blocking off my escape routes on all sides. The crystal chandelier, with its countless jagged edges, was like an assailant's weapon rather than a source of light. Even the floral bouquets and marble columns could be a source of danger – what if Lafayeedney had positioned his 'heavies' behind them, lurking in case he called on them to intervene?

I had learnt from our previous meetings that Lafayeedney was fastidious about punctuality, and so it proved today. We exchanged small talk whilst tea was being served, but both of us were eager to turn to more pressing matters. I was taken aback when, unexpectedly, he blurted out a damning verdict on the impact of the Olympics so far on development and regeneration in the area.

'The Olympics is bad for us. Prices have gone up, people's ambitions have gone up.'

'Stratford City was happening anyway,' I agreed. 'I don't think the LDA wanted the Olympics at all.'

'I think it's the last thing they wanted,' he said. 'Anyway, let's look at Hancock Road.'

Hancock Road had been on the periphery of my searches to that point, but I hadn't seen anything suitable that might be available.

It was a short stretch of road by the northern approach to the Blackwall Tunnel, about half a mile south of our current site. Yet suddenly Lafayeedney was fumbling around in his folder for some plans so he could point out precisely where he had in mind for us.

'Now, if you look at Hancock Road, it's gonna be industry all the way.'

'There's quite a nice modern unit there,' I said.

'That's a printer's, and that is going to be mixed-use residential. There's a couple of bars. I think they're putting a school there with a bridge across it.'

'Because that land's not under the CPO is it?'

'No, and I own all that.'

He then drew my attention to a site occupied by French Connection, a fashion warehouse, as well as three adjacent buildings. I explained that I had an imminent meeting with the LDA at which I'd be presenting the report from M&A on potential sites, but he cut me off. 'You want my advice? Forget it, you're not going down that route. You've obviously got to meet Blacker tomorrow.'

'And I don't know how I'm supposed to deal with this as far as he's concerned.'

'I'll tell you how to deal with it. You say to him, look, I've identified three sites, or five sites, or whatever you want to do. What you can say is there's a fastball solution. I'm asking you not to mention my name. Say to them there's another solution I'm working on, and it gives me what I want. It gives me the land and the factory and you do the fitting.'

Lafayeedney believed that, with the right assurances in place from the LDA, he'd be able to acquire a site on Hancock Road at an accelerated pace.

I said, 'Well, you'd need to own and control the site pretty damn quick.'

'So, what I want to do with you is say to your lawyers, "This is what we're going to do, confirm it in writing." Then we'll go out to the five sites, not just those two, and put the bids in. We've got offers for those two down, and they've been accepted.'

'And you're saying you need to do that with the other three sites because you then subsidise the land and the factory.'

'Of course. Where I can do it.'

I was unclear exactly what he was suggesting, so I probed the specifics. If he was proposing somehow to acquire a site in Hancock Road, and then sell it to me at a reduced price, I asked whether that might raise questions when the details appeared in the Land Registry records.

'No, no, no, no, no,' he said. 'I'm not selling it to you. I'm gonna do a land swap.'

'A land swap?'

'Because the values won't be there.'

'So, if you acquired the site, no idea, say it's costing you £4 million, and my site is valued at...'

He waved his hand dismissively. 'It's already been worked out. For Christ's sake, get a good firm of lawyers!'

I took this as a gentle implication that I should switch to different advisors. At that time, the same firm was acting on behalf of hundreds of threatened businesses. Was Lafayeedney concerned that presented an unacceptable risk that a 'land swap' deal might leak out and set a precedent?

'How quickly will you have control over those sites?' I asked. 'Are you buying them anyway, whether they're suitable for me or not?'

'There's only one I've lost in four years that I really wanted. So, seven days? Ten days?'

'So what you're suggesting is you would be the buyer, and we would have a back-to-back deal where you would swap with my land?'

There was one obvious flaw with a simple land swap, and that was I also needed a factory to be built. An acre of wasteland, whether in Hancock Road or elsewhere, wasn't of much use to me, and factory building doesn't come cheap, especially when so much of London's construction capacity would be swallowed up by the Olympics itself. I needed to understand if Lafayeedney's proposal extended to the build, but I also wanted him to appreciate a parallel issue that had been troubling me. Under CPO rules, I was entitled to compensation for the impact of the disturbance on my business' profitability during the period of upheaval (my 'Loss of Profits' claim), and my accountants had already developed a preliminary calculation. I put this to Lafayeedney.

'Isn't that anticipatory profits?' he challenged.

'It's what the accountants have calculated.'

'You might have some difficulty getting that. They could argue it's for other reasons, such as bad management.'

My reason for putting this on the table was that, in principle, I was open to a deal whereby my Loss of Profits compensation could be put towards the build cost of a new factory. For that to work, I needed to ensure the factory build and fit out was within the scope of his proposals.

'Either you would build it, or you would fund it and we would build it?' I said.

'I don't yet know how it would be done,' he said. 'But you would have to design whatever it is.'

'It would be what we have at the moment,' I said.

'You'd have a Heads of Terms. The property's easy – it's the building of the factory. I'm not saying it would take weeks or anything like that, that's not a problem. I want you to feel comfortable with what I'm telling you now. You won't be in a worse position.'

'If I can have a factory on one of those sites, then that's it!'

'You're not gonna be in a worse position,' he repeated.

Unlike the government employees with whom I'd been dealing for two years, at least Lafayeedney was talking the language of *solutions* rather than problems. But I still couldn't piece together all the moving parts. I asked, 'Is it worth me having a private discussion with Gareth or not?'

Lafayeedney leant forward. 'No. Absolutely not. Please don't do that.'

'Right. OK.'

'I never ever compromise people. You do that, and you're f****d. I have a hell of a reputation in certain sectors. You build a reputation with people who know you, stick by them and it'll work. You do something that makes them slightly nervous, or you become slightly unreliable, they'll steer clear of this space. Do not f*** it up by trying to be clever. It won't do you any good in the long term or short term. I'm telling you straight.'

'My only agenda is getting my business sorted so I can carry on trading.'

'You've gone to the media. Media for me is a complete anathema. I don't need any publicity. I don't want any.'

'In my position, you probably...'

'I'm just saying what's what, if I have to trade with you, Lance.'

Within moments, his tone had become confrontational and menacing. Suddenly, I was acutely conscious of the tiny microphone in my tie knot, and felt the need to wrap up the conversation quickly. Lafayeedney had sketched out a path whereby I could conceivably have a new site before the demolition vans arrived, and seemingly had the support of the LDA to do whatever it took to silence me. With time running out, I wasn't in the business of closing down options, even those with elements I couldn't yet piece together. My points about Land Registry records and Loss of Profits were still nagging doubts but both could wait until another day, when I'd seen how the LDA responded to the M&A shortlist. In time-honoured fashion, I closed the talk by putting matters into the hands of lawyers.

'We need to get the lawyers talking. I'll need to tell them what's going on presumably.'

'Say to your lawyers that you have a deal with Cleveland.'

'I'll tell them I've got another solution, Cleveland will acquire a site for me, they're going to pay to build a factory on it, I will then do a land swap with my site, problem solved. They don't really need to know more than that?'

'We'll need to cost that particular figure. At the end of the day, you've got a good solution here. Genuinely good.'

As he gathered up his papers, his eye was caught by a photograph of Gordon Brown, then Chancellor of the Exchequer, on the front page of *The Times*. 'We don't want that mad Scotsman in there, do we?'

'Takes one to know one,' I teased.

'Bloody right. Absolutely don't want that. I mean he's a real old socialist.'

We shook hands. As soon as he was out of sight, I raced for my car to check the recording had been a success. My device had lasted, undetected, the entire length of the meeting. Not a bleep, not a click, not a whirr, not a tumble from its perch. For five minutes I sat, breathing heavily. There was still enough time to sneak back to the Savoy and hear David Cameron's address to the Conservative Friends of Israel lunch. Or had there been enough excitement already for one day? Uncharacteristically, I found myself totally unable to decide.

CHAPTER 14

FORECLOSURE

I am in awe of inventors. Whenever they think of the surrounding world, it's not to determine how stuff works, but to figure out how it can be turbocharged.

For the rest of us, without the inventor's instinct or imagination, the huge majority of inventions represent a major step forward for humanity – for example, Jonas Salk's polio vaccine, or Wilhelm Röntgen's X-ray machine. Other inventions are simply annoying – such as Frank Marugg's wheel clamp. But the mindset behind all of them is admirable. To fix a problem, address a need, and generally make things better.

Except for one. The identity of whoever invented the 'business meeting' may have been lost in the mists of time, but I hope there's a special place reserved for them in the vestibule of hell, the ninth circle of Dante's *Inferno*, where Lucifer beats his six wings in a futile quest to break free from the ice flows whilst chewing upon anyone guilty of a treacherous act. And, to my mind, the cursing of humanity with 'business meetings' ranks in the premier league of history's greatest treacheries, alongside the betrayal of Caesar by Brutus, and the passing of Cold War secrets to the Soviets by the Cambridge Spy Ring.

'Business meetings' have consigned generations of sprightly

entrepreneurs to soul-sapping days around boardroom tables in windowless offices with pen-pushers and clock-watchers. In late 2005, my time was being consumed in preparation for the mother of all business meetings – the half-day session at the LDA. Lafayeedney's Hancock Road option had to be mercilessly shunted to the back of my mind. I needed to focus with laser-like clarity on the three sites selected by M&A Associates, which had been filtered in light of my criteria. If Blacker was true to his word, at this meeting the agency would review the options and finally come off the fence with a promise to endorse and support one from the shortlist. Either that, or, effectively, they would fire the starting pistol for my extinguishment. Whichever emerged, at least I'd have some clarity.

Word seemed to have gotten around the LDA that something significant was afoot. I had in tow almost every advisor I'd used in the last twelve months (I dread to think what it was costing if all the per diem rates were totted up). And as we were escorted through the open-plan area towards the conference room, a few heads looked up knowingly from their computer screens. I'm sure that by this time most LDA employees were heartily sick of the Forman's name, and had probably acquired a lifelong allergy to smoked salmon. I wouldn't have been surprised to learn a fully fledged 'Lance Forman correspondence department' had been established with its own section head and graduate recruitment scheme.

For a meeting of such import, the LDA's largest conference room had been pre-booked, but still every seat would be occupied. By the time we were ushered in, two sides of the conference table were already occupied by agency bigwigs. I whispered, 'It's a cast of thousands' to Mark Stephens. The attendee list was rounded out by the M&A project team, who had been positioned at the far end of the room next to the projection screen. My first task was to exchange handshakes with everyone present. I didn't want to offend anybody by overlooking them, but with so many in attendance it was hard to keep count, and I'm sure there were some I greeted twice just to make sure. Once introductions were over, everyone grabbed a strong coffee and a handful of biscuits, and settled in for the long haul. I figured I'd be lucky if we saw the outside much before dusk.

The M&A report had been copied and circulated to every delegate in advance of the meeting, and as I looked around the table, most people had annotated a half-dozen points they would be raising on the technical specifics. To my left, one of the older LDA reps was already muttering something about 'acceleration costs', as if rehearsing her first intervention. I could see the meeting becoming quite feisty. For my part, I was keen to force a conclusion but also not to make any rash commitments that I may regret in the morning. For this reason, I'd scribbled on an index card a list of items where I could be flexible, and others where I must hold a firm line.

Blacker was running a few minutes late, so Ian Rose from M&A suggested he spend the time providing some of 'the context'. He rose to his feet and was ten words into a self-aggrandising spiel about his firm's credentials, when Blacker burst through the door with such force that it hit the wall with an audible crack. He strode to the head of the table like the prize-winning peacock at the Newbury Agricultural show, but didn't even take his seat. Instead, he looked straight across the table at me.

'I understand we're here to discuss the three sites listed in the consultants' report,' he said.

People nodded their tacit agreement.

'But I know there's an additional option on the table, which Mr Forman has been considering with a third party.'

His look morphed into a stare.

My legion of advisors turned towards me, mouths agape. I hadn't breathed a word to them about the Hancock Road possibility, and so stared into the mid-distance to avoid eye contact.

'Isn't that right?' Blacker prompted me to respond.

Finally, there was nowhere to hide.

'Umm, yes, a fourth site,' I said sheepishly. 'Very early; exploratory, and I've been asked to keep it confidential at this stage. It's quite sensitive.'

I could feel every pair of eyes on my side of the table drilling in my direction in an accusatory manner, as if they were thinking, 'We are your trusted advisors, why have you been keeping information from us?' The perplexed expressions were shared by Blacker's team, who were no doubt wondering how their Director had access to nuggets of information which were not in their briefing packs. It felt like being the only people with headsets at a silent disco; the two of us gyrating wildly to the pounding music, yet looking mighty strange to all the onlookers.

'My strong recommendation', said Gareth, 'is that you should take the fourth option. But for the sake of completeness, let's just quickly run through the options in your report.'

The meeting lasted another fifteen minutes and each of the three solutions was dismissed for different reasons. But what did it matter? The Hancock Road option, whilst undocumented, was apparently the chosen one.

And with that, he turned on a sixpence and left the room. A four-hour meeting curtailed to just twenty minutes. And a roomful of highly paid professionals wondering what the blazes had just transpired. Everyone was looking at one another, dumbfounded. Then somebody – I think it might have been Mark Stephens – took it on himself to break the ice. 'If we aren't going to be doing any lawyering today,' he said, 'we might as well head for the pub. Anyone else up for that?'

A couple of hands shot up.

'And you, Lance. You're not escaping that easily. After all, we need you to decipher what on earth just happened.'

Whoever said the fish business was easy?

* * *

In the fading months of 2005 and early 2006, I was spending more time in government offices than most civil servants. If you couldn't find me in the LDA's meeting rooms striving to prise out a decision, your best bet was to check the Tower Hamlets town hall, where I was fighting to keep alive the Bow Lock option, having discovered that Emma Peters's reliance on a 'legal dispute' with Bellway Homes was without a scintilla of substance. With her proving impervious to my charms, I'd finally abandoned hope that she might show any flexibility of her own accord, and had taken the matter to the cabinet, who had reluctantly agreed to grant me a hearing.

My strategy was threefold. Firstly, I would pull on the emotional heartstrings. Forman's, I explained, had been founded and was resident in Tower Hamlets for much of its 100-year history, and had only moved to Marshgate Lane as a consequence of the River Lea flood. Secondly, provide a rational explanation for how our business could stimulate regeneration. And thirdly, show a spirit of goodwill and compromise: 'We are not necessarily seeking to acquire the whole of Bow Lock,' I said, 'merely about one-quarter of the site, at the awkward triangular southern tip, within the B1 planning category permitted by your draft Area Action Plan.' I ended by reassuring the cabinet that, with their blessing, I could move quickly and efficiently. We had a development partner lined up, Rugby Estates PLC, who already boasted a formidable track record in east London regeneration schemes.

I was pleased with my remarks to the cabinet – there were no evident flaws in my case, and, had I been in authority that day, I'd have certainly given the plan a robust stamp of approval. The acoustics in the cabinet room were excellent, and I'd been able to hold a polished and assertive tone without raising my voice. The only drawback was that my comments had been limited to a maximum of five minutes – less than three seconds for every year of Forman's existence – and so it was not possible to develop any of my themes in depth. This was a severe impediment, since I was forced to rush my speech, and I'm sure many forceful points blurred into one another.

After a few questions, the Chairman said the cabinet would 'consider the position', but in general he felt no decisions should be made regarding Bow Lock until the masterplanning work was complete. If only I was able to ruminate over decisions with such leisurely sangfroid – my blood pressure would be significantly lower!

I couldn't leave the future of Forman's at the mercy of a politically motivated schedule, so whilst the cabinet deliberated and prevaricated, I hustled the chance to deliver a lengthier version of the same plea to Tower Hamlet's Overview and Scrutiny Committee. The date was 10 January 2006, and this time I secured half an hour on the agenda to consider my case. This could be my defining moment, and I was determined to make the most of the platform I'd been accorded. In the hot seat, I didn't hold back. I told the committee I'd be making six points, each of which – in isolation – would be sufficient justification to overturn Peters's decisions. Combined, I felt the impact was devastating, and (although I didn't advance this argument) should lead to resignations.

I pointed out that 'legal issues' had been used as a feeble pretext; unless we were able to see and comment on the legal advice, it was impossible to take seriously such assertions, and my discussions with Bellway Homes had confirmed they were groundless. Masterplanning was also being used as a cover-all, like the last refuge of the scoundrel, and yet the most cursory glance at the council's vision would show it was compatible with my concept. I stressed that planning permission would not be an issue; that competitive tender procedures were not required due to the quantum involved; and that the pressure of the Olympic clearance timetable easily met the threshold that would deem this a 'special case'.

Above all, I reminded the Committee that the Olympic Planning

Application set very clear obligations on all relevant agencies, and neither the spirit nor the letter of these could be casually brushed aside. I entered into the record the following statement, which I felt captured our quandary beautifully:

> It is a condition of the Olympic Planning Application that the agencies involved should cooperate to help businesses relocate as close as possible to their existing premises. We have a site which would be ideal but we have been blocked by the London Borough of Tower Hamlets without due consideration, rather than aided. We feel our scheme for Bow Lock is superior to your previous one ... and it accords much more closely with your AAP too, so the cabinet's inflexibility is most unreasonable.

I looked around the faces of the committee, and was shocked by how few had maintained eye contact with me. A couple of officers were doodling on their pads, one was checking his phone, another had – I was almost certain – nodded off. Even my revelation about Peters's deception over Bellway – which BDO partner Peter Leach had described as a 'twelve-bore shotgun ... you should fire both barrels' – had failed to raise them from their reverie.

When meeting a chef for the first time, I can always tell from the body language (more so than their words) whether I'll walk away with a customer. A purchase order invariably follows when he's been sitting bolt upright, head raised, arms flailing wildly with excitement, eye movements mirroring my own. Based on the body language around the Tower Hamlets committee table, it was clear the next steps would be inauspicious if not hostile. I was irritated but unsurprised when, a few days later, and only in response to a number of follow-up phone calls, I was informed that both the cabinet and the committee had backed Peters's judgement. My appeal was denied.

* * *

My attention returned to the Hancock Road site. Despite Lafayeedney and Blacker's advocacy of this solution, I was struggling to understand exactly the money flows. A three-party land swap had been suggested, but nobody had explained how would this be accounted for on the LDA's books. Shortly after the 'cast of thousands' meeting, I arranged a one-on-one meeting with Blacker to work through the sequence of the transactions he envisaged. As far as I could make out, the suggestion was that Cleveland would acquire the Hancock Road site, and then sell it to me at a substantial loss, but at the same price the LDA was offering me for my site in Marshgate Lane, for which the LDA would then swap.

It didn't help my confidence in the land-swap arrangements when Lafayeedney left the strangest message on my voicemail. With 'Te Deum' playing in the background, he started out by explaining that 'Gareth is still trying to get you the Hancock site', but then digressed into a monologue about the meaning of the early Christian hymn. 'The monks came onto the battlefield at the end of Agincourt and, in the style of a Gregorian chant, were singing the prayer of Judea since it was a great prayer of the Catholic church.' I suppose it made a change from messages from insurance salesmen and ambulance-chasing lawyers.

The next day, I tried to draw a more detailed explanation from Blacker. 'I understand what you are trying to do here, Gareth, but I can't see how it's going to work in practice. The media are all over me like a rash. Property sales are a matter of public record in the Land Registry as soon as they're executed. How will the LDA explain to a journalist that a piece of land has just been bought for over £5 million and sold to Mr Forman for less than £1 million the following week?'

'Don't worry about how we'll justify the deal publicly,' replied Blacker. 'That's our issue. Just leave that to me. We'll deal with it.'

I couldn't make sense of the optics, but I was impressed by his confidence, so decided not to press the matter. After all, I told myself, Forman's wouldn't be culpable in any of the scenarios. Everyone knew we were innocent collateral damage from the need to build an Olympic Park, and all my energies were channelled into a workable property solution. If I was offered a site at an affordable price, how could I be criticised for pursuing it? I even had the hard evidence to prove how the scenario had played out.

Over the following week, I went to visit the Hancock Road site a few more times, to familiarise myself with the lay of the land, and even asked Phil Hudson to start drawing up some preliminary design plans. I was starting to feel some excitement, or maybe it was just relief, at the prospect of this arduous war-game reaching its grand finale.

But, within just a few days, it appeared to be yet another blind alley. Blacker called me and, without any warning, made a complete reversal. 'The deal's off,' he said. 'We can't work out how we'll justify it publicly.'

'But your words were: "leave that to me",' I said. My thoughts were unprintable. If there are two things in business that make me feel queasy, it's shady deals and rank incompetence. With Hancock Road, Lafayeedney and Blacker had contrived to fuse together both traits in a single unholy alliance.

Blacker skated over the incident, telling me not to obsess with the past when my focus should be the future. I'll have to remember that line next time a government agency chastises me for some arcane rule breach.

I spent a thankless morning making frantic calls that might salvage the deal. At one point, I felt a breakthrough could be imminent when Jeremy Fraser offered some warm words and promised to intervene.

'It's stupidity,' said Fraser. 'There is a total misunderstanding by Gareth because there is no price. The way we've managed this means he won't have to put the figure we pay through his books, if you see what I mean. Lafayeedney swaps his asset with your asset, how does that hurt? It doesn't.'

'I think the issue is that when you do your swap, it should be for something of equivalent value,' I said.

'No, we're not asking for that. It doesn't need to do that. It's what we achieve over the whole of the scheme that matters, not what we achieve on any one site. Provided Dan keeps to that, which he has done, then we're prepared to make a paper loss on this. That's the point I was trying to explain to Gareth.'

'So the price is irrelevant?'

'It's irrelevant, totally irrelevant. It's not the first time a developer has decided to make a loss on one site to make money on another.'

'So where do we go from here?'

'I'm gonna try to meet with Gareth today – I'm in Canary Wharf for another meeting. I want him to get his head around how we'll solve this. I feel that's my role for the next twenty-four hours.'

I'm unsure whether Fraser ever made it to Canary Wharf, or whether the proposed conversation ever took place. But, next time I spoke with Blacker, he was more resolute and obstinate than ever – despite his early and effusive endorsement – that Hancock Road would not be happening.

'Lafayeedney tells me he's ready to exchange right away, and just needs a decision from you,' I said.

'The fact he's having to pay £5 million for it is a big problem.'

'But Jeremy Fraser said it shouldn't be relevant at all.'

'There are two reasons. We don't want to encourage the inflation in land values, and £5 million per acre takes things to a new extreme. And we don't want to set a precedent.'

'But there have been other deals on Hancock Road that have already set the tone, surely?'

'There was the French Connection site, but that was a rogue deal. When you start doing more than one, you have a cumulative effect.'

The ground seemed to be shifting every time I raised a point. Firstly, he couldn't set a precedent. Then, when I pointed out that a precedent already existed, I was told it was 'rogue'.

Having spent three years at Price Waterhouse valuing businesses for privatisation, I thought I had a pretty good grasp of the concept, so I persisted.

'But there's bound to be loads, Gareth. Last week I was sent details of a site in Dace Road on Fish Island – 0.88 of an acre, they've already had an offer of £5 million.'

'Which isn't what an industrial building on that site is worth, if you work it out.'

'But that's what he's selling it for!' I always believed value to be the price agreed between a willing seller and a willing buyer, but Gareth, with his legal powers of state-sanctioned robbery, gave the game away.

'Well, that's what CPOs are for,' he said, adding as an aside, 'and regeneration.'

'I can't get my head around the conflict between a perception of market value and the "compensation code", which talks about the presumption of value. What if the market value includes a disturbance element, because the deal needs to be done quickly due to the CPO? It's like buying a theatre ticket. If you buy a year in advance, the "market price" is different from buying on the black market at the last minute for a sold-out show.'

'It all comes back to how much we know about the ultimate end game, and how that will look as an auditable transaction. There are issues with developers being in land-trading mode. We really are trying to find a way to do something, but it's very frustrating.'

In my next call with Fraser, I lamented that I couldn't just get Blacker and Lafayeedney 'to sit in a meeting room together and just thrash it out'. When I spoke with Lafayeedney, he'd be brimming with confidence and persuade me that his latest wheeze would see everything slot into place (one week, it was 'a share swap rather than a land swap, so there's no record at the Land Registry'). When I spoke with Blacker, he'd dismiss the scheme as a non-starter ('it's still an HMRC event'). The chumminess and bonhomie between Cleveland and the LDA had vaporised as soon as I'd started asking basic, albeit awkward, questions.

With Bow Lock and Hancock Road seemingly off the table, I had to take seriously the possibility that Forman's would close its doors in just eighteen months. I was fixated on the July 2007 eviction deadline; it was impossible to sweep it from my consciousness. It was like being aware of the date of your own death. I suspect that part of the explanation for the LDA's lethargy was that, to them, eighteen months just didn't sound that imminent. But fully functioning factories don't build themselves overnight. And if there's one area where Britain leads the world, it's in the dazzling cornucopia of rules and regulations inflicted on food businesses – from the vital to the well-meaning, the draconian to the absurd. The move from Queen's Yard to Marshgate Lane had taught me many lessons, and foremost amongst them was that eighteen months can whizz by in a flash. It was a little easier for start-ups in the era when Harry Forman placed his first salmon in his first smoker, and, eureka, was in business.

This raised a gruesome prospect. If closure was to be the outcome, my next ordeal would be negotiating an extinguishment value with the authorities.

Under CPO legislation, a business owner is entitled to receive compensation from the government – known as 'extinguishment value' – if a major project such as the Olympics is the direct cause of the firm's failure, on condition that the owner has made all reasonable attempts to find a 'going concern' solution. For months, I had kept up the pretence – even to myself – that closure couldn't and wouldn't happen. But in truth no business is invulnerable or eternal. Research has revealed that eight of the largest ten businesses in America in the 1950s fell by the wayside in just over half a century – through either severe downsizing, being acquired by a hostile predator, or simply running out of cash and collapsing. One-time giants of the American corporate world such as US Steel, Amoco and Goodyear have been replaced at the top of the rankings by companies such as Microsoft, Walmart and Hewlett-Packard – firms that are more attuned to the changing societal landscape. There is no law of nature that dictates Forman's will last for ever. The 'too big to fail' mantra may apply to merchant banks, but certainly not to the last of East End's original salmon smokehouses.

'Is it really possible you could go down that route?' asked my architect and erstwhile partner Phil Hudson.

'I might have no choice, Phil.' We were meeting over a glass of wine in a basement bar near Paternoster Square, and I could barely look up from my drink.

'It flies against everything you stand for.'

'Do you know what's hardest to stomach?'

'I could guess lots of things.'

'I could almost accept going under if it was because our customers hated our product. Or our competitors developed something better value. Or the tastes of the market change, and we fail to keep pace. Or we make a foolish investment that doesn't pay off.'

'I think I know where you're going.'

'What really grates about this situation is we face collapse not because we run a bad business or have made bad business decisions. We face collapse because, to all intents and purposes, the government and two weeks of sport has destroyed us. Ironically, the LDA helped us move to Marshgate Lane in the first place; couldn't someone in the Olympic bid team have tipped them off this might be a problem down the track?'

'And that's why you need the extinguishment report, I suppose?'

I commissioned our accountants, BDO, to study our financial

records, assets and liabilities, and future potential. Their remit was to place an extinguishment value on Forman's that I could share with the authorities. When it arrived, it was a tidy sum – certainly sufficient for my family to enjoy a comfortable life, even if I was never again able to work. But that wasn't really the point. I adore the smoked salmon business, and thrive on the daily challenges it presents. I couldn't think what else I'd do, and I was too long in the tooth to retrain as a barrister or a heart surgeon, even if I'd had the inclination or ability. Perhaps I'd write a book?

Equally important, every member of my staff relied on their Forman's payslips to settle their mortgage and household bills at the end of the month. What would the future hold for fifty smoked salmon folk, suddenly let loose on the streets of east London? It's not like the mackerel smoking business would enjoy a renaissance any time soon or herring was in heavy demand from Mayfair's clientele.

I presented the extinguishment valuation report at my next meeting with the LDA, hoping that the sight of a number with a few zeroes after it might propel them into action. But they couldn't have been more dismissive. It was as if I'd handed them an analysis of a stranger's hourly belching habits, rather than the compensation cheque they'd need to cut in the event I went under.

'If Forman's fails, the charge to the taxpayer will be more than double the cost of paying and renovating Bow Lock, or any other site,' I emphasised. 'You'd be crazy to go down that route.' Cue a row of furrowed brows. It was as if they were all thinking, 'It's not my money, I don't care. Now how much longer until we can get out of here?'

* * *

Tower Hamlets' intransigence over Bow Lock hit me hard. Until that point, I'd assumed the government machines comprise well-meaning professionals working constructively towards the general good. I couldn't fathom any legitimate motive behind their refusal to engage with me about a derelict site, whilst blathering on about masterplanning and Area Action Plans. It seemed the triumph of bureaucracy over employment and trade. Jim Sneddon summed it up when he said to me, 'Far too much masterplanning goes on at the expense of actually doing something!' I was so low it was hard even to share my frustrations with René, lest I double the number of depressed family members from one to two.

Wild animals are most dangerous when cornered, and – if Forman's faced its final curtain – I would go down fighting. I wrote to BDO's Peter Leach, whose firm had led on the extinguishment value calculation, venting my anger. 'They lie to me like this because they are arrogant idiots who completely underestimate their foe,' I said. Extinguishment was the last resort; I needed to be ready for it, but it was far from being my Plan B. Plan Z, perhaps. I needed to exhaust all other options before I'd accept its inevitability. If those options required me to be obstinate, stubborn, bellicose, bull-headed, cantankerous and bloody-minded, then so be it.

I asked my advisors about any 'dogs of war' I had yet to unleash, and Linda Saunders, who was a colleague of Mark Stephens at Finers Stephens Innocent, said in passing, 'Well, you could always threaten a judicial review.' I'm not sure she expected me to take the suggestion literally, but I spent the next two hours becoming a lay-expert on judicial review procedures courtesy of various legal helplines and websites. Twenty-four hours later, Emma Peters and Tower Hamlets was given notice of my intention to refer their behaviour for judicial review. It gave me a wicked satisfaction to think of their expressions when they were appraised of this development. I know from countless episodes of *Yes, Minister* – which I regard as documentary not fiction – that the nightmare for every bureaucracy is open scrutiny of its inner workings. If power without accountability can be an aphrodisiac, then being investigated and second-guessed by a cynical judge trawling over long-forgotten emails must be a passion-killer. 'All I'm doing is throwing dynamite at the bonfire,' I thought. 'What happens next isn't my fault!'

What did happen next, within hours of the legal notice arriving at Peters's desk, was that I received a phone call from the LDA's Chief Executive, Manny Lewis, who shouted down the phone.

'Why have you issued legal proceedings against Tower Hamlets? How do you think they're going to help you if you are taking them to court?'

I responded calmly. 'Well, they certainly haven't been helping me for the last six months, so I am not sure why you think they're going to be helping me now. And in fact, Mr Lewis, I think the LDA should join me in this action, since they were not only lying to me, but also to your Mr Winterbottom, who sat through that entire meeting.'

Lewis slammed the phone down.

Peters still seemed to regard Leyton as a suitable solution, despite the fact I'd dismissed it for numerous commercial reasons months beforehand. She had written to my solicitors in response to the legal threat saying,

> It is our clear understanding that your client has been offered a site in Leyton in the London Borough of Waltham Forest, which is just under two miles from his existing site, appropriate in size (indeed allows for expansion) and is within a designated employment area. Moreover it is the primary location where various authorities working with businesses affected by the Olympics are seeking to relocate all those businesses engaged in food related industries.

I was prepared to overlook her misrepresentation of basic facts (the distance was three miles not two), and the cavalier way she grouped together all food businesses as homogenous (as if supplying artisan-crafted smoked salmon to central London hoteliers had the same operational requirements as an Asian and Afro-Caribbean cash-and-carry business). What really incensed me was the audacity and presumption of a public official to assume they knew the best commercial solution for my company better than I did. If the move was a disaster, I was the one who would spend the next decades dealing with the consequences – I didn't notice them offering to forfeit their salaries if their bland and inane assurances failed to materialise.

Another frustration related to industrial land values, and my hopes were high that the judicial review would expose the inconsistency being shown by the authorities. Both Blacker and Peters had made vacuous comments about the going rate being 'around £1 million an acre'. My response had been terse: 'If that's so, please advise me where there is available land at this price that suits our needs.' For the emptiness of the silence, I might as well have been speaking in Aramaic to mute polar bears in the middle of the Sahara!

At first, Peters used the fact of the judicial review to retreat further from any confrontation with the issues. She wrote to me stating, 'In the circumstances, I think it would be appropriate to wait until your proposed legal action against the council has run its course before engaging further on any of these matters.' I was incensed at the opportunism. She was exploiting my discontent over one matter to refuse me cooperation on any others. Having spoken with my lawyers, I replied forcefully: 'I am advised you cannot refuse to engage with me on separate sites and this, in itself, would be a matter for further judicial review.' Prudently, she backed down, and her next correspondence was more conciliatory.

However, another month had passed. It was now mid-February and the window to nail a solution was fast-closing. Another few days, and it would be latched. Another couple of weeks, locked, with the key flung into a lake. I emailed Manny Lewis, LDA Chief Executive, hoping he had got over my legal torpedo and had the influence to break through the logjam. He promised to speak with Michael Keith, the Chief Executive of Tower Hamlets, and that gave me some comfort, but I was exhausted from placing my trust in a series of false dawns, and in my heart resigned myself to similar disappointment this time. It only took a week to learn that Keith would not be sticking out his neck on Forman's behalf. An insider in the borough told me that the council leadership had their own political agenda, which took precedence over my concerns. The borough to this day remains fraught with treachery and double-dealings. I will never know the truth, but rumour held that a huge split had emerged in the New Labour ranks within the borough. George Galloway's Respect Party was gaining strength amongst the Muslim Labour voters which would split the party locally, and one of the chips being used to prevent Muslim councillors from defecting was the prospect that large homes for Muslim families might be built on the Bow Lock site.

The adrenalin rush of the judicial review gave me a degree of satisfaction, but I knew it was momentary and fleeting. Exchanging rancid comments with my professional advisors might be fun; and launching proceedings was fun-on-steroids. But I was still no closer to a realistic solution. I was finding it harder to sleep. I would roll restlessly in bed for hours, my mind filled with scenarios and numbers and property specs. In addition, the burning sensation that would race up and down my forearm became more intense whenever my thoughts turned to the Olympics (which was often). There were a couple of people I trusted enough to share my health worries. Lloyd was not impressed that I was being cavalier about the matter, and ordered me to see a doctor.

The GP referred me to a cardiologist, who took blood tests, scans, had me wired up and running on a treadmill to see if the physical symptoms were the cause of something physical rather than stress. I lost yet more sleep as I waited for the results, which – when they finally arrived – confirmed that I was generally healthy, thank goodness (to which Mike Finlay remarked: 'Who says that a diet of rich food is bad for you!'), but suffering from an occasional heart flutter. 'You must keep an eye on this,' said Lloyd. 'You need to be careful.' I vowed to spend at least a few hours every weekend with my family, avoiding all mention of property and relocation and Olympics. The words Blacker and Lafayeedney and Cleveland would be forced to the back of my consciousness. Nobody would be helped if, on top of everything else, I suffered a 24-carat nervous breakdown.

CHAPTER 15

FORMIDABLE

Finally, Sebastian Coe was in my sights and ready to be javelined.

The LDA's planned acquisition of land throughout the River Lea area, so that it could be transformed into the Olympic Park, rested on its ability to use Compulsory Purchase Order powers, and this was subject to the outcome of a public inquiry, which was being rushed through to meet an immovable date – the 2012 Olympics – and ignoring all precedents along the way. Due process was being sacrificed on the great altar of sport. Terminal 5 at Heathrow and the Olympic Park CPOs had each received a similar number of objections. The former required six years; the latter was being dealt with in six weeks, because you cannot host the 2012 Games in 2018. And time-sensitive decisions were being steamrollered through, with John Prescott – deputy Prime Minister and human steamroller – having the final say. So much for sportsmanship being synonymous with fair play.

I had been one of those to lodge an objection against the CPO powers, and now had the opportunity to cross-examine witnesses to the inquiry. Sebastian Coe, in his capacity as Chairman of the London Organising Committee, was one of those called to appear. The stakes could not have been higher. If the public inquiry found in my favour, the LDA would have no legal ability to seize privately owned land. This could, in extremis, mean the entire Olympics would be called off, and the bidding reopened. Either that, or the delivery authority would have needed to erect the stadium around our factory. At least we would have had an unmatchable view of the men's 100m final. I knew this was a last resort – my own WMD to save our business. Realistically, if Forman's had nuked the London bid to protect itself, I wonder whether many customers would have returned to purchase a pound of Forman's finest ... perhaps I would've needed to set up a branch in Paris!

By 2006, Coe had already chalked up enough achievements to fill a dozen lifetimes. He had won four Olympic medals, set eleven world records (including three in the space of forty-one days), served as a Conservative MP and been made a life peer. Even without the London Olympics, he could have looked forward to many well-remunerated years serving in pleasing sinecures on sporting body boards, and regaling light-hearted anecdotes to adulatory audiences on the international after-dinner-speaker circuit.

But all this exemplary service counted for nothing when appearing as a witness at a public inquiry. Such events are great levellers. No matter how blue-blooded, famous or wealthy one may be, there is no immunity or privilege in the eyes of the law. One is still obliged to answer questions fully, honestly and to the best of one's ability. Coe would no longer be in his air-conditioned office or chauffeur-driven car. He would be a man, like any other, required to give straight answers.

* * *

No wonder he appeared slightly nervous as he entered the inquiry room and sat at the witness table.

Architecturally, the room was a bog-standard conference room in a glass-and-steel office block, but it had been given the trappings of an Old Bailey-style courtroom, with the inspectorate seated at the head of the room in the manner of a judge, and designated areas for witnesses, barristers, examiners and members of the public. Witnesses were also sworn in under oath before being asked to give evidence. I'm sure these were the reasons that Coe appeared more ashen-faced than I'd ever seen him before. I noticed his right hand was shaking slightly as he poured lukewarm water into a plastic cup and took a sip. And I'm sure there was a glisten of perspiration on his brow. These were all tell-tale signs that he feared the scrutiny that awaited. And, that day, I was certainly in the business of exposing home truths. If I had my way, by the time I sat down, he would be revealed as a devious manipulator, prepared to run roughshod over legitimate grievances and wreck livelihoods and businesses.

For two years, he had evaded me. My correspondence had been either ignored or treated to vacuous responses that bordered on the contemptuous. Now, he was at my mercy, and I was in no mood to be merciful. As we travelled together to the inquiry venue, City Aviation House in the Royal Docks, I'd joked with Mike Finlay, 'They say, don't kick a man when he's down. I say, well, if you don't have the guts to kick him then, you never will!'

My strategy was centred on the issue of regeneration. The Compulsory Purchase Order had been made on the premise that the desire to acquire land in the area was driven by the need for regeneration, not just sport. The LDA had to make that claim, notwithstanding it being self-evident nonsense, because their constitution at the time of the order did not allow them to acquire land for a sporting event. If I could prove that the only logical reason for the CPO was to make way for the London Olympics, the entire event could collapse like a house of cards, and Marshgate Lane could continue as the home of the world's oldest salmon smokehouse.

The official narrative was that 'this is a derelict area which will be regenerated by the Olympics'. However, the area was not derelict. I admit, it wasn't pretty with architectural masterpieces like the late Zaha Hadid's Aquatics Centre, but it was a wealth-creating zone and London's greatest concentration of manufacturing land. What's more, the LDA had a commercial interest to characterise the area as 'derelict', to depress the value, like a canny house-buyer keeping his enthusiasm under wraps when meeting his dream home's vendor. In any event, regeneration was already happening. Aside from our new smokehouse, there were brand new business parks, a new Eurostar terminal was under construction and the massive Stratford City development had received planning permission. When we raised this with the LDA and asked, 'If this is about regeneration and not about sport, why are you doing it? It's already happening,' they responded that, it was such a large project, if left to piecemeal development by private developers, it would take around twenty years, and with government involvement they could speed things up. Interestingly, when we speak to the planners today and ask them why the post-Olympic regeneration is not happening with the same urgency as the Olympic clear-out, they respond, 'It's a big programme, it will take twenty years.' The reality is that the Olympics delayed the ongoing regeneration activity by seven years as no real regeneration could take place until the Games were over.

Establishing the myth of regeneration had meant misleading the IOC, the media and even the monarch in the run-up to Singapore. On the eastern side of the Olympic Park was a 1960s council housing block called Holden Point. When the Olympic bid team took visiting dignitaries to the viewing platform on the twenty-first storey, so they had a bird's eye view of the area proposed for the park, they pointed in the wrong direction! Not west, towards the Marshgate Lane manufacturing hub, but south, towards derelict railway land cleared for Stratford City, not for the Olympics.

There had been no stipulation that questions must be submitted in advance, which meant I had the flexibility to take my inquisition in any direction I chose. David Rose, a member of the Royal Town Planning Institute, had been appointed by the Secretary of State to manage the proceedings, and seemed intent that everything should function with brisk efficiency. After rattling through his opening remarks at breakneck speed, he called on me to begin the interrogation. I figured I may as well go for the jugular from the outset.

'Lord Coe, you are on record as stating that acquiring land compulsorily "is not a decision that can be taken lightly, or in anything other than exceptional circumstances". Do you stand by that belief?'

'I do. It's integral to how I think government should behave.'

'You have also said that 11,000 jobs will be created by the Games. I assume that is part of your definition of "exceptional circumstances"?'

'Yes, we should all welcome 11,000 new jobs. It's incredibly good news. Each one of those 11,000 jobs represents a real person, somebody who will be able to put food on the family table.'

'Are you aware, Lord Coe, that the businesses you're destroying collectively employ 14,000 people?'

Coe looked through his briefing notes in search of support.

'Perhaps I could ask something else whilst you're looking through your papers. Would you care to enlighten us about how many of those 11,000 jobs will still exist after the Paralympics closing ceremony?'

'A few, I think.'

'Isn't it the case, Lord Coe, that you propose replacing 14,000 skilled and well-paid jobs, with 11,000 temporary, minimum-wage jobs. And even those won't exist once the Olympics has left town. In fact, by 2013, I suspect the only permanent employment you'll have created will be for a few security guards to watch the entrance to an empty and unused site. Good news for retired police officers, but not so good for the rest of us.'

'I think that's unfair.'

'And what's the source, by the way, of your 11,000 figure? You can't just invent numbers in order to impress the inspectorate.' I looked at Rose. 'We can all invent numbers to suit our case. You won't beat me, if we're allowed to play that game.'

'It was in the Arup report.'

'Ah yes, the Arup report. A document paid for by the public – and I'm sure it cost a tidy sum; these consultants don't come cheap – but which the public isn't allowed to see.'

'You can't blame me for that. It wouldn't be my call.'

'But luckily for me, and for the public, I do have a copy with me today. Provided to me by an insider who felt it was outrageous to keep such important information confidential.'

I waved the Arup report above my head for dramatic effect. There was an audible gasp within the room, and Rose started rifling through some folders. I suspect he was trying to locate any guidance about the admissibility of leaked information as evidence at a public inquiry. After a few moments, he glared at me as if to say, 'Why have you put me in this tricky position?' I took the absence of an unequivocal order to stop as unfettered permission to continue.

'And do you know what the Arup report says about new jobs, Lord Coe?'

Coe was now grabbing the side of his chair in a failed attempt to control his shaking. 'N-no, but I'm sure you'll tell me.'

'Three thousand, Lord Coe. Less than a third of the figure you're claiming.'

'Oh.'

'Don't you feel ashamed, Lord Coe, at giving fictitious, tendentious numbers to this inquiry about such a significant matter, especially with billions of pounds of public money at risk?'

'Not really. I mean, that isn't how I'd express it.'

'Let us now turn to some of the other material contained within the Arup report.'

Coe turned to Rose, fear in his eyes. 'Isn't this meant to be about the CPO, not the Arup report,' he pleaded.

'A good point, Lord Coe.' Rose turned to me, relieved he'd found a potential escape route. 'Mr Forman, unless you can demonstrate that the Arup report has an explicit bearing on the matters before us, I'll ask you to make no further references to it.'

I had anticipated this challenge, and relished the chance to deploy my devastating riposte. 'Sir, it's not me making the connection. Paragraph 2.3 of the Statement of Reasons, appending to the CPO, says – and I quote – "In light of the Arup report, the Cabinet decided to support the bid." I think that's an irrefutable reason for me to draw upon it.'

Coe looked deflated. Rose said, wearily, 'I suppose so, Mr Forman. Please proceed.'

I turned back to Coe. 'The Arup report was guided by a steering committee which comprised representatives from government, the Mayor, the LDA, the British Olympics Association, UK Sport and Sport England, and I note that in the opening paragraphs the Arup authors state that, during their review, they did not consult with any business landowners on how the Olympics would affect them, nor the consequences for them of relocation. Why would the steering committee have given Arup that direction, Lord Coe?'

'I've no idea,' he whispered meekly.

'An accurate observation, in many ways,' I said. 'Now, let me now turn to the four explanations in the documents before us that are offered as the "rationale" for the CPO. Firstly, it is argued that the land is needed to "secure the economic development and regeneration" of the area. Yet the Arup report clearly states that in Stratford, "development is planned and can be expected to be implemented within ten to fifteen years irrespective of the Olympics". Isn't that true, Lord Coe?'

Coe mumbled.

'Answer the question, Lord Coe,' pressed Rose.

'It's true,' he said.

'Moreover, Richard Sumray, Chairman of the Steering Committee, in his evidence to the GLA, before the location decision had been made, said that, "Stratford ... is less interesting because it's less regenerative and housing will be built there in any event. I don't think that's the one we would want to consider." Is that true?'

'It's true.'

'Even Glennys, advisors to the LDA, confirm that east London was already enjoying an "exponential" surge in development, and cite numerous infrastructure improvements that are taking place, or in the pipeline, such as the new A12 Blackwall Tunnel link road, the Channel Tunnel rail link, CrossRail, the Thames Gateway Bridge, and the duelling of the A120 from Stanstead to Braintree. True?'

Coe sighed. Again, Rose forced him to be explicit. 'Yes, that's true too.'

'And to trump it all, the London Borough of Newham planners submitted an official objection to the choice of Stratford for the Olympics on the grounds that it would actually damage pre-existing regeneration plans. Let me repeat that: *actually damage*! It would cause them to be shelved. It was submitted that "sacrificing the long-term redevelopment for a short-term gain is contrary to good planning". Ironic, certainly. And also true?'

'I suppose.'

'Is it not the case, Lord Coe, that the entire reference to regeneration in the CPO is spurious and without foundation?' I slammed my fist on the table for emphasis. 'Stratford has never lacked good transport links or employment prospects. This rationale was no more than a cynical attempt to sequestrate assets through fine-sounding words disconnected from reality. Propaganda worthy of *Pravda*.'

'There are still three other reasons,' spluttered Coe.

'Ah yes, rationale two: "To promote business efficiency, investment and competitiveness." And rationale three: "To promote employment and enhance the development and application of skills relevant to employment."'

'Exactly.'

'Let's see what Arup says about these. Firstly, investment. On page 60, entitled "The Effect of Blight", Arup conclude inward investment would be adversely affected by the uncertainty of the CPO. Next, business competitiveness. On page 55, the authors outrageously propose acquiring and redeveloping land "on a staged basis to reduce the potential for compensation ... [and to] assist with the negotiation with the particular remaining tenants in terms of any compensation payable". On page 58, they propose acquiring Decant Land "to mitigate acquisition costs and reduce the likely compensation payments". How is a plan that deliberately sets out to deprive property owners of fair value compatible with making businesses more competitive? This is the thinking of a totalitarian state! If seizure of assets was a sure-fire way to commercial success, the Soviet Union would have been an economic powerhouse.'

Coe glared at me and said, 'Is there a question inside that ramble?'

'Here's my question. We might have been faced with the destruction of our businesses, but at least we got a helpline. Are you proud of the helpline, Lord Coe?'

'Absolutely. Don't mock it. We didn't need to set up a helpline, and you should be grateful.'

'So, here's the strange thing. When we called the helpline, managed by the Royal Institution of Chartered Surveyors, we were referred to two separate firms of surveyors – neither of whom had any idea they were meant to be a helpline. Would you like the details of what they said?'

Coe stared at one of his aides. I assumed it was the aide responsible for the helpline programme.

'Which brings us neatly to the point about employment. Would you agree that many of the businesses in the Olympic Zone are already growing? Mine, for example, has expanded from twenty-eight to fifty employees in three years.'

'Yes, I would concede that.'

'The Arup report estimates that 380,000 square metres of industrial workspace will be destroyed, and only 160,000 square metres created by the Olympic Park. When I was at school, 160,000 was a lot smaller than 380,000. Was that the case at your school?'

Rose reprimanded me: 'There's no need for sarcasm, Mr Forman.'

'My apologies, sir. I'll rephrase the question in a neutral way. Is 160,000 smaller than 380,000? Regardless of whatever you may have been taught at school.'

'It's smaller.'

I turned to Rose. 'Sir, there is one further rationale for the CPO. But I think it's already clear that the entire case rests on bogus assertions, sweeping generalisations, implied falsehoods, and the reckless misuse of statistics. In fact, throughout their report, Arup acknowledge that their costings are "not definitive". That's their terminology, by the way. I'd use "outdated and subjective". For example, on page 29, they state that more discussions need to take place which could "lead to quite significant changes to the disposition of land uses and other elements of the proposal, and could significantly affect the cost".'

Rose looked shocked. 'Is that really what it says?' he asked. 'In the document the government used as the basis for its decision to bid?'

I walked from my table to stand directly before Rose and Coe. I wanted to be able to look into their eyes as I administered the coup de grace.

'Sir,' said Coe, 'would it be possible to adjourn for the rest of the day so I can consult my notes?' He must have sensed that he'd been snookered with shrewd and meticulous precision, as if he was playing a grudge match with Steve Davis.

'Man up,' said Rose. 'Request denied.'

I continued: 'On page 53, Arup are explicit about the treatment being meted out towards business owners. They state, "Whilst we have made broad assumptions to establish an estimated cost of acquiring the sites, the final costs will depend on the individuals in question and the nature/position of their land investment." Do you see anything wrong with that, Lord Coe?'

'I'm not quite sure where you're headed, but I'd still like the court to indulge me in a short adjournment.'

'I said it already: man up,' said Rose.

I was so close to Coe that I could see the sweat stains spreading on his shirt. 'I put it to the inquiry that land and property values should not relate to "individuals in question". A state authority should not be seeking to negotiate the lowest deal individually with every landowner depending on their circumstances and whether they find themselves in desperate straits. It should be making a fair appraisal of the value of the land and apply this even-handedly to all those affected.'

At the back of the room, Mike Finlay shouted, 'Hear, hear!' Sitting next to him, Seamus, who was not to be outdone, stood up and applauded loudly. Moments later, the entire room was on its feet, whistling, clapping and stomping. Rose tried to quieten the room, but to little avail. 'Order, order,' he kept repeating, but his aged voice was drowned out by the raucous, delirious cheering from all around. It was a full five minutes before it abated, at which time – facing my audience, but addressing my witness – I said five simple words: 'Isn't that right, Lord Coe?'

When there was no answer, I repeated the question.

Still silence.

'Answer the question, please, Lord Coe,' instructed Rose.

This time, the request was greeted not with words, but with the sharp sound of a crash. Three dozen necks craned to see what had happened. Lord Coe had collapsed from his seat, and was lying prostrate beneath the table, one arm hooked around his briefcase, his legs akimbo like

Katie Price in a photoshoot. He looked less like a pillar of the British establishment and more like a teenager sprawled in the gutter after too many vodka shots on a Saturday evening in the town centre of Hull. Wiped out, passed out – out for the count. I folded my arms in satisfaction and looked forward to tomorrow's headlines: 'Sacré bleu: Olympics heads to Paris after all', 'Fish man triumphs over fishy man', 'Marshgate businesses propose Forman for knighthood'.

* * *

This, at least, was how I dreamt my cross-examination on Coe might proceed.

In the event, I was to be cruelly denied the chance. In the weeks leading up to the CPO, a new site had emerged which might meet our needs. Credit goes to Emma Peters who, under pressure after the judicial review notice had been served on Tower Hamlets, thought laterally about potential sites in the borough and made us aware of three that might create the opening for a deal. After the months I'd spent chasing the slightest hint of a deal in far-flung corners, whether it be Bow Lock or Hancock Road or Channelsea House, it was ironic that this opportunity – on Stour Road – was literally just a few minutes' walk from the factory.

Stour Road runs for much of the length of Fish Island, a fifty-acre area bounded by the River Lea Navigation, the Hertford Union Canal and the East Cross Route. For centuries it had been a thriving residential and industrial community, but much of the housing was destroyed during World War Two bombing raids, and the island was now primarily occupied by factories and warehouses, including a large concentration of artists' studios. Contrary to popular belief, the name does not signify an abundance of fish in the nearby waterways; it derives from the bizarre assortment of streets with fish-related names:

Dace Road, Bream Street, Monier Road, Roach Road. It had often been portrayed as having 'the great potential' for a residential resurgence, and with that hope the Community Housing Association had acquired a plot of land on Stour Road, on the edge of the River Lea and overlooking the future Olympic Park.

The Association's vision had been to replace these with a modern, vibrant residential block, and with feckless abandon had handed over £4 million for a three-quarter-acre plot of land with three derelict factories. At that time, they'd understood planning permission would be a formality, but with the arrival of the Olympic Park, Tower Hamlets had revised its policy towards Fish Island, and designated it as a prime area for relocating businesses, meaning the site's market value had plummeted back to industrial-use level. Realising it had no use for a former black cab repair shop, the Association was prepared to offload the site if it could recoup its initial outlay. If not, it would sit on the site for five, ten or twenty years until residential developments resurfaced as a planning priority for Fish Island.

After so many false starts, I knew exactly how to complete a rapid-fire assessment of Stour Road's suitability as a smokehouse. My lawyers checked out the existing consents to determine what planning applications would be required. And, crucially, the ever-reliable Phil Hudson conducted a high-level technical feasibility study. On 8 March 2006, he sent me one of the most important communications received in the 100-year history of Forman's. His conclusions were forthright:

> I feel the Stour site is much better than Cleveland's in Hancock Road. It has massive street frontage, being at the turn of the road offers a long view of Forman's main entrance, there is plenty of loose space for your vehicles and parking. If the LDA is prepared to proceed with Stour Road, I would do nothing that might cause them to hesitate. I would go hell for leather. I am concerned you

> may feel there is some advantage with Cleveland, and I fear by reaching for it you risk complicating the current excellent option for a less good one.

Already, my gut had been telling me to chase after Stour Road, but once Phil had bestowed his blessing there was no going back. Hancock Road was dead, there was no way I could settle for a secondary solution after so many sleepless nights and cardiologist consultations. The location was appropriate, the size was ideal, there was a willing seller, and – uniquely – none of my advisors had been able to identify a downside. It was a perfect match with the CPO promise that affected businesses should be left 'no worse off'.

When I passed on my observations about Stour Road to Blacker, his immediate response was, 'We might be able to trade very quickly', and suggested he 'find out tomorrow' as much as possible about the Association's wider dealings with the Housing Corporation (the public body, since abolished, that funded new affordable housing) and the Greater London Assembly. Initially, I was rebuffed by the Association, who were reluctant to crystallise their write-down. But I proposed a three-way, merry-go-round deal to Blacker, whereby the LDA would find another site to which the Housing Association could relocate, which would provide them with the residential planning permission they needed, and swap it for their existing site. This would free up the Stour Road site for us which the LDA would sell to us at an industrial land valuation of £750,000 (equivalent to £1 million per acre), equating to the value of the land they had set for our site in Marshgate Lane. If I could exchange contracts on this basis, honour would be satisfied all round. The Association would be able to extend its affordable housing provision. The LDA would not have set an unwelcome precedent for Olympic zone land values. And I would have acquired a site that, at its previous valuation, would have been far out of reach.

The train had left the station, but the risk of derailment was still high. If not for the leverage provided by my planned cross-examination of Lord Coe at the public inquiry, I suspect my Orwellian nightmare would have continued right up until the moment the first bulldozer started smashing down my factory walls, with my final action before eviction being to press 'send' on an email to clients explaining that Forman's had ceased trading. But then events took an unexpected turn. Less than one week before Coe was scheduled to take the stand, my lawyers received an electrifying call from the LDA, offering to 'sort out' Stour Road for me if I consented to pull my questioning. Emotionally, I was reluctant to forfeit my moment of glory. I was pumped up and had spent the previous weekend rehearsing my lines of attack with Michael Finlay, so took it as a personal affront that anyone could suggest I sit this one out. My lawyers had been advising to keep the threat on the table until a deal was secured, but now insisted I was close enough that I dispense with such thoughts. They reminded me that the CPO objection, like the judicial review, was a means to an end, rather than the goal itself, however satisfying the prospect of humiliating those who had tormented me and underestimated my resolve. We agreed that I would indeed relinquish the chance to question Coe, but only on one categorical and unflinching condition – that contracts for the purchase of Stour Road were signed by noon on that very day (5 May) complete with a statement that the LDA would meet all our costs for a like-for-like facility, pay any costs thrust upon us as a result of planning requirements, pay for the accelerated construction costs for having to build a factory in half the time needed, settle our loss-of-profit claim and support us fully to ensure our planning application could be fast-tracked. I was not in a trusting mood. If I was going to sacrifice my public platform, the deal needed to be watertight.

For the first time in my endless dealings with them, the machinery of government moved with blinding velocity and agility. I was receiving emails from my lawyers with queries from the LDA lawyers for action to take as though they were trying to stave off some major terrorist attack. They were employing adjectives such as 'urgent' and 'immediate' in place of 'deliberation' and 'reflection', which had been their preferred *bon mots* to that point. Tricky points were being conceded or air-brushed away in the race to sign. If not for my continuing dread that everything might fall apart, I would have savoured my newfound (and temporary) power.

I remain dazzled by the pace at which everything fell into place. The transaction was negotiated, drafted, signed, counter-signed and exchanged in less than one day. Our 'high noon' deadline was missed, but only by a few hours. Two and half years of pain, for one day of gain. Before I left my office, I grabbed a compliment slip and an envelope from my filing cabinet, wrote the London 2012 address, which I knew by heart, and penned nine sweet words to Sebastian Coe. 'Dear Seb. You can run, but you can't hide.'

On 9 May, the day before my cross-examination would have been delivered, the press reported the news that the Forman's fight was over and our business saved. 'The future of Britain's oldest salmon smoker had been secured after its owner agreed to make way for the London Olympics,' wrote Matthew Beard in *The Independent*. 'The LDA has spared Seb Coe embarrassment by striking a deal with the most aggrieved of the businessmen forced to relocate,' was *The Guardian*'s take. And the *Daily Mail* commented that 'The LDA have agreed a last-minute Stratford land deal with their most vociferous opponent, salmon smoker boss Lance Forman, just before the public inquiry into the compulsory purchase orders.' A number of the newspapers picked up on the symbolism of Forman's being moved to 'Fish Island', and let rip with groan-inducing puns, but none chose to publish my rejoinder that 'it wasn't nearly as appropriate as the LDA's recent location, to the Isle of Dogs'.

* * *

My old sparring partner Dan Lafayeedney almost vanished from my life when my lack of interest in Hancock Road became apparent. But he did resurface in a couple of unexpected situations. As news seeped out of my pursuit of the Fish Island site, I learnt that he coincidentally had exchanged contracts on the land on either side of it, which he hoped to repurpose as residential accommodation. Since few people, he assumed, would wish to live adjacent to a fish factory, my sudden interest in Stour Road for the Forman's revival threw a mammoth spanner into his machinations. The first hint of trouble came in a call with Richard Fieldsend, the agent who first introduced me to Lafayeedney, who had been blunt in his warnings that I should steer clear. 'There's a lot you don't know, Lance. You're better off leaving it to Dan, because he has strings he can pull.'

After every promise about Hancock Road had turned to dust, I wasn't minded to 'leave it to Dan', so mobilised my team to proceed with the offer and exchange documents. When Lafayeedney learnt of this, he realised his investment in the neighbouring sites – already precarious – was on the verge of crumbling into a substantial loss. He reached out to me, with words reeking of anguish and gloom rather than his customary swagger.

'Can you please call me,' he wrote, 'as our interests would be severely damaged should you go ahead and build your factory on Stour Wharf without cooperation between us.' I told him that I needed to honour my commitment to the LDA, but would help him out if possible. Until the very last moment, I was nervous he might gazump us, or stymie us through a deal with Blacker that operated to our detriment. In the event, there was nothing I could do to assist, and his options proved worthless. But he didn't seem to bear a grudge. (Admittedly, that last claim is supposition not fact, my only evidence being that, three years later,

Lafayeedney contacted Forman's to ask that we cater for an event at one of his newly acquired properties in Sugar House Lane. I'm never one to turn down good business, regardless of any historical entanglements, and was pleased to accept Lafayeedney as one of our ever-growing collection of satisfied customers.)

I never did fathom every piece of the Lafayeedney jigsaw, but there was one conclusion which, I felt, I was safe in drawing: the Olympics was an event of global significance, taking place in the planet's oldest democracy and fifth largest economy, and its spokespeople paraded the virtues of sportsmanship and integrity without a hint of hypocrisy or shame. Nevertheless, with the eyes of the world watching, its site-clearance programme was managed with a mixture of incompetence and worse – the worse being a blatant land grab, in the knowledge that, post-Olympics, much of it could be reconfigured for residential schemes with the commensurate uplift in values. Transparency and straight dealings were not, to put it mildly, its greatest legacy.

CHAPTER 16

FORMING

The saga of compulsory purchase and relocation had brought me into conflict with almost every corner of the British establishment – national government, local government, quangos, the legal system. The sole exception had been the police – whether through luck or judgment, I'd been spared any visitations from Inspector Plod during this entire period. In the two decades since forensic detective work had blown the lid on my student shenanigan – when I'd been part of the gang busted for possession of looted rolls of Andrex Classic White – I'd had no further run-ins with the boys in blue. As far as police records were concerned, I was an upstanding citizen with an unblemished record of law-abiding behaviour. Unfortunately, those credentials would not remain impeccable for much longer.

Ever since London's anointing as the Olympics city, media interest in anything remotely related to the Games had screeched into dizzying overdrive. I was now on speed-dial for broadsheet and tabloid hacks whenever they'd needed a pithy quote close to a copy deadline. In a 'penny-drop moment' writ large, the public generally, and journalists especially, were waking up to a number of shocking clauses in the London Olympic Games and Paralympic Games Act 2006, many that overrode 1,000 years of legal precedence. And the BBC itself was not to be outdone. As factories started crumbling in the path of wrecking balls and demolition crews, a three-part observational documentary was commissioned entitled *Building the Olympic Dream*. The second episode, subtitled 'The Last Stand at Stratford', was trailed as lifting the veil about the winners and losers:

> After unexpectedly winning the bid to stage the Olympic Games in 2012, the authorities waste no time in clearing the land for the Olympic park in east London – inevitably there are winners and losers. The ambition and scale of the project is huge – and resistance to the plans comes from some unexpected quarters.

So much for the propaganda about every business being restored to a *no better and no worse* position – even the Beeb now accepted that the Games was creating a pool of 'losers' with legitimate grievances. It's a credit to their journalistic integrity that they were prepared to delve beneath the surface hoopla. Both government and opposition benches were a closed shop in their uncritical, frenzied joy that the greatest show on earth was coming to town. Thank goodness for a (mostly) free press prepared to treat politicians' claims and promises with a healthy dose of cynicism.

Debbie Hartley was the showrunner assigned to the BBC project, and we struck up an immediate rapport. She had a nose for a great story, and was determined the nation should be told about the Games' fallout, about the damage to employment and livelihood in the local community. Throughout her months of involvement with the story, she acted with uncompromising professionalism. She'd meticulously cross-check my claims and allegations with information from other sources before reporting them as facts. She created a programme which – as well as being a gripping narrative with sensational visuals – gave a voice to all sides, both the Goliaths and the Davids, so that viewers could make up their own minds about the events portrayed.

Our showdown with the police came towards the end of her time covering the story. Most of Marshgate Lane had been turned to rubble, with our factory one of the few still standing. Since it remained a functioning place of work, only our delivery vehicles, together with both Lloyd's and my cars, had permission from the LDA to journey through the perimeter to our loading bays and back. They referred to this as a 'special dispensation' – how typical of the authorities that, in destroying our building, they found terminology that suggested they were doing us a favour. After this edict had been issued, the only way Debbie could reach our factory was if I personally escorted her from the Olympic Park's security gate in my 'approved car'.

By now, most of the future Olympic Park resembled a war zone, strewn with the smashed remains of once-proud buildings. Parts of the scene were heart-rending; small vignettes that encapsulated how a once-mighty manufacturing hub had been laid to waste. Debbie unhooked her camera, rolled down the window and started filming. In the foreground was the signage for a repair shop that had once employed three dozen people. Elsewhere were scattered company documents and files, half-buried in the mud like a herd of bathing rhinoceros – many businesses had given up the fight, chosen liquidation over relocation, and never gotten around to emptying the paperwork from their offices.

Which is when we ran into trouble with the Olympic police.

Rather than travel directly to Forman's, I thought it would help Debbie, the BBC and the programme's audience if I took a more circuitous route, which might reveal some more interesting and varied views. Although, if the truth be known, there was very little of interest. It was like driving through a country lane where all you can see is mud, some mustard yellow farm equipment (in this case, demolition equipment) and one lonely farmhouse in the distance (in this case, our soon-to-be-demolished smokehouse). She had been filming for perhaps a minute or two when a squad car – its blue lights flashing and sirens blaring – came screeching down after us, and the officers spilled out, stony-faced and determined, as if they were about to bust a major drug deal. With it being a really hot and bright sunny day and the police wearing sunglasses, the whole thing seemed as preposterous as being landed in a scene from *Dukes of Hazzard*.

The lead officer, probably thirty-five but with the face of a teenager, stared at Debbie: 'What the hell do you think you're doing?'

'Just taking some GVs. I didn't think that would be a problem.' If we had actually been on the *Hazzard* set, her acronym for the production term 'general vistas' might have been intelligible – but to the ears of a London copper it probably sounded extremely dangerous.

'It's against the law,' he said bluntly.

'There's nothing here except rubble. How can that be…?'

'Don't get clever with us. Do you know where you are?'

'I think everybody knows.'

'And how do I know you're not a terrorist?'

'Really? Do I look like a terrorist?'

'They come in all shapes and sizes.'

'Maybe so, but I'm not one of them,' she said, brandishing her ID. 'In fact, I'm from the BBC.'

'I don't care where you're from, you're handing over that film.' He came closer and attempted to grab the camera.

'No, you're not. Not before I've spoken with BBC lawyers.'

Unfortunately for Debbie, the BBC wasn't at its most efficient that day. With the officers growling impatiently, the switchboard operators took painful minutes to reroute the call. I grimaced at Debbie's discomfort and cursed myself for putting her into such a vulnerable position. On the other hand, at least the experience gave her first-hand insight into how impotent one becomes when the Olympic powers decide to turn their fire in your direction. At the last moment, when surrender of the footage seemed inevitable, Debbie was finally connected with her boss, and given the BBC's full support to stand firm against intimidation. Her camera was retained and the programme aired, although none of this footage made it through to the final cut. To this day, I'm perplexed that such an innocuous, scene-setting shot could have been deemed a threat to national security.

What struck me most about the police action against Debbie's reportage was not simply the fact of seeing her pictures almost destroyed, but the arrogance with which authority was being exercised. There was no hint of apology or regret. Throughout the years of the Olympic Park's construction, it was like dastardly lobotomisation gases had been pumped into the Stratford air, stripping anyone connected with the Olympics of their humanity, humour and sense of perspective. 'It's because of the Olympics' was the catch-all justification for reams of arbitrary rules, an upsurge in bossiness and the suspension of common sense.

* * *

With our new Stour Road site secured, I was determined that it would be our durable, catastrophe-free home for decades to come. After ten years of upheaval and disruption, we had surely tested to destruction the patience of our clientele and the fortitude of my incredible Forman's team. I couldn't risk another ten years tottering on the brink of perennial downfall, my time preoccupied with disaster management rather than leading the business forward. Having a decent site, in a good location, at no risk of flooding, was a solid start. Next, we needed a factory. And it needed to be a factory that would not only function efficiently – but also inspire, impress and astonish. It must be a showcase to our standards and values. In fact, I didn't want it to look like a factory, feel like a factory, or even be a factory. Years later, Boris Johnson referred to Forman's as being a 'smoked salmon theme park', four simple words that summed up my vision to perfection. What a gift Johnson has for a pithy, evocative and memorable turn of phrase (and probably why he's a lead contender to be our next Prime Minister, whilst I have never surpassed the glittering moment I enjoyed in the political firmament when I served as a special advisor in my twenties).

Speaking of my early career, Phil Hudson had drifted out of my personal orbit since we went different ways after our East8 exploits, largely due to being physically separated by the 1,300 miles between Ukraine and the UK. But with our various property woes, he had re-emerged as a vital figure for vital times. I'd already been using him on an ad hoc basis to advise on miscellaneous sites that had cropped up, but with Stour Road confirmed, it was time to firm up the arrangement. He remains to this day the most daring, visionary architect I've ever encountered. If I wanted a bog-standard factory box, there were hundreds of architects in London I could've appointed. But he was the only single person to whom I could ever entrust the creation of something exceptional.

Of course, for a project of this scale, I needed a team of professionals with a range of skills. My project manager was the Barrie Tankel Partnership (now the BTP Group), a thirty-year-old firm of quantity surveyors and cost consultants based in the West End. My builder was Phelan Construction, who had wide experience of complex new-build projects in the commercial sector. With construction due to commence in October 2006 for completion by 2 July 2007, they had just eight months (I repeat, *eight months*) to build and fit out a fully functioning factory from scratch – both recoiled with horror at the accelerated timescales, but promised to pull out the stops. Construction projects are notorious for over-running deadlines, and in fairness to those involved there could be numerous elements beyond their control (the weather, the performance of sub-contractors, approvals from various authorities). However, in our unique situation, the repercussions of a delay were almost inconceivable. The LDA had given us a fixed date on which it intended to take possession of our old factory. If Stour Road was unable to accommodate us from the moment of our eviction, then the Stratford air would be pierced with two unforgettable sounds – a stream of expletives from my lips, and the clanging of the death knell for our business.

In any adventurous new build, especially one not following a common template, there will be complex calculations involving weight distribution, foundations, walls, beams and roofs. In the case of Stour Road, our concertinaed timescales meant that Phil was working without complete information to hand. The soil conditions were unknown – a particular concern when building on insecure land adjacent to a canal – and we weren't even entirely certain of the boundary lines because the local authorities insisted they be allowed three weeks to retrieve the records. We faced an unenviable choice between sitting idly by whilst losing anther three weeks, or proceeding on the basis of hunch and intuition rather than irrefutable fact. Phil made a number of pragmatic recommendations. With the laying of the foundation soon underway, he told the builders to pile heavily enough that even a California-type earthquake wouldn't dislodge the building. And he brought the structure in from the boundaries, using a truss system rather than the portal frame structure, which is the usual solution for large open factories or barns.

In the event, we were able to turn adversity into advantage. It would after all be possible to extend the truss right up to our neighbour's land and this gave us a large curved roof and a vast and unexpected loft space, which we christened our 'ghost floor' until such time as we could figure out exactly what to do with it. With the curved roof and the building sitting adjacent to a canal, Phil sent me some sketch designs, showing the reflection of the building in the water and the comment: 'It looks like the cross-section of a salmon.' We carried this theme throughout the architectural design. The 'guts' of the salmon was where we located the smoking, the truss became the bones, the external walls were finished in salmon pink stucco resembling the flesh, and to top it all was the salmon skin roof in a scaly pattern with two tonnes of silvery grey. The roof effect is almost impossible to detect from ground level, but I was mindful that airplane passengers on the final approach into City airport also eat salmon!

The aquatic-style imagery wasn't confined to the building's fabric; there were numerous maritime touches to the interior fit-out, such as rope handrails, porthole windows and oversized portholes creating a viewing gallery into the smokehouse, which Phil often described as 'the engine room', with its stainless funnels and flues proudly on show. There was hardly a corner of the factory where nautical sizzle couldn't be applied. When we learnt from the health and safety officers that every internal door must have two glazed viewing panels (eye level and low level) in case someone swings opens a door into a wheelchair-bound employee or visitor, we made a point of upgrading these windows too, to thick circular glass encased in metal frames in the style of the portholes in a ship's hull. Everyone would be getting the vibe.

The contract exchanged in haste with the LDA obliged them to fund the construction to the extent it matched our previous building. Tenders had been issued but during our crunch talks about the finances, one word took on a life of its own. I wanted the legal documents to quantify a sum for 'contingency' for the build and fit-out, and I felt that 10 per cent would be customary for a property project of this complexity and speed. 'Contingency' proved to be the solitary matter on which the LDA could not bend, not by an inch. 'The government does not pay for contingency,' was the unambiguous rejoinder from Gareth Blacker. 'No contingency, it will not happen. Just keep within the approved spend.' I reconciled myself to this condition, albeit reluctantly. It later hit me that contingency represented a major slab of the budget for the Olympic Park itself; £2 billion, according to contemporaneous press reports, and rising – indeed, more than 100 per cent of the original budget. Once again, one rule for the tax payer, another for the tax receiver.

Of course, being a *Forman's* relocation, it was never going to proceed without a crisis or two. One of the most absurd was the appearance from left field of Rob McCarthy and his colleagues from the Environment Agency, who objected to our plans for the site on the grounds that an eight-metre 'buffer zone' should remain between our building and the canalside. Losing such a large element of our floorplate would have destroyed the viability of our new factory, and for the only time in my life I fired off an email to my team of advisors in which every word was in bright red and capitalised. 'I AM READY TO EXPLODE, HAVE A HEART ATTACK OR EMIGRATE,' I raged. The tone epitomised my mood at the time. I was more restrained in my dealings with the EA officers.

'Why do we need to set the building back and lose almost 20 per cent of floor space, on land which I now own?'

'It's Environment Agency policy,' was the response. No explanation, no consideration, just some dreamt-up policy.

'But this strip of land leads to nowhere. It's not a canalside walkway and indeed plans are afoot to tear down the adjacent building and build a bridge, which would then make our private canalside space the end of a cul-de-sac. I can't understand why you're forcing this upon me?'

Eventually the answer was revealed. It was to provide sufficient space to allow various aquatic insects to mate.

I calmly pointed out that should the buffer zone remain the nesting grounds for fleas, fruit flies, hornets, ticks, arachnids and the rest, none of said insects would enjoy a long post-coital lifespan, given that our factory was obliged (by a different arm of government) to zap any that came within proximity of the food preparation areas with our obligatory blue-lighted insectocutors. We could show no discretion, no mercy – like a sniper ordered to take out any stalker breaking a restraining order.

The same Environment Agency officials took a real shine to our new riverside and attempted to press their vision of my land with a wild and natural look. They insisted that the canal edge should not be 'hard', and should be planted with reeds, insisting that all plants must be indigenous species. I resisted the temptation to remark on the irony of being told that 'indigenous species must be protected' by inspectors who all hailed from Down Under. In the end we compromised with a hard edge, four-metre setback and a solitary, yet British, Acer Crimson King.

Aside from the desire for our new home to provide for an insect orgy, there was a second motivation behind the Environmental Agency's objections. Apparently they felt it was imperative to protect the area 'against increased urbanisation'. I had spent the last six months fighting a CPO that explicitly sought the 'better utilisation of land' through development and regeneration. So I appended my 'capitalisation' email with this blunt assessment: 'THESE PEOPLE ARE FULL OF INCONSISTENCIES. THEY DO WHAT SUITS THEM AT THE TIME. IT'S A FARCE.'

As the designs were finalised, there was hardly an arm of government that didn't find an excuse to lecture and patronise us. It had been my early vision that our factory would benefit from a shop – what would be more natural for visitors than, after a tour of the premises, to purchase a pack or two of Forman's London Cure? I set aside a portion of the ground floor for my retail ventures, but soon found out that whilst England may be a 'nation of shopkeepers' (according to Napoleon), there's rather more involved than hanging an 'Open' sign on the door. Before I knew it, I'd lost days of my life in meetings about my duties and obligations. The factory floor was a few inches higher than the pavement, which raised issues of disability access, and led to interminable meetings with inspectors about precisely where to locate the step. It would, I was told, be a flagrant breach of the law for the step to abut the pavement, since this would deny entry to anyone in a wheelchair. But, in that case, where? In my naiveté, I assumed the safest spot would be at the rear of the store, behind the counter, where no customer would ever tread, but this modest suggestion was greeted with furrowed brows and looks of dismay on the far side of the table. I was reprimanded for displaying an inconsiderate attitude towards any disabled worker I might employ in future who would enter the shop from inside the factory.

I explained that health and safety, and possibly food hygiene rules, would make it highly unlikely that a wheelchair-bound salmon carver could ever be employed in this situation. They would need to unhook a side of smoked salmon from a rail, seven feet off the ground, lay it on a high countertop and then carve slices onto a set of scales. One slip of the very sharp knife and it would act like a weapon, so stability is critical. 'You'd be amazed what these people can do,' I was advised. We suggested as a joke that a feasible solution would be sitting the edge of the serving counter above the step, and installing a diagonal chute which my serving staff could use to propel products from high to the low ground. The inspectors misunderstood our attempt at humour and endorsed the plan – the ridiculous is probably the norm in a world where practicality counts for nothing.

Another frustration came from our friends in the planning department of Tower Hamlets. Despite most of my staff driving into work at 3.30 a.m., before the wheels of public transport start to roll, the borough's planning transport officials advised that we would be restricted to fourteen parking spaces, of which two had to be reserved for disabled use. Our yard had sufficient space for double that number. Why the local council wished to stunt the growth of our business when they expected to seize expensive business rates is beyond me.

However, another irony later appeared after our relocation. The very first event hosted in our ghost floor, later named 'Forman's Fish Island', was the annual conference for the CEO of Tower Hamlets. Over 200 delegates would be arriving for this important event. Everything went very smoothly, but there was one complaint: 'We could have done with more parking spaces.'

These issues were minor compared with the traumas that had preceded them, but they still niggled, like a scratch you can't reach. We were going full guns blazing to build a new factory at the behest of the state, and yet they were throwing obstruction after obstruction in my direction, with no concern that I still had a business to run. Mating insects, British plants, salmon chutes and underutilised parking – it reminded me of the craze for speed humps in the 1990s; there were side streets in Herne Hill with speed bumps every twenty feet.

We hadn't appreciated until late in the day quite how fortuitous was our new location, but as the park's excavation programme began, we noticed that a stadium-shaped hole was emerging just across the river, about 100 yards from our frontage. As it turned out, we were to be the closest building to the Olympic stadium – not just the London stadium, but its equivalent in any Games in living memory. I had never wanted Forman's to be just a factory, and was already planning to set aside a proportion of our space for ancillary activities, but with the stadium's proximity confirmed, my mind was abuzz with the spinoff opportunities. In hindsight, I'd been so preoccupied with our own travails that I'd paid little attention to updates and announcements about the actual Games. This needed to be rectified rapidly, so I despatched one of my team to search out any and all rumoured visuals, which Lloyd and I pinned to the wall of my office. Although the final design was not confirmed for another few months, it was already clear it would be a magnificent showpiece. Designed by Populous, and to be built by Sir Robert McAlpine, it eventually comprised a series of tiers, with a permanent sunken elliptical bowl containing the track and around 25,000 seats, as well as a demountable lightweight steel and concrete upper tier to house the rest of the spectators. The stadium's most distinctive and iconic feature was the arrangement of fourteen lighting towers, seventy metres above the track, each weighing thirty-five tonnes and containing up to forty-four lamps. The building's exterior was almost as remarkable, being wrapped in 2.5m-wide fabric panels, twisted at an angle and held in place with tensioned cables. It was a design that would soon be seared into the collective consciousness of generations.

Back in 2006, it took a bit of imagination to conceive how the sea of mud just across from our new factory would be transformed over the next three years. But the opportunity was too good to miss. There was no longer any doubt in my mind about how the ghost floor should be deployed. When complete, the ample 1,000 square metre area beneath the roof would stretch the entire length of the factory, and with its exposed trusses and load-bearing columns would vaguely resemble a 1970s discotheque before the revellers are admitted. With the east of the ghost floor directly overlooking the future stadium, we used toughened-glass windows, built a roof terrace and created arguably the most unique venue-for-hire in the borough. In fact at the 2015 London Venue Awards, Forman's Fish Island was awarded the prize for being the most unusual and unique venue in London for over 200 guests. I hadn't yet figured out *who* would hire it – that was a challenge for tomorrow. It could be global corporations holding a jamboree for their staff, or sports broadcasters yearning for a spectacular backdrop, or award events trying to justify the £1,000 cost of a table, or the planners of weddings, parties and bar mitzvahs who wanted something a little different from the usual recycled list of hotel chains. There were countless possibilities – which is naturally a sweeter issue to face than too few! I mentioned the idea to a few loose-lipped friends, confident that word would seep out. I realised my cunning plan was working when unsolicited enquiries were forthcoming before I had spent so much as a bean on marketing the service.

Hosting the occasional mega-bash was exciting, but I also wanted a memorable service to offer any loyal Forman's customer who happened to be in town. Once again, the vista over the Olympic Park gave us an edge. I allocated space for a small restaurant – later expanded into a larger restaurant with a lounge bar – that specialised in our London Cure smoked salmon as well as seasonal British food and drinks. The regeneration of Stratford, especially with the Westfield Shopping Centre, would inevitably gentrify the area and give thousands of tourists an excuse to travel east of St Paul's. Everyone needs to eat, especially after a tough day in the office or touring around the capital's sights. Our restaurant would, I hoped, provide the perfect ambience for bringing the day to a relaxing close. And, in addition to its spectacular stadium view, I can't think of a restaurant in the world that's reached via a more unusual walkway, one that doubles as a viewing platform for the factory. Diners can watch the kilns in action (at least, as much action as a kiln can muster; there aren't many moving parts), before taking their seats to enjoy the produce. Whenever guests arrive at the restaurant today they are often taken aback by our proximity to the stadium and comment, 'What an amazing view!' My standard riposte is, 'Yes, it's the best view that any Olympics has ever had of a fish factory!'

One evening I was checking over the Stour Road plans at one end of the kitchen table whilst Oliver was at the other, hunched over his homework. I must've started whistling to myself, because Oliver put up his head and said, 'You seem a lot more cheerful these days, Daddy.'

'It was an important day at work. They laid the first bricks of our new factory.'

'Does that mean you're not going to lose your job after all?'

'It looks like we're finally safe. Your father will be the smoked salmon man for a few more years.'

'I'm so happy about that.' Oliver was running towards me, his arms flung open, ready for a huge bear-hug.

'It means that, one day, when you're old enough, you can be the fifth generation of Forman to run the business,' I said.

At which point, Oliver stopped dead in his tracks – hug undelivered – and stared at his shoes. I swear a tiny tear was welling up in the corner of his eye.

'That's not funny, Daddy.'

'It wasn't meant to be.'

'Well, it wasn't. I would never, ever, want to run that horrible place.'

I was taken aback by such a forthright declaration. 'It's been in the family for 100 years,' I said.

'I don't care.' He wiped away the tear with his sleeve, and I saw that his cheeks were turning an angry shade of red.

'Why ever not?'

'Because I never want to come home smelling of fish!'

'In running a smoked salmon factory, this is the very least of your problems,' I thought.

* * *

With ground broken, the construction of the new factory proceeded with remarkable speed, but, as with any building project, there were snags. Lots of them in this case, with more haste and more speed. Some were the fault of the builders (the right- and left-side drainpipes mysteriously connected underground in the shape of a U; we only discovered this when the gutters quickly filled to overflowing during the first heavy rainstorm); others were beyond their control – the late delivery of our kilns, and some Tower Hamlets red tape. None of this meant an earth-shattering delay, certainly nothing that would imperil the wider Olympic timetable, but the ODA (Olympic Delivery Authority, formerly the

LDA) kicked up the almightiest fuss when I gently requested that our eviction date be pushed back from July to September and then again just another couple of weeks to mid-October. From the stream of venomous letters I received from senior ODA executives, accusing me of reneging on a signed agreement and having poorly managed the construction programme, one would think I'd asked for the Olympic stadium to be shifted to the Blackpool Pleasure Beach. For days, they were intransigent, and I faced the horrendous scenario that – with one factory destroyed and the next not yet completed – I'd be left incapable of supplying a single slice of smoked salmon to a single customer.

Fortunately common sense prevailed, especially after I put in a legal objection to the local authority stopping up the road to prevent me getting to Marshgate Lane, which would delay them in any event. The threatened date was grudgingly relaxed, although the lukewarm display of generosity was coupled with the severest warning that not a single additional hour delay would be countenanced under any circumstances, 'so please don't ask'. Throughout this correspondence, there wasn't a scintilla of recognition of the double time that both Lloyd and I had been working. It was an aggressive display of power by small-minded people suddenly given authority over the lives of others. With a fast-looming deadline, my micro-management of the construction became even more obsessional. This was not a situation where one could follow the management textbooks and delegate to good people the complete freedom to deliver the tasks for which they are accountable, because there was a subtle but crucial imbalance between my incentives and those of my builder. A slippage of a few days might deprive them of a nice case study to post on their website. For me, it would mean curtains. However, the speed of construction led to some bold design decisions which, with the safety of time to reconsider, might have resulted in a building that was more restrained. Forman's is an architectural masterpiece worthy of a food factory museum, if such a thing exists.

In line with the threats, the ODA was insistent to the last that we vacate on schedule, and after gruelling weekends and night-time working, we hit our deadline. The irony was that, having been bullied into getting out because of their desperate need to build a stadium, they then left our factory untouched for over a month before they got around to demolition. Oh for a job where one can be so cack-handed with no career consequences.

Debbie Hartley felt that filming me being interviewed against the backdrop of the demolition of our Marshgate Lane factory for the *Building the Olympic Dream* documentary would make for powerful television, and on the prescribed day directed her camera crew to a viewing location (this time, safely outside the perimeter) where the moments could be captured for posterity. It would have been emotional for me (and, in fairness, also for Debbie) under any circumstances. But, since Forman's was now the only remaining building in the park, the melodrama was unparalleled. It was a black and wet November day. Despite being ten in the morning, the sky was so dark it felt like ten at night. The rain was lashing with such ferocity that the prospect of gathering meaningful footage was slight veering towards non-existent. The entire crew, Debbie and I sat in my office waiting for the rain to subside. Many cups of coffee later and the crew, prebooked out to their next job, could procrastinate no longer and accepted we would simply have to get drenched. We all were. We left the warmth of my office and trekked the five minutes to the Greenway where we had the perfect vista to watch the bulldozers smash our former smokehouse to smithereens.

I stood, umbrella in hand facing Debbie, when – just as the cameras were about to roll – the rain sensationally subsided. A dark cloud that had been obscuring the sun floated away and, moments later, a vibrant and shimmering rainbow lit up the sky. Its arc was unusually angled. For all the world, I was sure one end of the rainbow was pointing at our old factory, as it collapsed beneath the might of the ruthless demolition vehicle fleet. I pinched myself; was the other end really hovering over Stour Road? Even Steven Spielberg, with all the computer-generated effects at his disposal, couldn't have produced a scene suffused with such symbolism and beauty.

CHAPTER 17

FORTUNE

'I am interested in imperfections, quirkiness, insanity, unpredictability. That's what we really pay attention to anyway. We don't talk about planes flying; we talk about them crashing,' said Tibor Kalman, founding editor-in-chief of *Colors* magazine, which (taking a lead from its sponsor, Benetton) spent much of the 1990s promoting cultural empathy and reconciliation through the use of striking, unnerving and controversial imagery.

Readers who have, in Kalman's words, been 'paying attention' to my saga of quirkiness and insanity will hopefully realise that we've now all caught up with my opening scene, way back in the 'Foretaste' chapter. During the intervening pages, Forman's has survived an unremitting series of catastrophes: the destruction of most of the factory in a raging fire; the disappearance of my General Manager when I uncovered financial irregularities; the contamination of our facilities when the River Lea burst its banks; and the decision of the British government to dump an 80,000-seater Olympic stadium on the exact spot where we operated.

Ever since the last of those setbacks, we had teetered on the brink of collapse. We had faced down deception, intransigence and incompetence. We had fought for our rights – and those of many other businesses – in the courts of law and the court of public opinion. We had ignored pressure from figures of authority who wanted to shield the Olympics' nasty underside from public view. We had constructed and fitted out new premises, compliant with reasonable as well as irrational regulations, at whirlwind speed. Now, finally, we had a modern, spacious facility in a location that was practical for our purpose, equipped with state-of-the-art kilns that would last for generations.

All that remained was the little matter of our product. With Stour Road open for business, our customers were looking forward to their first deliveries – and, with them, irrefutable evidence that Forman's could still be trusted to cure and smoke unbelievable smoked salmon, delicate in flavour and remarkable for its texture. A food whose delights never overstay their welcome on the palate after being consumed – the stuff of discerning gastronomes.

Except that, as I wrote in Chapter 1, the first slice I carved on our first morning in Stour Road displayed none of those virtues. What happened was that:

Lloyd, who had been shifting uneasily throughout my remarks, could keep his counsel no longer. He stepped forward and interrupted me mid-flow, 'Lance, can I just have a couple of words please?'

Sensing something was amiss, René had ditched her champagne duties, and was standing by my side. She threaded her arm reassuringly around mine. 'You'll work it out. You always do.'

'I can't understand it,' said Lloyd.

The slice was wet, for sure. Slimy, without doubt. And, above all, there was a disgusting bitter aftertaste. So unpleasant and intense that I might need to gulp down the contents of both champagne bottles just to cleanse the palate. This was like that cheap supermarket smoked salmon that I despise … only worse.

I was worried. And Lloyd was worried. And Lloyd doesn't worry. Which was worrying.

Had all my speeches, letters, meetings and interviews been in vain? Had I, so overwhelmed with desire to emerge bloody but unbowed, somehow contrived to snatch defeat from the jaws of victory? There is clearly no value in a magnificent smokehouse building if the product itself is sub-standard. Our new factory might as well be an empty shell – four walls, a roof, and a sign out front announcing 'space to let'.

I was having visions of the life that might lie ahead. No longer the fish man, I would slink back to PWC, begging their indulgence, hoping they'd allow me to resume my accountancy work – but, this time, fifteen years behind my peer group. My next decade could see me hunched over the books of liquidations in Hartlepool, trying to make sense of ramshackle ledgers, lodging for the night in the only nearby flea-bitten B&B with a short notice vacancy. Then returning home on the Friday sleeper service, to be greeted with a hug by a sympathetic wife whose first words would be: 'Did you manage to sort out the reconciliations this week, darling?' In future, my every New Year wish might be that, please God, could I be let loose on a semi-glamorous audit account? Like a software business. Or a firm headquartered in the Caymans. Or even a hotel. One day, hunched over my spreadsheets, perhaps I would spot a clerk in the client's finance department staring at me with puzzled expression. 'You look familiar,' they might murmur. 'Didn't I see you in the papers once? Weren't you involved in the Olympics somehow?' If I'm lucky, perhaps they'd buy me a sandwich at lunchtime so I could retell the circumstances of my downfall for the five-hundredth time. A future, I imagine, that would be not dissimilar to how Pete Best spent his twenty years as a civil servant after Brian Epstein fired him from the Beatles.

But enough of daydreams. René had been spot-on with her coaxing. I needed to get myself together and 'work it out'. The first thing was to call the technicians at Reich, the kilns' German manufacturers.

'We have no future as a premium brand if we can't guarantee an unforgettable culinary experience,' I said.

'I don't understand it. You were quite happy when you tested the fish over here.'

'Yes and that's how I need it to taste right now. Anything less, and you can have your kilns back. Anyway, this isn't the time for a blame game. What are we going to do to fix the problem?'

'Perhaps it's a one-off. Perhaps it was a bad batch of salmon.'

'Can I verify the settings we used for the test batch at your plant? Then we'll just try again tomorrow.'

We re-checked all the settings and they were precisely as Lloyd had programmed the kiln, but we had no option to try once again. We needed to smoke the salmon for the next day's deliveries and, being a 24-hour process to cure followed by a 24-hour process to smoke the salmon, any test products would be the ones we would need to supply to our customers.

I was impatient to have the matter resolved, so the prospect of inaction – albeit for a single day – didn't overwhelm me with joy. By way of compromise, Reich agreed that tomorrow they would fly over their two most experienced engineers, on the first departures from Schechingen, if there were no detectable improvements in quality. In the event, the taste on the second day was even worse. Hideous, drab, sliding around the mouth, indigestible, exhibiting all the diabolical features of mass production smoked salmon that I've publicly eviscerated. Our customers were loyal enough to forgive one, even two, sub-standard results. But a third day without a transformation and we'd be buried.

Nervousness was spreading around the workforce. Every one of my employees knew how Forman's smoked salmon should taste, and was painfully aware we were falling far short of our standards. One or two averted their eyes as I walked past, hoping to keep their fears hidden. Everyone was on edge, less patient and more irritable. I overhead supervisors snap for the mildest reasons, and, for the first time I could recall, an entire day passed without a light-hearted moment, let alone a joke being shared. It was like the moment the tightrope walker steps onto the high wire at the circus. We were all spooked and apprehensive about where it was leading. Fifty jobs depended on getting this right.

But my intrepid sleuth Lloyd, never one to languish at the mercy of events, had developed a theory.

'If you recall, one of the advantages of Reich's Airmaster kiln is tightly controlling the quantity of smoke,' he said. That was true; rather than igniting a stack of sawdust, the smoke in the Airmaster came from a wheel spinning against an oak log. 'It worked perfectly when we tested the process in Germany, yet the same settings have been a disaster here. So what other variables have changed?'

'Beats me,' I said. 'The factory conditions are similar; the fish were laid out in the same way on the trolleys.'

'Which leaves only one other factor,' said Lloyd. 'And that's the *number* of fish. At Reich, we tested a dozen. Yesterday, we filled the trolleys to capacity. Identical, computer-controlled settings, but a different concentration of product. What if that affects the rate of dehumidification? It could mean no longer the 10 per cent weight loss we've always targeted.'

Lloyd's explanation seemed plausible; in any event, a drowning man will grasp at anything. When Reich's engineers turned up at the factory gate, they had barely paid their taxi fare, let alone taken off their coats, before we were relaying the theory, fearful they would debunk it on technical grounds, but desperately hoping they'd nod sagely and scratch their chin stubble in an approving sort of fashion.

The next day, I took it upon myself to programme the settings, using instinct and experience to estimate changes that could deliver the optimal humidity and weight loss. I was in the factory at 4 a.m. to sample the results – I couldn't sleep, so the early start was no hardship. My first task was to weigh the salmon sides, to measure the impact of the additional drying. The result was not bad. The next day, a further refinement.

And an additional improvement. For the next ten days, we added or took away a few decimal points from each number we programmed, like a golfer fine-tuning his swing until he finds the consummate arm movement to land the ball on the green. I was convinced that one final tweak would result in perfection and I gave the programme the name 'Lucky Smoke'. The following morning, my judgement was rewarded and Lucky Smoke has provided Forman's with the world's finest smoked salmon from that day forth. My relief was as palpable as it was undiluted. That lunchtime, I insisted on a three-course celebration at my desk – a smoked salmon starter, a smoked salmon main course, and a smoked salmon dessert. That's how thrilled I was at having, however belatedly, a sample I could savour.

It only takes Usain Bolt nine seconds to move 100 metres. It had taken us six years. Being distracted by three-letter acronyms such as CPOs had prevented us from exploiting the economic boom of 2003 to 2008 for revenue growth. But we were intact – that could not be overstated. In the decade since our relocation, I've come across the heart-breaking stories of once-viable businesses which were not so fortunate facing the threat of the Olympic CPOs. Some of them, to this day, are still skirmishing through the courts in the fading hope of eventual recompense.

With a functioning factory, the improvement in my own temperament was quickly apparent. There was widespread fascination with my escapades, and from time to time I was invited to address business audiences, usually hosted at our venue, about my experiences and the lessons I'd learnt. Now that our future was secured, I felt able to pepper my remarks with a degree of humour (laughs had been notable by their absence when I'd been reciting my woes before the Tower Hamlets cabinet or the London Development Agency AGM). Speaking before the Food and Drink Exporters Association, I began by picking on a 'safe' target – US President George W. Bush and his rhetorical frailties:

'Bush was asked to say a few words to the New York bid committee to wish them luck before they headed to Singapore. Standing at the podium, he was in upbeat mood as he said simply: O, O, O, O, O. It was left to his Chief of Staff to point out he'd been reading out the Olympic logo ... his actual speech was further down the page.'

There were guffaws around the room, and some banging of fists on tables. I felt emboldened.

'It was under Gordon Brown's leadership that we were relocated to these new premises. Thank you, Gordon, we are for ever in your debt. As are our children, and our children's children.'

More chortles. I had their attention. I've always preferred the adage *Don't stop when you're on a roll* to *Quit when you're ahead*, so figured it was time for some darker, more caustic wisecracks:

'I didn't come here tonight to be cruel and vicious about the Olympics. No, no. I was already here!'

An intake of breath as the room sensed I was straying into more contentious territory, and wondered whether I'd start exploding any landmines.

'When I realised the writing could be on the wall for my business – and I'm not referring to the local graffiti artists – I had to fight like a tiger. But I'm pleased to say that Sebastian Coe and I have since made up, and I've gotten to know him quite well. So, ladies and gentlemen, let me tell you something about Seb ... intelligent, sophisticated, eloquent. These are just three of the words Sebastian Coe cannot spell.'

I was on fire that evening, and my delivery was pitch-perfect. From every table, spontaneous applause. Or, to be technically accurate, from every table bar one. A member of Coe's team, LOCOG Head of Catering Jan Matthews, was in the audience that night and no doubt her bosses expected a report back that I'd been syrupy and gracious; but when I reached the 'cannot spell' punchline, she ostentatiously stood up and stormed towards the exit doors. Apparently, mocking the

US President was *de rigueur* (I'd noticed she chuckled at my George W. Bush quip), but taking a pot shot at the Chairman of LOCOG was a grotesque impropriety. Until that day, I'd been casually acquainted with her, having been invited to attend the last two meetings of the London Olympics Food Committee. Following my after-dinner speech, I was never invited back. It seems some transgressions are so irredeemably offensive that their author must be permanently exiled to the dark side. They overlooked that a more devastating punishment by far would've been inviting me back to another of their committee meetings!

* * *

As with the rest of the Forman's service range, the philosophy was: we'll only do it if we can do it well. We agreed we should cause a stir by pushing at boundaries, rather than playing safe. We had a team of chefs, great ingredients, kitchen equipment, and knew that in the coming years 10 million people would be landing on our doorstep. If we didn't seize this opportunity, I'd for ever wonder 'what if...?' and 'if only...' We knew we could successfully deliver food in boxes to people's homes and to leading catering establishments, so it couldn't be that complicated to deliver it on plates to tables. And so Forman's Restaurant was born. And, contrary to popular perception, not every single item on our restaurant menu involves salmon. One could, of course, dine in that fashion – starting with London Cure smoked salmon with buckwheat blinis and accompaniments, before moving on to the seared Scottish salmon with smashed peas and button onions, and winding down with smoked Scottish salmon and Cornish crab salad with fennel and apple. But there are other selections as well. A potted chicken liver parfait, or a poached turbot with scallops, clams, chorizo froth and baby carrots. But of course smoked salmon is our signature dish, the popular choice for most of our guests, and the first words on our waiter's lips in the unlikely event that he or she is asked to name the 'speciality of the house'.

To attract punters, a start-up restaurant needs to take risks – especially in a city that's home to over 5,000 already. One of the unorthodox decisions I took was to serve only English wines. This wasn't quite as bizarre as it sounds; we had been long-term champions of the glories of British food. Nevertheless, it was idiosyncratic – I wasn't aware of any other restaurants operating a similar policy at the time. Tony Laithwaite, arguably the country's top wine merchant, was one of our early diners, and remarked on our 'small' wine list. I justified it by explaining we were a 'small restaurant with a small menu', to which he laughed, 'It's a genius idea, but still very brave.' Once we were established, we were able to extend this philosophy into our selection of spirits – we can conjure up a fabulous Negroni with Sacred's Spiced English Vermouth, Rosehip Cup Liqueur and London Gin. I felt my decision to focus exclusively on English wines was vindicated earlier this year when the renowned champagne house Taittinger acquired a vineyard in Kent.

Whenever I'm tempted to 'let bygones be bygones' over my tussles with Livingstone and the LDA, I pinch myself and remember how very close we came to losing everything. He had once made a quip that the Olympics would cost Londoners the equivalent of a 'walnut whip a week'. Rather than argue about semantics or mathematics, we chose to endorse Livingstone's calculations – by adding a 'gourmet walnut whip' to our menu, priced at five pounds, 'to prove Ken really did know what he was talking about'. Livingstone gamely attended the three-year 'Countdown to 2012' event at which we first served the Forman's version of a walnut whip (the rest of the menu was priced at a symbolic £20.12), and he joined me as my dinner guest at Forman's and agreed to pose with me for a souvenir photograph to be taken whilst his own serving was standing tall and proud on his dessert plate. I'd been keen to meet with Livingstone so I could informally probe about any knowledge he might have had about the dodgy dealings within his organisation, but, despite some cunningly phrased questions, he played a straight bat.

In fairness to Livingstone, when I'd requested a favour shortly before moving into Stour Road, he'd responded graciously and with a more generous sense of humour than had ever been evident amongst his Olympic sidekicks.

Oliver's bar mitzvah was approaching and I was still struggling to find that killer idea that would be remembered decades hence – both by him, and by our guests. I had bought a pocket-sized notepad that was following me around, and whenever a crazy scheme hit me (whether in the shower, or whilst dozing off to sleep) it was jotted down, however outlandish it might seem. With a month to go, and half a dozen pages filled, still nothing was grabbing me. All my guests, friends and family knew I'd been preoccupied with building a new factory at breakneck speed, having fought a high-profile battle against the former Mayor worthy of column feet in the press and hours of TV coverage.

What a coup it would be if Livingstone could appear as a surprise guest. I wrote to him in the expectation of either being ignored, or receiving some bland apology, but perhaps the way my request was drafted was sufficient temptation for Ken the politician. The attendance would be by way of video and I would draft the thirty-second script. I concluded my invitation: 'I think this would be immensely funny, would demonstrate that our battle with you is now well and truly over, and perhaps be an informal sign to the Jewish community that you have no prejudices against them.'

Four weeks later, my extended family and Oliver's dearest friends were gathered at a venue near Canary Wharf to celebrate his coming of age as an adult member of the Jewish community. As the dessert plates were being cleared away, and the coffees served, the lights dimmed, and a video screen descended at the far end of the room. Two hundred pairs of eyes turned to gaze. The opening shot was of the River Thames, close to Tower Bridge, and as the camera pivoted a long stretch of the South Bank came into view. That's when I appeared, holding a microphone, and for the next couple of minutes I approached any random passer-by – Japanese students, Norwegian pensioners, office workers on a cigarette break. Not all of them had a strong grasp of the English language, but somehow I managed to persuade each one to face the camera and string together the words, 'Congratulations on your bar mitzvah, Oliver.'

The effect was quite surreal, but nothing compared with the grand climax, when Mayor Livingstone himself strode towards the camera ('Who on earth is this bedraggled fellow?' was my subsequent voice-over), and uttered the immortal words: 'Congratulations, Oliver. I'm delighted at your coming of age. Please don't turn out like your father. He caused me so many problems and life isn't fair. I'm sure he'll get the smoked salmon contract for the Olympics anyway. The very best to you and have a great life. Oh, and by the way, ask your mum to get rid of the Land Rover.' He finished with a trademark Livingstone wink.

For a full five seconds, there was a stunned silence throughout the room. No one was quite certain what they'd just witnessed. Had it been a lookalike? Had the audio been dubbed? When the realisation dawned that every frame had been genuine, there was virtual pandemonium. Cheers, roars, hooplas – it was quite a rumpus. In fact, had Livingstone squeaked in at the next Mayoral election due to a handful of Jewish votes switching to Labour (rather than suffer an ignominious end to his career beneath the Boris steamroller), that might have been the evening that sealed it. Although had I thought the result was going to be so close, the invitation would not have been proffered.

* * *

Boris Johnson – shortly to play a pivotal role in Forman's history – is one of life's irrepressible, flamboyant, eccentric personalities, and shortly after our factory move, I came into contact with someone else with the exact same traits. Since the individual concerned didn't have a day job running our capital city, I was able to persuade the Hon. Arthur Somerset to join our refreshed and revitalised management team.

A real-life aristocrat, Arthur was a former President of the International Special Events Society (in the years before their acronym starting raising eyebrows), and had spent the past few years putting the East End on the map as a credible location for the corporate shindig through his own event management business, Mask Events. He was introduced to me by the brilliant Pat Holmes, who looked after Inward Investment and Business at Tower Hamlets, and who, I later learnt, lost her job – not despite her talents, but because of them (she showed up everybody else!). Arthur was a remarkable discovery; I liked him immediately and hired him almost as quickly. With Lloyd taking care of the smoked salmon production, I now had a leader of equal integrity and ambition to develop the hospitality business. Arthur and I had everything that makes for an ideal business partnership – a shared goal, an insatiable work ethic, a sense of humour and an obstinate refusal to accept that some things can't be done. And let us never forget that the band Arthur Somerset and the Turkeys of Sloane rocked the charts in 1984 with the classic anthem, 'OK. Ya!' If he wasn't always twenty years ahead of himself, people may have thought from the song title that it was something to do with a Japanese sushi chain.

Arthur joined the team in 2008 on a contract which would culminate when the Olympic Games came to town. All our efforts in the intervening years would be directed towards this unprecedented opportunity on our doorstep. Having been distracted from our core business for five years, and spending much of our first year at Stour Road dealing with a mile-long snag list caused by over-hasty construction, it seemed the best way to recoup our losses was to focus our creative energies on 2012. In the meantime, I'd allow salmon sales to tick along, ready for an upsurge in demand post-Games on the back of our soaring – and global – brand awareness.

Around a year after moving in, Arthur asked why we hadn't gotten around to organising a launch party. It was a curious omission, he suggested, 'Unlike most businesses, you don't need to get quotes for venue hire, or fret about whether your catering contractors are reliable.' As Boris Johnson had now replaced Livingstone as Mayor – a towering achievement in a city with huge Labour heartlands which, according to conventional wisdom, cannot be reached by 'elitist' Conservative politicians – Arthur suggested I reach out to his private office, asking if he'd be prepared to cut the proverbial ribbon at our grand opening.

There was a little nagging voice at the back of my head reminding me that the last time I'd used a Conservative VIP guest (also with a colourful personal life, and the aspiration to make a mark as Mayor) to open a factory, it had ended in fiasco. But what's life without the occasional risk? Jeffrey Archer's arrest on perjury charges was not enough to deter me from revisiting the exercise.

But Boris's crammed diary was a major hurdle – according to rumour, he receives over 500 invitations every day – and it was proving impossible to tie down a date. On the verge of abandoning the idea, I sent him a side of smoked salmon as a Christmas gift, but also as a gentle reminder. In early January a thank-you note landed on my desk, for the '*bottle* of smoked salmon'. And a week later a call from Boris's office gave me just four days' notice that his itinerary 'means he can swing by' early on Friday morning, 'but will only be able to stay for twenty minutes, max'. That meant I had four days to compile a guest list, design an irresistible invitation and do everything possible so that, when the Mayor arrived, our ghost floor would be heaving and buzzing with energy. 'The perfect launch for our venue,' Arthur deftly noted. 'Twenty minutes of Boris is worth hours of just about anyone else.'

Archer had remained at Forman's for over two hours back in 1999, enough time to shake the hand of every guest, make himself available for photos and deal with the formalities. So how could I make best use of Boris's time? For him to deliver a speech and cut a ribbon and for me to condense a five-year journey into just a few minutes, I knew it would be tight. I wanted Boris to experience our smokehouse, taste our smoked salmon and also, if time permitted, visit a photographic display we were exhibiting, by Marion Davies and Debra Rapp, named 'Dispersal', which dramatically recorded the hundreds of businesses devastated by the Games owing to the LDA's high-handed attitude towards their eviction.

Boris arrived on the dot of 8 a.m. accompanied not only by his advisors but also by the press and TV media. He apologised that his schedule was tight because, upon leaving us, he was being whisked to a media event at the Olympic Stadium where Prime Minister Gordon Brown would be gushing and eulogising about the jobs that the Olympics would be creating.

On hearing this, Arthur and I looked at one another – he was thinking what I was thinking – and we made an immediate and unscheduled change to the itinerary. The expectant guests on our ghost floor would have to wait a few minutes longer.

I ushered the Mayor to the 'Dispersal' exhibition, and showed him some of the more harrowing images. He could scarcely believe what he was seeing. He kept muttering. 'Nobody told me this; nobody told me this.' His characteristic bonhomie and mirth vanished in an instant; as he gazed at photograph upon photograph of businesses that had survived the Blitz and struggled through the three-day week, but been destroyed by heavy-handed officials, he shook with a mixture of sorrow and rage. He made an off-the-cuff decision to jilt the PM, and let his twenty-minute commitment to Forman's morph into three hours. We escorted him around the factory floor, recounted the near-legendary chronicle of the installation of our kilns, and let him loose on a fine salmon with a carving knife. It gave me a frisson of pleasure – and, I suspect, for Boris as well – when the papers castigated Brown for failing to ensure he was joined by a senior Tory at a supposedly apolitical celebration of sport.

Whilst starting the day with champagne and the world's finest smoked salmon might have been the clincher for some, I'm sure it was Boris's name on the invitation that tempted over 400 guests to make the dawn trip to Stratford. I was relieved that, with the Mayor's extended stay, far more of them would have the chance to shake his hand.

'Would the Mayor like a glass of fizz?' I asked as we headed into the reception.

'Err… no,' I was told by his advisors. 'If the media get a photo of him with a glass of champagne, it'll be splattered all over the front pages.'

'Oh,' I said. 'In that case, perhaps a cup of tea?'

'No, no. He'd love to have some champagne. But in a mug, please, not in a glass.'

If only Archer's minders had been so streetwise, he might never have had reason to publish *A Prison Diary, Volumes 1–3*.

Boris was in ebullient form. The bubbly gave an extra sparkle to his impromptu address, when he congratulated us on defying the 'smoking ban', chuckled that we'd both enjoyed the pleasure of defeating Ken Livingstone, labelled us not only as a 'shrine to smoked salmon' but as 'the Olympic legacy in advance', and said that he'd use the speed with which we'd constructed our factory to bludgeon the Olympic Park contractors to 'up their game'. Then, ruffling his hand through his famous blonde locks, and conscious that we'd already been operational for over twelve months, he declared our factory to be 'even more open than it was before!'

Boris has remained a stalwart friend to Forman's during his mayoralty years. He launched his manifesto in our premises when running for his second term as Mayor in 2012, and agreed to spend an hour playing table tennis at Forman's Fish Island against the winner of a fund-raising auction, with £40,000 donated in the process. Lustre was added to the ping-pong challenge due to Boris's mischievous association with the sport – at the time of the Beijing Olympics, he'd riled the Chinese by claiming it was originally a Victorian invention called 'whiff-whaff'.

I became an avid follower of Boris's reflections on political history, our cultural heritage and global affairs, and almost fell off my chair when I read him responding to a series of ten quick-fire questions in a glossy magazine interview. One of the challenges was to name his 'ideal bagel filling' – 'Forman's smoked salmon of course. It's absolutely delicious.' I needed no further encouragement. We now produce London's finest bagel, the 'Boris Bagel', made from a traditional Brick Lane boiled bagel and filled with Forman's London Cure and a schmeer of cream cheese infused with lemon and chopped chives, available from Whole Foods, from branches of Chop'd and for home delivery through Forman & Field. Boris was kind enough to give his official blessing to the nomenclature, and in return we donate 10p from each bagel sold towards the Mayor's Fund for London, so that it can be channelled into feeding over 2,500 disadvantaged school children daily with a free, healthy breakfast.

As the Olympics drew closer, Arthur's entrepreneurial zeal and thirst to experiment took us into an array of bewildering new directions. We hosted the semi-final of *Celebrity MasterChef* – at the time, the UK's second most viewed show after Simon Cowell's *X Factor* – with Dame Kelly Holmes, Dame Tanni Grey-Thompson, and (of course, the ubiquitous) Sebastian Coe in attendance. We hosted corporate events for many of the Olympic sponsors, including Coca-Cola (who filmed a pop video featuring Mark Ronson and Katy B), Panasonic and the Olympic Delivery Authority itself. Christmas parties were held for Olympic Stadium builders, Sir Robert McAlpine, and the global advertising company Ogilvy; soon, the unrivalled view of the park meant Forman's

Fish Island was a sought-after place for anyone involved in the Olympics to host their showcase event. A particular moment of history was when steel magnate Lakshmi Mittal, who had funded the bright red looping observation tower called the Orbit (often mistaken for a helter skelter), chose Forman's for the Topping Off Ceremony to celebrate the completion of its construction. Within thirty months, from a standing start, our hospitality business became our most profitable venture. We were making up for lost time, and even agreed to sponsor one of the British Olympians, handball athlete Louise Jukes. Whoever claimed that Forman's was anti-Olympics?

In promoting our sponsorship of Louise, we inadvertently fell foul of the Olympics' obsession about brand protection. Arthur created a wacky Christmas-time visual – 'five gold rings', with salmon leaping through a pattern of hoops that bore an uncanny resemblance to the classic Olympic symbol. In our naiveté, we'd assumed the authorities would applaud us for taking seriously their warm words about benefiting the host community. The 'cease and desist' letter we received about our harmless promotional piece was a taster of the increasingly aggressive stance being taken towards anyone displaying a bit of ingenuity around the Games.

At the same time as LOCOG lawyers were forcing me to tone down my innocuous marketing campaigns, other members of the Olympic family were encouraging me to be bolder. 'This place will be a goldmine,' said a senior official during an event we were hosting. The 'goldmine' word was used repeatedly by guest after guest – by senior figures in the worlds of the Olympics and of hospitality, and I had no reason to doubt their wisdom. This was not a world Arthur or I knew, but we became convinced the odds were stacked in our favour. If I'd been a slot machine, the spinning reels in my brain would've frozen at that very instant to reveal a perfect row of dollar signs lined-up where my eyes used to be. Would our grim determination to survive finally pay off? Was an unqualified bonanza just around the corner? In the immortal words of Cuba Gooding Jr, was somebody finally about to 'show me the money'?

We went 'all-in'. We invested all our earnings from two years of hard-slog hospitality on our ghost floor to acquire the adjacent land – the very site on which Lafayeedney had allowed his deposit to lapse since it was too close to a fish factory (with Cleveland now hitting hard times). The challenge was to convert an unremarkable plot into a beach and hospitality destination that could dazzle 8,000 guests per day. We brought in truckloads of fine sand to build our very own beach volleyball court, imported sixty palm trees from Italy, acquired 300 sun loungers and wicker sofas, commissioned the Maddox Club to set up a beach bar, erected a 75-metre double-decker hospitality 'tent', displayed a twenty-metre-wide screen to relay Olympic Park action, and dropped a fifty-foot Sunseeker yacht on the canal side, showcasing the best of British luxury.

Moët & Chandon were so impressed with our tenacity that they agreed to sponsor the Forman's awards podium, where Olympic medal-winners could, according to the colour of their medal, receive either a free bottle, magnum or jeroboam of champagne. Simon Cowell's then-girlfriend suggested we name it St TropE3. I've always been a sucker for crafty puns, but in this instance decided to keep it simple. Fish Island Riviera. Catchy, evocative, and – if all worked out as planned – the key to gazillions and a doubly well-deserved payback for seven years of bad luck, followed by seven years of bad luck.

CHAPTER 18

FORTNIGHT

'None of us wants to build facilities that local people can only press their noses up against.'

No wonder politicians' promises are treated with such universal disdain. Tony Blair assured us that Iraq could deploy weapons of mass destruction within forty-five minutes, Gordon Brown promised an 'end to boom and bust', and David Cameron spoke with a straight face of his fundamental reform of the EU in the run-up to the 2016 referendum. Grandiloquent rhetoric delivered with confidence and panache. Statements that were all a million miles adrift from reality.

It was Lord Coe who, in his evidence to the CPO public inquiry, made the 'press their noses' remark. With such a colourful turn of phrase, his audience might have assumed that, through the hearts of the IOC, LOCOG and the rest, ran a vein of pure determination to share the joy of the Olympics with the local community. And certainly there was a lot of joy to share: 10,568 athletes who set ninety-nine Olympic records, in front of 8 million ticketholders. A media centre the size of six football pitches that transmitted the events to an estimated 4 billion viewers. And America's Michael Phelps becoming the most decorated Olympian in history after earning his twenty-second medal. Even the sceptics were forced to acknowledge that the London Olympics wasn't doing things half-heartedly. From the 'Journey Along the Thames' sequence that launched Danny Boyle's Opening Ceremony, to the Festival of the Flames on the final day of the Paralympics, the organisers redefined the meaning of extravagant bombast and flamboyant ostentation. The sets, drama, music, costumes, lighting, dance, actors and humour meshed into a vivid and powerful celebration of the world's most oddball country. It assaulted the senses on every level, and those incredible summer weeks remain etched in the minds of everyone who experienced them. Having proven to the world that Britain knows what it takes to throw a great party, there weren't many naysayers mumbling, 'Perhaps it should've gone to Paris after all.' The country had made a statement – loud, dazzling and unique.

Except that, despite Coe's fine words, local people could only share the fun by 'pressing their noses' from the other side of a stark divide. The authorities might as well have stamped the words 'not welcome here' onto the front door of each residence. They stymied and undermined every attempt I made to bring the Games to local citizens who hadn't struck lucky in the ticketing ballot, but who still wanted to eat, drink, sing and revel. They were determined that, throughout the weeks of the Games, any fun in Stratford must be confined to places within the Olympic Park perimeter. When this attitude became obvious, I sighed to René, 'For all they care about the surrounding area, they might as well stage the Olympics on the moon.'

Our first idea was to erect a 'non-sponsors' tent to accommodate firms who couldn't afford the £50 million-plus forked out by the official sponsors such as Coca-Cola, Visa and McDonald's, and who were therefore ineligible to use the 'partners tents' in the park. In our naiveté, we had assumed that we could generally do as we wished on land that we owned and had paid for, so long as it wasn't illegal, offensive or dangerous. But that was before we were exposed to the wrath of those connected to the official sponsor programme, who evidently saw us as a threat – which of course we were, but the world would be an odd place if commercial enterprises were able to shut down any competitor they deemed to be a 'threat'.

Since imperilling the sponsors was a political minefield, we needed to think more laterally, and create ideas that worked with and not against their interests. We proposed that we could install a 100-metre screen (the dimensions chosen in honour of Usain, of course) on our newly formed Riviera, the largest TV in existence, that would relay live footage of the Olympians as it unfolded. But apparently the Games' calendar meant we'd just fall outside the definition of a 'temporary structure', and hence we'd need to apply for full planning permission, which was not forthcoming. At the same time local authorities across the country were installing huge screens in public parks to broadcast the Games, LOCOG uniquely came to the view that such an idea in any way near the stadium would gravely endanger public health.

If we were being forced to seek planning permission, I reasoned, we might as well be bold. Phil Hudson created the schematics for 'London's Living Room' – three fibreglass structures, up to fifty feet in height, that would stand on top of our Riviera hospitality block, and be shaped and coloured as a sofa, an armchair and a TV, to mimic how most of the population would be enjoying the Games. The idea would be overtly sponsor-friendly, by incorporating the relevant brands and logos within the design (the TV would be a Panasonic, a Coke can would be lying on the floor). We were excited about the concept, but no one in authority shared our enthusiasm. Apparently, we were told, the canvas at the back would be 'inappropriate' (the catch-all phrase wheeled out whenever bureaucrats are snookered) in a conservation area. It wasn't often that you'd hear Fish Island's mixed bag of ageing and renovated factories described as a conservation area, but regardless, when we called their bluff – by proposing the canvas should depict

Venice's Piazza San Marco – the argument shifted. The actual concern, it now emerged, was that the building would be too large and ostentatious. I asked whether, that being the case, they'd be knocking down the large and ostentatious stadium on our doorstep. Next, the planning authority fired a series of technical questions, at a level of detail that would never normally arise when seeking outline planning permission. Eventually, they gave up attempts to rationalise their decision. London's Living Room was, they said, 'inappropriate', and that was the end of the matter. Period – no evidence, no explanation. To its credit, the *Evening Standard* went apoplectic on our behalf, but to no avail. LOCOG now had so much momentum and power that media scrutiny was like a squashed bug on a windscreen.

We jettisoned the grand, high-profile gestures, and pressed ahead with less contentious hospitality packages. But even so, the Olympic authorities blocked and stifled us at each turn. Every day, I was putting in cold calls to the marketing and events departments of major brands with what I thought was an irresistible offer:

> Forman's – The closest venue ever to an Olympic stadium, with three magnificent hospitality options to experience the Games.
>
> Option One: An existing building with fully kitted-out hospitality space
> Floor 1: 180 sq. metres, seats 100, standing 200 guests
> Floor 2: 1,000 sq. metres, seats 480, standing 750 guests
> Both spaces have private entrances, natural daylight, roof terraces and the best views of the Stadium and Olympic Park.
>
> Option Two: 5,500 sq. m of open land, adjacent to its headquarters
> On this flexible space, a temporary hospitality facility will be able to accommodate up to 8,000 guests. This will be broken

down into units according to demand and be fitted out to clients' requirement.

Option Three: Riverside

Forman's also has 150 metres of mooring along the River Lea. Sunseeker will be mooring 6–8 of their hand-crafted boats to add to the glamour of the occasion. For smaller events these can be hired – rather like a box at the theatre.

My pitch was simplicity itself: 'Invite your clients for the type of day that comes once in a lifetime; they'll never forget the experience.' I figured it was a slam-dunk. I'd be fending off a veritable stampede of brand and customer relationship managers desperate not to miss out. We'd have a wait list to get onto the wait list. In fact, nothing could've been further from the truth. With exquisitely bad timing, the government chose 2010 – just two years before the greatest hospitality opportunity of all time – to pass their bizarre Bribery Act, packed with vague definitions and tantalising ambiguities. The penalties were eye-watering: ten years' imprisonment, unlimited fines, the confiscation of property and the disqualification of Directors. With insufficient time for case law to establish boundaries, firms were understandably nervous about the consequences of an inadvertent breach, and preferred to remain whiter-than-white. But even with firms prepared to risk fines and jail and disqualification, there was a further objection, yet more unyielding than the first.

The Olympics brand police and their legion of lawyers forbade any use of terms relating to the Olympics for commercial purposes by anyone other than the official sponsors. 'How can we invite our clients to an event next to the Olympic Park to celebrate the Olympics without mentioning the Olympics?' I encountered this refrain, time after time, whilst cold-calling prospects to generate interest. In the event, from a prospect list numbering hundreds, just one major brand succumbed to my smooth-talking. So let's hear it for Speedo. To quote their website: 'Why so serious? Come join the fun! From educational games to kids' swimwear, we've got all the tips and kit you need have loads of water-based family fun, whether at the beach on holiday or in the pool with friends. So what are you waiting for? Dive in!' My philosophy on life precisely.

Increasingly, it seemed to me that the Olympic sponsors had stitched up the deal of the century. Their combined investment was around £1 billion, which represents less than 10 per cent of the bill for staging the Games. And yet they'd seized for themselves 100 per cent of the commercial spinoffs. The hard-pressed tax paper, who has stumped up for the lion's share, was being denied any such luxury. Churchill's famous observation that never in human history 'was so much owed by so many to so few' could be handily twisted to describe the relationship between the frugal general public and the voracious sponsors, alternatively known without a hint of irony or self-awareness as the 'Olympic partners'. The firms themselves are, in my view, blameless. What is hard to accept is how the Olympic movement has ensnared them into contracts that lock out any hint of entrepreneurial innovation in the host community.

Whilst my hospitality proposals were being roundly rebuffed by corporate Britain, I consoled myself with at least one cheery thought: I had been asked to host the Opening Ceremony after party for 400 VIP guests! This was both a humbling privilege and an unmissable opportunity to raise our profile with some of the most glamorous people in the world. There are, after all, a maximum of twenty-five Opening Ceremony after parties every century. The request had come from Anita Zabludowicz, who with her husband Poju could have invented the phrase 'power couple', and whose interests encompassed defence contracting, early-stage technology investments, art collecting and philanthropy. Anita has become one of the world's foremost art patrons, having founded the Zabludowicz Collection in 1994 which now contains in excess of 2,000 works by 500 emerging artists, spanning forty years. But, crucially for my purposes, she was joint Chair of the Legacy List, a charity seeking to deliver £2.8 billion in economic value to Stratford through pump-priming a 'new cultural district on Queen Elizabeth Olympic Park' and advancing the causes of art, culture, education, heritage and science in the area. The after party, modelled on the *Vanity Fair* Oscars party, would be the hottest show in town. The guest list would be a *Who's Who* of everyone you've ever heard of; a fusion of most-medalled Olympians with G20 world leaders, Davos Economic Forum keynote speakers, Oscar-winners, Milan Fashion Show catwalkers and Glastonbury headliners. I was thrilled, bewildered and honoured that my little fourth-generation family business was felt worthy of such a prestigious role.

With a billion dollars' worth of talent in attendance, security would of course be paramount. That was, I'm sure, one of the most important reasons for our selection. Being just 100 yards from the stadium meant there was no risk to the VIPs as they were escorted from one venue to the next. I obtained a quote for a temporary steel pedestrian bridge so they could cross the River Lea – I suspected some of the celebrities might never have learnt to swim – choosing a style with eight-foot-high sides and non-slip floors in case any of the attendees were literally giddy with excitement about the pleasures in store. Moreover, I was enormously supportive of the Legacy List's purpose, and agreed to donate our ghost floor for the party on a pro-bono basis, a gesture which resulted in an invitation to be one of the charity's patrons. My first summons to join the hallowed ranks of the great and good – perhaps a knighthood wasn't a pipe dream after all? Or membership of the House of Lords? I'd always fancied relaxing my posterior on the crimson upholstery of their Lordships' benches. All was running smoothly – Anita was publicly thanking me for hosting the event at donor meetings, and describing it as 'Boris's Party' – and I was turning my mind to the attendant publicity. Of course, this being Forman's, I should've known to be wary of anything that seems too good to be true.

A few months before the Games, LOCOG Chief Executive Paul Deighton was at our smokehouse for a separate occasion, and I happened to mention that 'I'm overjoyed to be involved with the opening night party'. His brow furrowed and he gave me one of those peculiar, quizzical looks – the kind suggesting the person behind the brow hasn't the remotest shred of a clue about the topic you've just raised. 'Whoops,' said an inner voice, 'that wasn't the reaction I anticipated.' And, with the proverbial menagerie of cats out of the bags, it was inevitably downhill from there.

'Thames Water own the land beside the canal; they're bound to object to your bridge,' said one jobsworth.

'Actually I've spoken with their Chairman, and he thinks it's a fantastic idea.'

'It might be unsafe.'

'The manufacturers specialise in temporary bridges. That's what they do! They've been installing them for fifty years without incident. And their engineers will be on-site on the night.'

'People might get lost en route.'

'It's 100 yards, for goodness sake. They're far more likely to get lost if you disperse them to lots of different venues in the West End.'

The excuses were increasingly outlandish, and I half-expected the next objection to be that our interior décor wasn't to their taste. The truth, when it came, was even more preposterous. In their dubious wisdom, LOCOG decided to cancel the after party – kaput, on the basis that the VIPs would be 'too tired to drink or dance' after sitting through the four-hour-long Opening Ceremony. I was with Arthur when the news came through, and after we'd got over our initial dumbfounded speechlessness, we both collapsed into laughter at the absurdity of it.

'Let me paraphrase what I've just heard,' I said. 'Four hundred Masters of the Universe – your ultimate 24/7 gang – used to all-night partying at the flashiest clubs in places like Monaco and Verbier, all pumped high with adrenalin and talent. Yet, after the Olympics Opening Ceremony, they'll want nothing more than to be tucked in bed for a snooze? With some cocoa no doubt.'

'Will the Opening Ceremony really be that boring?' said Arthur. 'In that case, they should've put us in charge of the whole thing.'

It was February 2012, and I was sanguine but not impressed at having the rug pulled from under the event so late in the day, having committed the space at least a year beforehand. Plus, having offered the space gratis, there wasn't even a non-refundable deposit to keep in the event of cancellation. Predictably, that was the last I heard about becoming a Legacy List patron, although for the next year, whenever I scoured through the day's mail, I half-expected to find an invitation to the next patron's meeting. After all, I'd remained willing and able to the very end; it hadn't been my decision to abort.

With or without the after party, I like to think that the Fish Island Riviera was one of the 'places to be' on the 27 July opening night, when 1,500 guests joined us to soak up the atmosphere. (No doubt it would've been double the number, except that for weeks the crazy official decree to the public had been 'Stay Away From Stratford'; it takes a cantankerous type of killjoy to send out that type of message about the biggest celebration of the century.) With the ceremony visuals relayed via our big screen, as well as the actual sounds of the event audible from just 100 metres away, and scores of added extras that were not available inside the stadium – such as cocktails, beach volleyball and the finest fast food in town – I like to think that nobody went away disappointed. From the initial countdown, when images of Britain with the numbers sixty to one on street nameplates, London buses, supermarket labels flashed across the screen, to the final scene, when Paul McCartney led an estimated global audience of 900 million in singing 'Hey Jude', the Riviera was a mass of laughter and childlike wonder. I don't think I've ever been embraced by so many effervescent strangers; as McCartney warbled, there was a spontaneous outbreak of hugging the length of my beach. Whatever happened next, I told myself, it was a memory that will live with me for ever.

The only sour note came when we were dependent on others to fulfil their duties, and were badly let down. I had arranged for a number of ticketholders to dine with us before heading across to the stadium to view the live ceremony, with transportation provided by a fleet of canal boats. You can imagine my embarrassment when my guests were left waiting by the side of the River Lea, with not a canal boat in sight, and less than a quarter of an hour remaining before the ceremony was officially underway. Disastrously, the police had refused the canal boats admission to our stretch of waterway for unspecified security reasons, despite all the necessary permits having been obtained weeks in advance. Of course, I was the easy target for my guests' fury, with most of their insults involving acts of considerable anatomical dexterity and imagination. Poor Jackie Chan was almost in tears at the likelihood of missing out; I think if we'd been in one of his movies, he'd have attempted to cross the river by launching into a spectacular cartwheel off the edge of our roof.

Five of my senior staff stopped everything they were doing as we executed a multi-channel strategy to resolve the problem – phone calls, emails, racing round to the security cordon to beg with whoever was in charge. At the last moment, someone in authority thankfully relented and the boats were released from Limehouse Basin, and I never got to see whether Jackie would've resorted to desperate measures. In recounting this tale, I trust, one of my lasting services to humanity will be that anyone relying on canal boats for future Olympic hospitality events will remember to build in oodles of contingency time.

After the mixed fortunes of the opening night, the priority was to raise awareness of the Fish Island Riviera amongst the hundreds of thousands of daily visitors to the Olympic area. As soon as the day-one pyrotechnic display had finished illuminating the Stratford night sky, and with the tincture of gun powder still alive in the cold air, I despatched four members of my staff to attach signs advertising our presence to high objects throughout the area. Perhaps 90 per cent of park visitors were being herded along a single route to the main entrance, and that provided fertile grounds for our signs. Lamp-posts, drainpipes, overhead cables, flag-poles. If it was taller than six feet, it was a prime candidate to have a laminated 'Fish Island Riviera – This Way' flapping in the breeze before dawn.

I hardly left Fish Island for the next two weeks. I was working at least twenty hours every day to ensure we exceeded expectations with each event we hosted and the service we provided. Typically, I wouldn't crash out until around four in the morning – treating myself to a berth on the Sunseeker, our moored yacht, of course. Then, it would be up before seven, to review any lessons learnt from the previous day's festivities, remind ourselves of what lay in store during the hours ahead, and then switch straightaway into delivery mode. The pressure was relentless. It was impossible to be a hands-off executive during those days, because we were making it all up as we went along (there aren't huge numbers of workers available who have in-depth experience organising an Olympic Riviera). Each day, we identified aspects to fine-tune and issues to finesse, so that every guest left with a spring in their step, ready to spread the word to friends and family.

We had capacity for 8,000 guests daily, and needed 1,000 to break even, so I was a little disconcerted when, by noon on the second day, there had been barely a trickle through the front door. Bemused, I wandered the streets to see whether our signs had perhaps been hung in locations that were too obscure; or at least so I could eavesdrop on conversations people were having when the signs caught their eyes.

Thirty minutes later, I called in my staff to berate them for their incompetence. 'I've walked the entire stretch from the park to the Tube,' I said, 'and didn't see a single sign. Where on earth did you hang them?'

'Like, everywhere.'

That was how it hit me. Having thwarted us at every turn in the build-up to the Games, LOCOG was up to its old tricks. Quite clearly, no sooner had someone spotted one of our signs, than a crack squad of removal experts had been ordered to undo our fine works. Somewhere in the deep recesses of LOCOG's headquarters, a broom cupboard had doubtless been converted into a storeroom for requisitioned Forman's ads.

We had plenty in reserve, and, undeterred, my team was instructed to repeat their mission, but to reach a little higher so the signs would be that much trickier to tear down.

Ten minutes later, they returned, almost in tears.

'We'd barely unfolded the step ladder', said Jack, 'when we were surrounded by at least ten Games Makers ordering us to buzz off.'

'Games Makers' was the official nomenclature for the 70,000 volunteers tasked with assisting visitors with directions and information. They were all kitted out in an identical uniform – chinos, a purple-and-red shirt, a regulation bag, hat, jacket and trainers. It had been one of the more well-received innovations for 2012, although some of the Games Makers did get miffed by the incessant requests by American tourists for directions 'to the nearest McDonald's', having spent the past month swotting up on boutique restaurants and pubs serving exceptional British fayre.

On receiving this news, I knew immediately that we would be suffering a huge write-off for the Olympics fortnight. Our entire strategy had been predicated on generating a buzz and a vibe. If we were to be denied the oxygen of publicity, a tricky task became nigh impossible. I lobbied the media to report our plight, but by now the Olympics was in full swing, and we were drowned out by the latest from the Aquatics Centre, or the Greco-Roman wrestling, or the dressage. There was too much going on for anything other than sports to get a look in. Boris did valiantly spring to our aid at one point. He was being interviewed on LBC for a few sound bites, and one of the reporters raised our complaint about LOCOG's oppressive behaviour. He genuinely seemed unaware of the problem, and without a mealy-mouthed caveat or the scintilla of doubt, condemned the suppression of free speech. 'I opened Forman's on Fish Island,' he trumpeted. 'Everyone needs to get down there – in their millions.'

I've never dared to calculate exactly how much the weeks of the Games cost Forman's, but the bills kept mounting. In my stubborn determination to lay on a genuine extravaganza, I'd hired Ronnie Scott's to take charge of the late night entertainment, and whilst it became a conspicuous talking point, jazz doesn't come cheap. Arthur drafted the press release, announcing our special late-night jazz menu featuring a new Forman's recipe of 'Gravad-sax'. I'd also reorganised our shift system and committed to paying my drivers and factory staff tens of thousands of pounds in overtime to enable our fresh daily deliveries of smoked salmon to be made at two or three in the morning (did I forget to mention that we were still running our regular business throughout the Olympic weeks?), because LOCOG – who I assumed know all about these matters – assured us that London's roads would be clogged and unbearable once the Games hit the city. One of my staff spent almost a month obtaining keys and alarm codes from our customers so that stock could be left in their kitchen refrigerators even when there was nobody around to receive them. In the event, the precautions – and associated bills – were wholly redundant. The authorities had overdone their dire warnings, and the capital city was like a ghost town. I wasn't the only one suffering the financial aftershocks of the Games, which sucked the life out of the rest of London like a gigantic vampire squid. Hotels and restaurants reported that their takings had plunged. Many independent restaurants, lacking the working capital to operate at a sustained loss, put their staff on temporary leave, shut their doors, and pledged to reopen when the Olympic bandwagon had finally moved on.

I resigned myself to the financial hit. I'd gone 'all in' but I didn't even have a full house. So much for all those Olympic experts telling me I was sitting on a goldmine. It was fool's gold and everything I had earnt in the years since the move was blown – and more. My faith that I could start recouping the costs of five wasted years was shattered. Instead, there was nothing to do but chill and enjoy the Games fortnight as best as I could. We received great feedback from the many celebrities, such as Beverley Knight and Daley Thompson, who visited our Riviera and revelled in our hospitality (I had total strangers – many of whom were married – approaching me to proclaim their night at Forman's had been the 'best of my life'; for their sake I hope they didn't share the sentiment with their spouse). It was also comforting to think that, whether they knew it or not, Forman's had been a part of the arrival experience for thousands of the athletes and stars visiting London for the Games. A few months beforehand, the doyen of British chefs Heston Blumenthal had visited Forman's for a photoshoot on our roof terrace with fellow British Airways' Olympic Ambassadors, Richard E. Grant and Tracey Emin, and had complimented us on the gin-and-tonic cured smoked salmon we served as a canape. As it transpired, Blumenthal had been commissioned by BA to create a distinctive Club Class menu for its passengers that season. He must've ripped up his previous plans, because shortly after we received an order for our cure to be served on every BA flight in and out of London during the Olympic fortnight. It must've received rave reviews because BA continued featuring it on their menus long after the season wound up.

* * *

The few weeks of Olympic sport had cast a shadow over my life for nearly a decade, so it's hardly surprising that my emotions during the Games themselves ran such an astonishing gamut – rapture, despair, pride, frustration, exuberance, woe. I struggle to think of a parallel. Even making and losing half-a-billion-dollar fortune during a sleepless week in Las Vegas, with a drug-fuelled midnight marriage officiated by an Elvis lookalike thrown in for good measure, would pale by comparison. 'The epoch of belief, the epoch of incredulity.' However, none of the events I've described will be my abiding memory of that period. Not the controversy over London's Living Room, nor the fiasco over the Legacy List. Not my blind panic when it seemed my high-rolling guests would miss the Opening Ceremony, nor the business-killing actions of the Games Makers. Not the compliments of Boris, nor the privilege of Heston Blumenthal's endorsement. These are all fleeting and trivial, mere bagatelles, compared with what happened just two days prior to the opening night. That day eclipsed all else.

As part of our tribute to sporting heroes, we had created an exhibition, 'In the Rings With Ali', about the life and times of Muhammad Ali, who turned seventy in 2012. Boxing was undergoing a revival in east London, providing an outlet for disadvantaged kids to learn the values of sport, discipline and self-control. Having been world heavyweight champion on an unprecedented three occasions, and despite suffering from Parkinson's disease (which had sadly been the cause of my grandmother's death – the only grandparent I ever knew), Ali had spent many of the years since his retirement promoting religious and racial tolerance. He would be one of the bearers of the Olympic flag during the Opening Ceremony, although his illness rendered him unable to stand for much of the proceedings without the support of his wife, Lonnie. Ali's brother Rahman – also a former boxer, though not of Muhammad's pedigree – had been flown in specially for the launch of our exhibition and had lavished praise on the collection of iconic photographs, poems, writings and memorabilia that we'd assembled. We joked that it 'was great to get Ali and Forman back together once again – although the wrong Ali and the wrong Forman'. I mentioned that my great-grandfather Harry had been raised in Odessa, and Rahman revealed that was also the name of his mother – Odessa Clay. For the rest of the evening, every time we caught one other's eyes, he would mouth 'Odessa'.

Two days before the Olympic Opening Ceremony, Rahman unexpectedly reappeared at Forman's, once again with his wife, Cynthia. They were en route to Heathrow, and swung by for a final view of the exhibition – clearly expecting more personal attention as well as some smoked salmon sandwiches. Under normal circumstances, I would've dropped anything, but the day was already overwhelming and chaotic with two major events prescheduled. The first was a press conference we were hosting for the widows of the eleven Israelis murdered by Palestinian terrorists during the 1972 Munich Games, and who were campaigning for a minute's silence to be observed in honour and memory of their loved ones, forty years on. Jacques Rogge, on behalf of the IOC, had rebuffed their requests, exhibiting the same disdain towards the victims that had been shown for nearly half a century by his predecessors. In the presence of the Israeli ambassador to London, Daniel Taub, the widows would be announcing that their petition for a suitable commemoration had now reached over 100,000 signatures. The IOC's twisted logic was that a minute's silence would be 'political', a view made even more risible by the series of overt political messages Boyle was about to embed throughout the ceremony (including an entire sequence parading the virtues of Britain's National Health Service to a bewildered global audience). The media attention and security around the widows' press conference was of an intensity rarely seen in an east London smokehouse, and I was already being pulled in a dozen different directions by people who wanted me to comment on the campaign, express their thanks for making our facility available, or beg that I make yet another urgent and impromptu decision.

The second event was another press conference, this time for Speedo, which involved not only a photoshoot of the American Olympic swimming team, but also an interview with Michael Phelps for the *Today* show. So, charming though he was, Rahman's unannounced arrival had hardly filled me with rapture.

I was trying to juggle everything without the help of my trusted friend Arthur Somerset, who had collapsed the previous day whilst escorting a group of visitors around the premises, and had been recuperating overnight at Homerton Hospital before his planned discharge that morning. His absence was making itself felt, and I couldn't wait for him to return to his duties.

René and I were with Rahman and Cynthia, contemplating one of Muhammad's more evocative poems, when I felt Rita tugging my sleeve.

'Lance,' she said, 'can you pop downstairs for a moment?'

'Whatever it is, Rita, it will have to wait. I'm busy at the moment.'

'Lance, you need to pop downstairs. It's important.'

Again, barely looking round, I repeated, 'Rita, now is really not a good time. Tell them, I'll be down just as soon as I can.'

Rita intervened once again and, even in the dim lighting, I noticed she was ashen-faced. Then it struck me that Rita had never interrupted me before, let alone with such a blunt command. She was staring at me, and her eyes betrayed panic and dread. But also staring as a stern mother would face down a disobedient child. Whatever it was, it must be serious, and defying her instruction was not an option. I felt as if a shard of ice had been plunged into my spine. Two minutes later, I was in my office with Lloyd, who passed on the news he'd just been given by a friend of Arthur who had turned up at the hospital to collect him.

'Lance, you should sit down,' he said. 'It's about Arthur…'

From his sombre tone, I shuddered with a premonition of what was coming next.

'…he died about half an hour ago.'

My friend. My colleague. My inspiration. My trusted advisor. The person who would push the boat out when everyone else was begging to return to calmer waters. The person who had spent every moment of his working day, for the past four years, preparing for the Olympics fortnight. The fortnight which was now almost upon us. And he had … what? Why? It hadn't been a serious fall, it only seemed routine. We'd called for an ambulance as a precaution, not because we suspected the worst. Was somebody playing some kind of sick joke? Had I misheard or misunderstood? It surely wasn't possible. I banged the desk. The fire, the flood, even the whole blasted CPO mess. None of these mattered compared with what I'd just heard. Arthur was one of those immortal figures, larger than life in personality and stature, decked out in colourful suits and committed to the best of everything – at all times, in all ways. Why the hell are the greatest people always taken from us? And so bloody young. Fifty-two. With a wonderful wife Tanya. And three children – Iggy, Ivo and Oona. All under the age of ten and now without a father.

I muttered, 'Are you sure?'

It sounded so pathetic. Grasping. Of course Lloyd was sure.

'I'm certain, Lance.'

'But how? He seemed so…' God, did I really want to think about how? I couldn't think about how. Not today, not at a time like this. What would Arthur want me to do?

I swore loudly. René was looking in through my office window, a tear already sliding down her cheek. For the next five minutes, we stood in the doorway, holding one another tightly, as I trembled and shook and swore and cried.

Arthur's funeral was held the following week in the small Welsh village of Raglan, Monmouthshire, close to his family's ancestral home. It was the one occasion I left Fish Island during the Olympics fortnight, a time for calm reflection amidst the bedlam and confusion. The service was held in the fourteenth-century parish church St Cadoc's and was moving and beautiful, with an uplifting speech by Arthur's former business partner Tamsin Mitchell. I could barely focus on a word she was saying; my head was flooded with memories of his irrepressible spirit and unqualified friendship. Just a few weeks beforehand, Arthur and I had been selecting inspirational quotes from Muhammad Ali to line the walls of our main staircase, and I recalled the words of Arthur's favourite: 'I wish people would love everybody else the way they love me. It would be a better world.' The poignancy of the remark was stirring but also, I felt, agonising. It could have been written to describe Arthur himself.

After the service concluded, I went with Lloyd – who had travelled separately – to the Manor House in Castle Coombe, where we drank tea whilst overlooking the River Bybrook and shared anecdotes from our lives with Arthur. For once, my mind was not abuzz with a thousand thoughts about sports and guests and signs and broadcasters. Instead it was a simple image of Arthur's glowing smile as he rocked back in his chair that I couldn't let go. Less than ten minutes out of Castle Coombe, wending through country lanes and rolling fields that stretched to the horizon, I realised that in my grief I'd strayed onto the far side of the road. I pulled into a deserted lay-by and, with a flock of curious sheep gazing at me over the hedge, sat back in the driver's seat and sobbed uncontrollably.

Back at the office, the tributes had been flowing in from many people whose lives had been touched by Arthur. 'The bugger's probably gone upstairs to ensure we have good weather for the next few weeks.' 'He's escaped just in time as he knew how mad the Games would be.' 'He's having words with the big boss right now.' The teasing humour in the face of tragedy was exactly how Arthur would've wanted it.

He knew, more than anyone I've known, the power of laughter to diffuse hardship and adversity.

After the inquest, I learnt that Arthur's fall had been triggered by a hereditary condition called dissected aorta, and that the hospital had mishandled every detail of his short time on their ward, including a failure to identify the internal bleeding. His maternal uncle had suffered a similar incident a few years previously, but made a full recovery and was now well into his seventies. The misdiagnosis led to a pay-out of an undisclosed amount to Arthur's family, but of course the money was no consolation. They would've repaid every penny of it for the chance to spend just another few days in Arthur's extraordinary company.

As things were settling down, I exchanged a series of heartfelt emails with Tanya Somerset, Arthur's grieving widow. I wrote of the final night tribute we arranged for her late husband. 'It was our best night by a long way, and about 3,000 people showed up. Just before the closing ceremony started, we uploaded a picture of Arthur onto our huge screen, and everyone observed a one minute's silence. We'll all so miss him. Keep in touch.'

We still retain a picture of Arthur on the page of our website that lists our events team. That's how we still regard him – myself, Lloyd, our Head of Events, and Arthur. It takes all four of us to make great things happen, with Arthur egging us on with his spirit and willpower. In the photo, he's chilling on a pink lounger, flashing a cheeky grin in the direction of the camera. The picture will stay on our site for as long as I'm in charge.

Goodbye, Arthur. Some things are so much more important than a few days of sport.

CHAPTER 19

FORTHRIGHT

It was the wily diplomat Henry Kissinger who once remarked, in a meeting with the Turkish Foreign Minister, that 'the illegal we do immediately; the unconstitutional takes a little longer'. What he omitted to add was that trying to be helpful when a full-blown international crisis is about to explode is more time-consuming than either.

An almighty imbroglio had arisen due to the Russian Olympic chiefs' desire to convert Marble Arch into a showcase venue, called the Sochi Centre, to promote the 2014 Sochi Winter Games. The idea had been to spend upwards of £10 million on an ice rink, a VIP suite and a theatre, so that 8,000 visitors daily could experience a foretaste of what was in store. However, the proposals had run into difficulty, with security issues being raised by the Metropolitan Police, and Transport for London expressing concerns about the impact on traffic flow, followed by Westminster refusing to permit planning.

The problem had been brought to my attention when, following a conference for the young leaders of the world economic forum, hosted at Forman's, and which I was asked to address, one of the delegates, Russian Elena Barmakova, made a beeline for me. I had been speaking about our adjacent site and the wonderful opportunities it presented.

At that juncture, we were still pushing the Olympic Living Room concept but fighting an unwinnable battle against the dead hand of officialdom. Elena said she had all the 'right connections' in Russia, and our site would solve a problem that was brewing.

A week later I had been invited to a charity art exhibition at the GLA and mentioned to Boris that I thought our factory site could solve his Russian problem. He was supportive and pointed me in the direction of his chief of staff, Sir Edward Lister, to sort out the details. My main aim was to tempt the Sochi Centre to locate itself to our factory's land. I suggested that, during the Games weeks, Marble Arch would be on the periphery of the action, and presented innumerable logistical challenges. The Forman's option, by comparison, offered flexibility, access, outside terraces, food storage and (being privately owned) incisive and fast decision-making, all adjacent to the Olympic Stadium and hence within sight of billions of TV viewers and 8 million actual visitors to the park. Putting nuance aside, I argued, there was hardly any comparison. For reasons of viability, profile, prestige and commercial return, Fish Island should be the clear favourite.

With Elena's support and persistence, I was so convinced of the merits of my proposal that the Russians' caution caught me by surprise. When their representative visited and praised me for presenting this opportunity, he also made clear the real stumbling block. Apparently, Dmitry Chernyshenko, President of the Sochi 2014 Organising Committee, had given a personal assurance to President Putin that the Sochi Centre would locate an ice rink in Marble Arch, and if there's one principle for enjoying a long and happy life in Russia, it's not to renege on a pledge to the President. Even if the experience was superior, and the financials healthier, one would be pigeonholed as being 'unreliable' and 'unable to deliver' – not a good blot to have on one's copybook. Always looking for a solution, I contacted Lister and asked whether, in light of the Met's and TfL's concerns, Sochi could locate the ice rink at Marble Arch but construct the hospitality tent at Fish Island – after all, the police's concern was not primarily the ice rink, but rather the hordes of vodka-filled Russians celebrating Olympic medal wins. Ed responded that this seemed a sensible solution and I reverted to my Russian contact with the good news. Perhaps whilst gongs were being handed out throughout the UK for those who had contributed to a successful spectacle, my efforts in diplomacy would be rewarded by an Order of Alexander Nevsky medal from Putin. Was my persistence and investment in looking for hospitality opportunities about to pay off?

But the excitement was not to last for long. Within a week, despite the GLA believing I had found the solution to the diplomatic problem, Westminster was still saying *nyet*. Would I find myself on Putin's hit list, having given an assurance I could not deliver? Putting my own commercial efforts to one side, I felt it was important to prioritise my time to devise a face-saving solution. My initial proposal was to bring Marble Arch to Fish Island. 'Why don't we build a mock Marble Arch on Fish Island? If Muhammad won't go to the mountain…' However, this also failed because Sochi had already invested over £300,000 in the real Marble Arch project and didn't want to be seen to have paid something for nothing. Westminster's position was that Marble Arch could be used on a gratis basis, but only if the Russians installed a piece of genuine public art, and so in tune with the 'winter' theme. I suggested a giant snow globe, lit up around the clock, in which performing artists could demonstrate their talents in fields such as acrobatics and ballet. The Russians were positive, and the onus switched back to me to ensure the Greater London Authority's 'Look and Feel Group' was onside. (Readers can imagine the expletives when I informed Stratford's displaced wealth-creators, working 24/7 to cope with mounting tax bills, that the GLA operated a 'Look and Feel Group'. Seamus virtually suffered a cardiac arrest at the vision of bureaucrats swanning around London saying, 'That looks nice, can I have a feel?'

Michael Finlay said, 'Perhaps we'd have been left alone if we'd been more f***ing pretty.')

As events transpired, Sochi came to neither Forman's nor Marble Arch. The Met stayed resolute in their scepticism, refusing to budge even in the interests of East/West harmony. But Chernyshenko's blushes were spared. Her Majesty the Queen stepped in to offer Perks Field, in the grounds of Kensington Palace, for use by the Russian's Olympic Committee for seventeen days during the Games. I could accept being trumped by the monarch, and I suspect Putin wasn't too displeased either. An amusing coda was that Siberian-born Sergei Kolushev, who put together the deal with the palace, had once been heard to comment, 'There is a stereotype that rich Russians in Britain are all Mafia or billionaire oligarchs like Roman Abramovich. This is unfair. In fact, I'm just a millionaire.'

At least in the case of the Marble Arch ice rink, the authorities had followed due process and given the matter reasoned deliberation, even when the stakes were relatively trivial. What a contrast with my own experience fighting a Compulsory Purchase Order. Only when I got embroiled in the entrails of the legislation did I realise how the cards are stacked overwhelmingly in favour of the state. This isn't like a criminal trial, where court affairs have been structured to promote fairness and equitable treatment for all parties. Nor is it even a David and Goliath scenario, where the future king of Israel at least had recourse to a sling and a stone. In CPO land, a more apt comparison is shooting fish in a barrel. The victims are denuded, deprived of ammunition and trapped within their container. That's how it feels to be the recipient of a CPO notice.

The first of the inequities is the representation available – or, rather, not available. In my situation, the LDA had an in-house battery of personnel. With no other day job to distract them, their nine-to-five obsession with seizing land that didn't belong to them could be complete. On top of that, they could splurge taxpayer money – my money – on the most aggressive outside counsel, all well-versed in case law and precedent. I, on the other hand, in-between trying to make a fist of my day-to-day operations, had to be careful and prudent with any outside advisors I instructed. Whilst in theory public funding was available for lawyers, this came wrapped around with caveats and restrictions, and I know of many businesses who had to dig deep into their own pockets to fund their defence. For myself, I took the view nobody else, however professional they might be, would fight with the same fortitude and grit as I would to protect my interests, and hence I must be exceptionally hands-on in my own defence. Every hour I spent on letters to Tower Hamlets, or in meetings with the LDA, or in prepping for the public inquiry, or in speaking to journalists, was an hour I wasn't spending serving my customers and developing the business.

Legal fees are a practical issue, but there are also fundamental philosophical flaws in the CPO regulations. One is that, in quantifying compensation, the basis of calculation is to envisage a 'no scheme world'. The argument, if it can be dignified with such a term, runs that property-owners should not benefit via their compensation from the fact that the change is happening; in other words, that compensation should imagine a world in which a major investment project such as the Olympic Games had not occurred. This position might just about be sustainable if the property being acquired belonged to a business whose owner-managers were retiring, and who already planned to exit. For the rest of us, we were being forced to live in the 'scheme world'. We didn't have the option to flick the switch on our inter-dimensional transportation bracelets and continue our lives in this fantasy 'no scheme world'. In my general dealings with the LDA, I'd sometimes felt their executives were hailing from la-la land. Now, in their invention of a 'no scheme world', fiction became reality. They were literally forcing upon us a world that didn't exist. How could the displaced businesses –

any of us – approach the owners of alternative land, and say, 'Could you please price it as if the Olympics hadn't happened?' We'd have been laughed off the premises. I don't think it would get me very far if, the next time I file my tax return, I appended a note saying my calculations assumed a 'no customers world'.

The final outrage is the concept of betterment. Let's envisage a small print works operating in 5,000 square feet. Let's further imagine that only two viable alternatives are available: one at 3,000 square feet, the other at 8,000. Contracting the business by two-fifths would mean laying off staff and turning away customers, so that wouldn't seem sensible. One is therefore forced to move into the larger, 8,000-foot facility. In the judgement of the LDA, one has now benefited from 'betterment', through upgrading to a large plant. You don't actually *want* that extra room, you don't even have a need for it, it'll just be lying empty, like fallow land. To be frank, it'll be a bit of an irritation because it will need to be cleaned and maintained, despite not being used. Your overwhelming preference would've been for another 5,000-foot building, and the only reason you aren't in one is the inconvenient fact that one wasn't available. Yet, under the rules, one must pay for this unsought and unwelcome upgrade, as if it had been a conscious choice. It was as close to a game of 'tails you lose, heads you don't win' as you can imagine.

When I recount the story of our Olympic 'persecution', it can often be difficult for my audiences to appreciate how close we came to collapse. There are many episodes in history where the outcome has teetered on the brink, and events could easily have unfolded in a very different manner. We all now know that the Task Force despatched to the Falklands by the Thatcher government was victorious over Galtieri's invading troops, so it's almost impossible to appreciate the soul-searching that must have preceded the decision. We all now know that the Cold War ended in the collapse of an overburdened and over-stretched USSR, so how can we communicate to anybody who didn't live through it that, for years, the terror of nuclear annihilation was real and immediate? Hindsight colours our memories, making things that were random or longshots appear to be predetermined consequences. Back in 2005 and 2006, Forman's survival genuinely hung in the balance, causing me months of stress and nausea as I hoped for the best but expected and feared the worst.

To many, the severity of the threat we faced is brought home by the realisation that many, many businesses didn't survive. With owners and managers preoccupied with disruption for two years, ruthless competitors were able to steal business, promoting their own interests at the expense of the firms being CPO'd. Even now, nearly ten years on, I come across companies that didn't quite make it. I was recently introduced to one such organisation, Bluefoot Foods. Its owner, Julian Rosen, had sunk much of his personal wealth into the launch and expansion of this wholesale foods business, and after years of perseverance it had achieved critical mass, recording a modest profit on sales of £700,000. Suitable compensation was never offered, the firm lacked the deep pockets to defend itself, and Bluefoot died directly because of the CPO. The aftershock still rumbles through the court system (the cynic would say the lawyers are stringing out the proceedings in the knowledge they won't cave in first). When I learnt of this tragic tale, I was so horrified. I kept repeating the words, 'That could've been us; so easily, it could've been us.'

I still occasionally encounter the individuals who have appeared in this storyline. Jeremy Fraser is now a priest in Stratford and has visited our restaurant. Sebastian Coe, who used never to eat fish, confesses to eating Forman's smoked salmon. At a recent charity dinner, he shared how LOCOG had fiddled the traffic lights to create a misleading impression about London's traffic flows when the IOC was in town assessing London's bid and focusing on their number-one concern, being the speed at which athletes could get from central to east

London (in fact, the efforts were so extreme that – according to Coe – he once asked for a couple of lights be turned to red as the motorcade approached, so that the tampering wasn't too blatant). Unlike claims being bandied about now that numerous London 2012 athletes tested positive after reanalysis of their doping samples, there were certainly no illegal substances involved in the traffic light manipulation, to be sure. But to my mind the underlying morality and ethics in this case were even worse than those of the individual athletes hoping to get away with an illicit boost. Here, the entire city was being doped. Ken Livingstone, once so vitriolic, later confessed that, had he been in my shoes, he'd have acted in exactly the same way. On one level, his comment was flattering; but why on earth had a fight been necessary? If the LDA had not reneged on the New North Road deal, we could've been settled years earlier, at a far lower cost. Surely, when government is dealing with its citizens, we should all be wearing the same type of shoe? It shouldn't be like opposing football teams, one wearing Nike and the other Adidas, each trying to kick the bejeezus out of the other.

Despite the absence of regeneration or legacy (remember all the hyperbole about inspiring a generation and ending childhood obesity?) many of those who oversaw the Olympics have prospered. Lord Sebastian Coe and Dame Tessa Jowell have never looked back and – Coe in particular – command vast speaking fees. Ironically, the only person who lost their job due to mismanagement was Gareth Blacker, due to busting the budget on land acquisition by £100 million. He's probably the only one who should, in truth, have been knighted for services to the taxpayer, because the land was worth far more than that. If Whitehall in general was as savvy with the public purse, the Exchequer would've been running at a surplus for the last twenty years.

After the lights of the Olympics weeks had faded, my focus had to switch to the future – to the commercial opportunities and threats of the next decade, rather than the perils of having a stadium dumped on your land. But the fallout from those years continues to reverberate in unexpected ways. A few months after our move, I was chewing over the state of the world with a surveyor friend who had knowledge of the area. He happened to mention that, in quick succession, there had been three unexpected deaths in properties connected with land transactions in the area. Businessman Danny Mardell, a colourful Bentley driver who had raised hundreds of thousands of pounds for a Down's Syndrome charity through boxing (he was a heavyweight champion) collapsed whilst jogging and lay unidentified for several days in Newham General Hospital. A second local businessman shot himself. And a third, a factory owner, had a seizure and fell underneath a bus. After hearing these stories, I took the precaution of double-bolting the backdoor for a few evenings and, to be frank, this has been the main reason it has taken me four years to bring myself to tell the full story of our Olympic struggle.

There were a number of lasting effects on me personally from the Olympics debacle, and one of the most unexpected was that I had struck up a decent reputation with the national media. I have never had any formal media training. I still remembered observing my former boss Peter Lilley being coached in the dark arts of spin and messaging, but most of my practicals were learnt on the job. In the days before the London Olympics launched, TV crews the world over were pitching up at Forman's looking for interesting back-stories on the Games – and what could be more exciting than a small, heritage food business that had been based in this part of town for over 100 years, had fought a high-profile battle for its survival and had now put its money where its mouth was and invested in a venue fit for the stars?

One such broadcaster was Hong Kong TV and its presenter was a cute and flirtatious Chinese girl, Heidi Chu, a former Miss Hong Kong finalist. One glance and you could see why. Captivated by her good looks, I dragged out the interview for about twenty minutes before suggesting that she might like to talk to other members of my team.

The more publicity and PR we could achieve, the better the prospects for our Riviera success. Heidi was very accommodating and so I ran straight down from our roof terrace to find our Riviera Club's DJ, Maurice.

'You must come and see who'll be interviewing you ... She's a stunner,' I begged him when I tracked him down. 'If you're lucky you might get more than a bit of smooth talking.' (Yadda. Yadda. Boys' talk. There were a few more choice sentences which I'll leave to the reader's imagination.) When I returned to Heidi, she had the biggest grin on her face. Clearly I had not left what I said to her imagination as I'd been wandering around wearing a live mic for the past ten minutes. So, whenever the striking redhead from Bloomberg, Louise Beale, who based herself on our roof terrace for much of the Olympics, interviewed me, I made triple sure everything was switched off at the finish.

Forman's seemed to tick a number of boxes for the media. The interior of our smokehouse provided a ready-made and eye-catching visual for an outside broadcast – racks packed with sides of salmon; picture of our kilns; footage of our slicers in action – a more intriguing setting, for certain, than banks of office desks with workers at their computers. The Olympic stadium always made the perfect reference point for viewers, even if the news story wasn't primarily about the Olympics. As the sole owner, I could make decisions quickly; journalists on a tight deadline don't take kindly to being caught in the labyrinthine web of internal sign-off procedures before an interviewee is authorised to go ahead. And I'd learnt the art of the sound bite, extracting the core from a complex argument and expressing it with a pithy turn of phrase, without rambling, mumbling or hesitating.

As I became more confident in front of the camera, I sought out opportunities that took my fancy. I approached the shopping channel QVC, having established that they didn't yet have a fine food partner, and agreed a trial show. I was impressed by the wealth of demographic data on the QVC daytime audience; it seems that a large proportion of their viewers are in the social and earning bracket likely to be tempted by a gourmet range. The results of the pilot were sufficiently impressive for a return invite – with QVC, the trickiest achievement is often the second appearance, not the first. This is because the sales results are measurable in real time. A product that flops is quickly blacklisted and not granted a second shot.

There were a couple of important tricks. Longevity on QVC, certainly in the food category, requires a core speciality, but also product breadth. A portfolio of TV-friendly items is necessary to fill a ten-minute timeslot – it doesn't sound much, but it's a fiendishly long time to hold the attention of a channel-surfing audience. Multiple products also means I don't disenfranchise any members of my audience who happen not to like smoked salmon (such people do, I'm told, exist). Recently, I segued from my tried-and-tested opening spiel about fish into a sequence promoting our newly launched bread and butter pudding laced with Irish cream liqueur ('naughty but nice' was the motto). As I've become accustomed to QVC-style patter, colleagues have challenged me to stretch myself rhetorically. I once slipped in a comment that, at Forman's, we 'chase the noble taste of the salmon' in acknowledgement of a boutique consultancy called Chase Noble that's owned by a university friend.

At around the time my QVC profile was on the rise, I found myself being invited as a guest on terrestrial and satellite current affairs shows, sitting in the hot seat whilst people like Dermot Murnaghan, Gavin Esler and Kay Burley lobbed questions about the news agenda. In some cases, preparation has been nigh impossible; three minutes before going on air, a showrunner will hand over the business sections of the broadsheets and ask me to pick a couple of stories on which I'd like to comment. These are summarily disregarded by the interviewer, who prefers to throw a curveball than follow a verbatim script, and one is caught between wanting to pause for valuable thinking time (never a good choice on live TV), or blurting out something idiotic that will live in immortality in the digital archives – or, if it's really cringeworthy, on YouTube.

Over the years, our sales through QVC and other direct-to-consumer channels have steadily risen. But a Chinese journalist did once let slip that even the broadcast media has its limits. I had long nurtured an ambition to develop business in the People's Republic, and the perfect opportunity arose two weeks before the Olympics when a crew from CCTV, China's BBC equivalent, turned up on our doorstep. I agreed to allow them in, and after spending two to three hours filming in the smokehouse, the crew finally came to my office for an interview. After twenty minutes of questioning, the interviewer, drawing the session to an end, said:

'Mr Forman, I have one final question I'd like to ask you. What do you see as your personal legacy from the Olympics?'

I didn't want to talk about sports or even discuss how we had been treated. This was my fifteen-second window to market directly to the people of China. I put on a serious face, looked straight into the camera and said:

'My passion is not really sport, it is about my product, smoked salmon. What I would like as my legacy from the Olympics is for everyone in China to try Forman's smoked salmon.'

The interviewer seemed a little puzzled and then responded, 'Ah, but Mr Forman, maybe you do not understand, but not everyone in China watches China TV. But we do have 300 million viewers.'

'No problem. We'll start with them,' I quipped.

I became an occasional spokesperson for the 'Leave' campaign during the EU Referendum debate. By one of life's more remarkable coincidences, their headquarters was located in the same Albert Embankment office block as Biteback – the publishers of this book. I hadn't appreciated this fact until the day of my high-stakes introduction to Iain Dale.

I arrived early, and whilst waiting in the foyer, I spotted the VoteLeave name on the list of tenants, just three floors below the Biteback suite. If Biteback had blown the raspberry at my synopsis, I might've slunk back to the East End, my confidence shattered. As it was, I was so pumped with adrenalin at the positive response from Iain and his team that I couldn't resist the urge to drop by the VoteLeave offices and volunteer my services. I had grown incensed by the cynical tactics of the government as they campaigned for a 'Remain' vote, which – to my mind – primarily involved bludgeoning the population into voting for the status quo on the farcical basis that anything different involved 'uncertainty'. Surely, nobody in government genuinely believed the dire warnings about the economic and security damage to Britain of Brexit which they parroted with increasing stridency – because, if they did, they should never have called the referendum in the first place.

When asked for my comments about the encroaching 'EU superstate', my remarks were offered not from an ideological perspective, but as a medium-sized business trying to create employment and cope with red tape. On *Murnaghan*, I told the story of the day an EU Directive was adopted that forced us, at a cost of thousands, to reprint our smoked salmon packaging with the warning: 'Contains fish'. 'If they insist on transparency, they should erect a sign above the EU Parliament with the message "Contains nuts",' I said. And never one to resist a commercial spinoff, I created the 'Leave' hamper – packed with a 'sparkling array' (as it said in our promo leaflet) of exclusively British goodies, including: Kipper Pâté ('not an endorsement of the UKIPpers, just a delicious pâté'); pork pie ('better to eat Porky Pies than listen to them; these are the best porkies on the market from Melton Mowbray'); Montgomery's Cheddar ('Britain now has more cheesemakers than France. It's cheeses like this, made in Somerset since 1911, that make Britain great'); green tomato chutney ('made with heritage tomatoes; if our heritage is going to be chopped up, we'll do it because we want to, and not because we're told to'); banana bread ('made with bananas of all shapes'); fudge ('Yes there's been far too much already, we know; this fudge is definitely worth demolishing'); English Brexit Tea ('perfect for the morning after'); dark chocolate salted caramels ('we debated whether to go for milk chocolate, but thought you'd prefer a leap into the dark'); and Brussels sprouts ('we're only kidding; we wouldn't allow Brussels anywhere near this hamper'). I'm not sure it was the best-selling hamper in our history, but we had no end of fun crafting those explanatory notes.

I could never understand why so many of our political leaders felt Britons lack the attitude and aptitude to succeed independently. That struck me as a doom-laden and fatalistic charge, far adrift from the country in which I lived and worked. In the East End, I see a spirit of fearless, remorseless, determined ambition. I am surrounded by businesses and people who create, innovate, pioneer and dream, who fizz with energy and have no need of Brussels bureaucrats' blessing before they let loose their firepower. These are not people who cower in horror at the thought of making their own decisions. On the contrary, it is the dead hand of corporatism that stifles and inhibits. If what I see around Stratford is representative of all my countrymen – and I believe it is – then, let free from the throttling, choking grip of the EU, I think we'll somehow be alright.

The spirit of independence was never as starkly on display as in the numerous artists' studios that were dotted around Fish Island, many hidden away in attics or basements or converted storerooms. Despite often being at the opposing ends of the political spectrum, we do share many values, such as creativity, a free spirit, a pathological loathing of conformity and authority and an artistic streak with an eye for design.

Having built our ghost floor into a venue, 'Forman's Fish Island', I was approached by some local artists asking whether I would consider allowing them to use the space as a gallery to display their works. Whilst wishing to be supportive, I was also mindful of the recent arrival of some graffiti to adorn my new building. So I proposed the terms of a truce. 'Find me your best local graffiti artists to come and graffiti inside my building rather than outside and I will make the space a gallery.' I figured if I demonstrate respect for their art, they will respect our building. It worked a treat and our ladies' and gents' WCs are decorated with 'street art' which, with any luck, will be worth more than the building one day!

Within months, the Forman's Smokehouse Gallery had been born, and has grown in popularity as word has spread. I like to think it's now something of an epicentre in the Hackney Wick area for established and emerging local artists to raise their profile and generate cash flow which, in many cases, can be desperately welcome. Over the years, our walls have been graced by works from pop artists such as Marty Thornton, Jennifer English, former Saatchi curator Martin McGinn, Royal Academician Jeanette Barnes, extrovert Molly Parkin, paparazzo Alan Chapman and other notables including Jukhee Kwon, Arina Orlova, Xiao Bai, Matthew Booth, Busk, Zsi Chimera, Frank Creber, Rosie Emerson, Kimberley Gundle, Heretic, Ben Hopper, Nadine Mahoney, Yash Mali, Bill McCombe, Marion Musry, Qing, Gerd Sedelies and Jessica Voorsanger. During the Olympics, whilst we ran with the Ali exhibition, it was a close call between that and a retrospective by world-renowned photographer David Bailey, who would possibly have been our preference, except for his reservations about the space doubling as a dining area. Artists! He was gracious enough to allow me to take a photograph of him, though. Amazing how far a pack of Forman's smoked salmon will go...!

One of our recent exhibitions was by Sue Tilley, known variously as 'Big Sue' or 'Benefit Supervisor Sue'. Sue was the nude model who had sat for a painting by Lucian Freud which was sold at auction for $50 million, the highest price ever paid for the work of a living artist. He had paid Sue just twenty pounds a day to sit for him, so Sue concluded it made more sense to be an artist than a model and we launched her very first exhibition. Although the quality of the art, Sue would acknowledge, was not worthy of the Tate, it was commercially our most successful exhibition with visitors wanting to purchase the works of 'the living Mona Lisa' and just one degree of separation from Lucian Freud. I confessed to Sue that we had a common connection with Lucian Freud, as he was a regular client of Forman & Field. If only we framed his cheques rather than cashed them, they would have been worth so much more than our food parcels. I told her I would not make the same mistake with Frank Auerbach, another discerning customer who had been named as Britain's greatest living artist by the BBC. Blow me down, Auerbach placed an order the very next day, and his very large and unbanked cheque will be spending eternity on display in a resplendent gold-leaf frame.

There was some residual scientism about the relevance of an art gallery to the creating and promotion of the country's finest smoked salmon, and every now and then I'd be challenged to conjure up a convincing explanation. At Salon III, our third annual open invitation exhibition, a journalist from one of the Sunday supplements directly challenged me on this point. London has many fine galleries, he said; so what was our strategic rationale behind the diversification?

I wondered whether I should indulge in a lengthy exposition of my approach to business strategy, but, in truth, there had been no overarching vision or carefully enunciated strategic logic. I had been driven, as ever, by a yearning to invest my time with subjects for which I'm passionate, and an instinct which, whilst not infallible, has accumulated more credits than debits over the years. I see Forman's as a creative business. We may not be artists but we are artisans producing fine food entirely by hand, with fine craft and care.

As the journalist's pen hovered over his notepad in anticipation of some profound insight, I settled on just nine words to justify the initiative:

'Curing downstairs. Curating upstairs. What could make more sense?'

CHAPTER 20

FOREGONE CONCLUSION

'You really should write a book about it.'

I was mingling with students in the Windsor Castle, a privately run pub on the grounds of the London Business School. The pub had been designed and built as part of John Nash's nineteenth-century redevelopment of the area just north of Baker Street, adjacent to Regent's Park, and it retained many of its original Georgian features. The Business School itself was, architecturally, as far as you could imagine from either an Oxbridge college or a modern redbrick university. If anything, the façade was mostly reminiscent of an upmarket residential terrace, which was unsurprising since Nash's original purpose had been for twenty-six prestigious homes, ideally suited as London bolt-holes for the landed gentry. Today the area buzzed not with the well-heeled aristocracy but with hyper-ambitious business students eager to clock their first million before thirty. That's because London Business School is widely recognised as providing one of the top five Executive MBA programmes in the world, and arguably the finest and most prestigious outside of North America.

Invited by Professor Richard Jolly on his 'Managing Change' course,

I had been delivering a lecture in LBS's lecture theatres to a class of around 100 students. The room was arranged as an amphitheatre, which – as a speaker – certainly keeps you on your toes. Not quite as frightening as being thrown into gladiatorial combat or set upon by lions in a genuine amphitheatre, but not entirely dissimilar either. A hundred pairs of eyes bearing down upon you from front and both sides means that, if you're rambling, you can sense the immediate rise in hostility levels – especially in the age of the smartphone. There's nothing that's more guaranteed to upset a speaker's self-assuredness than spotting a member of the audience surreptitiously updating their Facebook status or retweeting a joke.

In my lecture, I'd given my usual recitation of the history of salmon smoking in the East End, and how Forman's had survived the challenge of mass production competition since the 1980s. Then I'd given a whistle-stop tour of what it felt like to be at the centre of a maelstrom when a government agency decides it has a greater need for your land, and mobilises the state's vast resources against you. I had been slightly concerned that, in raising our Olympics story, I might be criticised for 'sour grapes'. But, quite the contrary; my audience was captivated. Many of them had been vaguely aware of the site clearance issues from media reports, but memories had faded with the passage of time, or been drowned out by the sheer noise and imagery of the actual 2012 event. After my formal remarks concluded, fifteen minutes had been set aside for Q&A, and uncannily every single question related to an aspect of our displacement. Fifteen minutes? Given the forest of arms, I could've been taking questions until midnight! I'm told that, at the end of the typical early-evening guest lecture, students disperse back to their residencies or to the LBS gym. On this occasion, at least half the audience cajoled me to join them in the Windsor Castle, so they could eke out from me additional nuggets from the Forman's experience – what was it really like to stare into the abyss, with everything for which I'd worked and strived on the verge of collapsing – literally – into debris and dust?

'It is the most incredible story,' said one student, a brunette wearing Versace Aviator sunglasses even though we were indoors on a cold October evening. 'I've spent the last year learning all about business theory and long-term planning. Analysing the competition and studying the market and articulating a vision. But nothing that would prepare us for the real world that you've described.'

'I just wish I'd had time to explain some of the details,' I said. 'For example, there was a time when I was contacted by an intermediary to meet a developer whose name I couldn't quite catch, but who said he had the power and authority to find out a solution that...'

'Shhh, don't spoil it,' the brunette raised her index finger to my lips. Then she indicated for a group of her friends to join us by the fireplace. 'I've been telling Mr Forman he should write a tell-all book about how close he came to seeing his business destroyed. What do you think?'

'I'd buy it,' said a Japanese student in an anorak.

'Me too,' said a third, who pushed through the crowds to shake my hand. He had the man-mountain build of a professional rugby player, probably a front-row prop, a real brawler. His body mass would've exceeded that of the brunette and the Japanese student combined. With my knuckles throbbing from his vicelike grip, he added for good measure, 'And another for my nan. I'm always stuck for decent Christmas presents.'

I was somewhat surprised by the enthusiasm of so many wannabee business tycoons for the inside story on Forman's travails and triumphs, not least because I'd used much of my time in the lecture hall expounding my views that planning doesn't matter. For a group of people who were spending tens of thousands of pounds for a paper certificate confirming their competence in – ahem – things like business planning, I half anticipated a gigantic raspberry. I might as well have said,

'Don't waste your shekels. Think of a great idea, work hard and trust your instinct.' But they seemed to relish a different perspective from the regular professorial expositions of arcane business concepts by ivory tower gurus who've never had to meet a payroll in their lives. And, it seems, the LBS authorities didn't mind my mildly subversive take on strategic matters, because they've since invited me to reprise my remarks. It's a credit to LBS that they haven't succumbed to the fad amongst universities and colleges to provide 'no platform' for any speakers whose views diverge from the official manifesto.

In the opening paragraphs of this book, I quoted the Yiddish proverb '*Mann tracht und Got lacht*', meaning 'Man plans and God laughs'. Whatever your religion, or whether you're a person of no faith at all, you might agree with my premise that the world is an uncertain and unpredictable place. We can spend our hours and days devising the most exhaustive, painstaking and profound plans, full of vision statements and actions and milestones and dependencies. I once walked into a large meeting room at Price Waterhouse in which a forty-foot-long wall was awash with printouts of activities on a timeline (called a GANTT chart, as I recall). We can create these planning tomes, and how wonderful and incisive they appear – only to jettison them post-haste as soon as they encounter the real world. For so much that happens around us is random. Think of the United Kingdom just one decade ago, when Gordon Brown was still Chancellor of the Exchequer, proudly repeating ad nauseam that 'We have abolished boom and bust.'

Who could have predicted that, within ten years, the country would've endured the most painful recession in living memory, real incomes would've stagnated, the banking system would've been nationalised, Woolworths and BHS would've collapsed, a little Californian company called Netflix which had just streamed its first content would be on its way to becoming a more powerful media brand than the BBC, and West Ham United Football Club would've negotiated the deal of the century – occupying a stadium (built on your dime and mine) for the next 100 years at a peppercorn rent.

In such an environment, I think the belief that planning holds the key to business success is a tragic blend of delusion and folly. Far better to build an organisation filled with talented people who understand their markets and their products, and are able to duck and dive, to dodge and weave, in response to events. Who have the versatility of mind and flexibility of skills to respond positively and rapidly when *stuff happens.* No strategic plan on earth could have envisaged any of the half-dozen major things that have affected Forman's since my arrival. We have suffered a fire that devastated most of our factory. We were victim of a flood that forced us to abandon a building that became unsuitable for food preparation. We exploited a chance encounter with a direct-to-consumer business that had run into trouble to give birth to Forman & Field. We saw our assets sequestrated by government diktat. We procured state-of-the-art kilns which, after installation, smoked a seemingly horrendous product. And we moved just 100 metres to a site with massive untapped potential due to its proximity to the Olympic Park. I could've spent half a million pounds in 1998 with a boutique such as Bain or McKinsey to produce some fine words on a page, with lots of complex algorithms and matrices. But not a single page, not a sentence, not a bullet point, would've envisaged any of these challenges.

Running a small business has enormous rewards. After twenty years, I still feel a frisson of pride at a complimentary letter from a customer, or when I can offer a grafter who's fallen on hard times the chance to rekindle their career. But it can also cause stress, anguish and anxiety. I've lost count of the number of times I've woken in a cold sweat, my mind abuzz and restless about some thorny business dilemma. Or been in virtual tears about the looming payroll bill, particularly when the LDA was doing everything in its power to obliterate us like some bulbous cold sore. Nobody in the public sector, and few in the private sector, can really appreciate the toll it can take, both mentally and physically. Sometimes I want to wretch when I hear patronising politicians trying to express empathy with the country's legion of entrepreneurs. This was David Cameron, in 2011:

> The spark of initiative. The courage to make your dream happen. The hard work to see it through. There's only one strategy for growth we can have now and that is rolling up our sleeves and doing everything possible to make it easier for businesses to grow, to invest, to take people on. What drives us is getting things done – and what drives us mad is the bureaucracy, the forms, the nonsense getting in our way. Back small firms. Boost enterprise. Be on the side of everyone in this country who wants to create jobs, and wealth and opportunity. The enemies are the bureaucrats in government departments who concoct those ridiculous rules and regulations that make life impossible for small firms.

Fine, uplifting words from the Prime Minister; I'm sure his scriptwriter received an extra pat on the back that day. But I hope no young pup took his words literally, remortgaged their house, cashed in their savings, thinking that – after the master had spoken – starting-up as an entrepreneur would now mean a life devoid of strangling, stifling 'rules and regulations that make life impossible'. Because, Prime Minister, they are all still there. Like an uncontrollable virus, immune to the latest antibiotics, they multiply. And knock you out. And, left unchecked, can kill. Speaking on behalf of the entire community within the Marshgate Lane Business Group, I can tell the Prime Minister that, ten years on, wherever we've succeeded it's been *despite*, not because of the bureaucrats. And whenever we've failed, its often been because planners and form-fillers were more interested in the purity of their checklists than common sense or doing the right thing.

The real heroes of this story are not to be found in the Forman's boardroom, however, but on the shop floor. I cannot praise highly enough the people who have stuck with me on this rollercoaster journey. Working for a family-owned business isn't easy. There's no guarantee your employer will still be around in the next decade, or even the next year; there is no gold-plated final salary pension scheme; your bosses can't afford to turn a blind eye if you're taking excessive sick leave. And yet, despite the uncertainties, my team has over-delivered. Reliably, professionally, cheerfully, producing the best quality smoked salmon in the world, and much more to boot. I could never have fought such an effective battle with the authorities if I hadn't been confident that ongoing operations were in safe hands. I could never have committed to such a fast relocation programme, except for the fact people were willing to muck-in, and not squat on their haunches moaning 'it's not my job, guv'.

A number of magnificent, stalwart characters have shown up during the course of this narrative: Lloyd Hardwick, respected throughout the London catering community as a General Manager of the first degree; Rita Law, a one-woman powerhouse who embodies Forman's gung-ho, knock-'em-dead ethos, and knows how to pep us all up whenever we were flagging; Darren Matson, still the Guinness World Record-approved salmon slicing world record holder; Arthur Somerset, who packed more joy and creativity into a week than most people do in a lifetime.

But my cast of heroes stretches much further than these four. When I took over Forman's, there were sixteen staff on the payroll. Last Christmas, we exceeded 100 for the first time. In a complex smoke-house operation, we employ accounts clerks, curators, curers, carvers, packers, cleaners, chefs, customer service staff, delivery drivers, events professionals, food safety personnel, store managers, restaurateurs, maintenance staff, marketers, quality controllers, sales people, trainers... Unfortunately there is no space here to list every one of those hundred, but perhaps readers will indulge me if I namecheck all those who have reached ten years of service – Lloyd, Candice, Cliff, Darren, Irena, Laima, Lorraine, Loretta, Louis, Matt, Richard, Sauda, Vitalija, Harvinder (who just retired after twenty-two years) and Rita (who also recently retired at the ripe young age of seventy-nine). To every one of these amazing souls, I say thank you for your hard work and your perseverance. I salute you, one and all!

The other heroes are of course my family, who spent the prime of my life being absent from most of it, as I spent every hour fighting for my (and their) survival. They say life begins at forty, and that's certainly when my life started to become 'interesting', as the Chinese would have you believe. René, with her right-hand assistant Clara, kept us all sane and in check; I'm proud of each of them and their successes. I crossed my half-century a few months after the Olympics, a year which was notable for many family milestones, including René's and my silver wedding anniversary, Oliver's eighteenth, Matthew's twenty-first, and (remarkably, without any disasters, despite being in October) Annabel's bat mitzvah.

The Forman's story is unusual in many ways. Not many mid-sized businesses have suffered so many threats to their existence, each fast on the heels of the previous one. Nor experienced becoming, almost overnight, such high-profile players slap-bang at the epicentre of an event of global interest. But there is one other feature, unmentioned until now, that is to my mind even more exceptional about our narrative. According to the Boston-based Family Firm Institute, typically just 10 per cent of family-owned businesses survive to the third generation. The cliché, which has much truth to it, is that the first generation starts the business; the second runs it and grows it; and the third wrecks it.

Or, as the somewhat more colourful aphorism runs, 'Shirtsleeves to shirtsleeves in three generations.'

There are numerous theories as to why this truth is near universal, from the over-long tenure of CEOs, who are therefore unable to cope with new technologies or market shifts (George Stalk, *Harvard Business Review*, 2012), to the inheritance by gilded and cosseted offspring who lack the 'scratch and claw' drive of the founder (John Warrillow, *Wall Street Journal*, 2010). For Forman's to have made it, not just to the third generation, but to the fourth, is an occurrence so rare that, as far as I can tell, the survival rate statistics are not collected. Most people see Halley's Comet more often in their life than come across a 4-Gen firm. I have often wondered if Forman's has been the exception to this rule, assuming it's not pure happenchance and good fortune. I can't speak for my father, but in my own case, I feel it was a huge advantage and, to that end, thank my parents that I wasn't groomed from infancy to ascend the throne. In that scenario, I might've taken over Forman's knowing everything about curing techniques and central London delivery routes, but without a hinterland – without a mix of skills to deal with unforeseen challenges.

In hindsight, the experiences I acquired during my 'away' years were vital to dealing with the existential threat to Forman's future posed by the Olympics. The three terms I spent as an officer of the Cambridge Union Society gave me the ability to present an argument to a large and sometimes hostile audience – which is a starkly different skill from composing fine words for a written report. My training as an accountant at Price Waterhouse meant that I could grapple with complex financial scenarios, and sniff out when situations seemed awry. My time as a special advisor to Peter Lilley gave me an unparalleled insight into the murky and treacherous world of politics (to be clear – that's a comment on the vipers' nest around Peter; his own personal conduct was scrupulous and impeccable). And my East8 adventures with Phil meant

I could find my way around real estate issues. So when it came to sorting out the aftermath of politicians' decisions to requisition property at knockdown rates, my résumé was almost tailor-made for the challenge. Had I spent all my years grafting for the same enterprise – as was the case with many other business owners in the area – I might have been overawed by the situation and dazzled by the numbers being bandied around by the LDA's representatives. When said quickly, the payoffs were eye-catching; it was only when they were subjected to actuarial analysis that one realised they were derisory, and one was being screwed over by one's own government.

It has taken me four years until I can look back on our Olympic experience with enough objectivity and dispassion to do justice to the story. I also hope I've set the record straight about one matter that has occasionally been irksome. Politicians, journalists and VIPs who visit our smokehouse often make a sardonic aside along the lines of 'You did well out of the Olympics, didn't you?' Not only is this remark inappropriate from anybody who hasn't seen our previous building – which, although differently configured, was equally striking and impressive; but also they aren't seeing the downsides – the years of stress and heartache and terror. People sometimes ask me to imagine a *Sliding Doors* moment – if I could click my fingers for Paris to have won the hosting rights, would I roll back time and follow that path instead? It's an impossible question to answer – I'm not one to wallow in regrets or dwell mournfully on 'what ifs', and our rollercoaster ride has given me endless stories to tell the grandchildren when in my dotage. So I'll sidestep the *Sliding Doors* scenario, but I'm happy to state for the record that under no circumstances could I ever be tempted to buy a ticket for a repeat journey!

With the Olympics consigned to the history books, I've finally been able to think about the future. I have no idea whether there will ever be a fifth-generation Forman in the hot seat – perhaps we might skip a generation, especially if the monarchy sets the precedent when it comes to Prince Charles's turn to wear the crown. In any event, I don't intend to vacate any time soon. As actor Charlton Heston often said in a wholly different context, 'I'll give you my gun when you pry it from my cold, dead hands.' With so many opportunities ahead, that's exactly how I now feel about my humble smokehouse.

My immediate priorities congregate around three broad themes. Firstly, I'm keen to develop business overseas. My quip about China TV's 300 million viewers in the last chapter had a serious undercurrent. As the levels of wealth rise around the globe, consumers are becoming more selective and discriminating in their eating choices. Forman's is well-positioned to take advantage. Our international pedigree can only be helped by the recent award of PGI (Protected Geographical Indicator) status to our London Cure, placing us on a par with champagne, Parma ham and Stilton. Ironically, the rubber-stamping of PGI status rests with the EU – a body I've been campaigning to leave. Some might say that I'm acting against my own best interests; I'd reply that I don't need an EU award to tell me something that my taste buds confirm every morning. But, if and when it does come through, 'London Cure Smoked Salmon' will be the first London-based food or drink to achieve such status.

Secondly, Forman's must assume a leadership role in educating the public about the taste of great smoked salmon. I was stunned at a recent seafood trade event that, in a blind tasting, a number of leading chefs who should have known better were critical of a slice of smoked salmon (not a Forman's slice) because 'I can't taste the smoke'. It was with a degree of exasperation that I said, 'But you're not meant to taste the smoke! The smoke is to seal the outside, so that you can properly taste the fish! If I served you grilled salmon, would you complain that you couldn't taste the grill?' They looked at me with the same gobsmacked expression that pervades the room whenever Hercule Poirot reveals it's the butler wot done it.

And thirdly, to continue raising awareness of the Forman's brand, because that unlocks so many other opportunities. It's why we're now stocked in selected supermarkets, and it's why our Forman & Field database continues to grow. I'm conscious that, in the food business, I can't match the multi-million-pound advertising budgets of the large corporations such as General Mills, so awareness will come from being smart, being quirky (for example, with our annual calendars), and reacting fast to any chances for free media – especially where the national broadsheets are planning their features and need a photograph or a quote. Will we survive to see our bicentennial? As Daniel Hannan MEP said in a somewhat different context (he was discussing the prospects for Britain outside the EU): 'With so many strengths, I think we'll somehow be OK.'

PETIT FOURS

February 1985. I had been procrastinating over an infernal economics essay – something to do with inward investment into the stuttering economies of South America – in favour of composing a full-page article for the inaugural edition of the Cambridge University Very Nice Society magazine. I'd been asked to submit a piece about life as Union Society President, and with typical immodesty, had headlined it, 'The US Presidency'.

The Very Nice Society was something of a crash-and-burn phenomenon. Set up by an archetypal British eccentric from Jesus College, it had soared in membership until it became the second largest society in the university, behind the Union Society itself, partly driven by its predilection for handing out hugs and Cadbury Cream Eggs at the Freshers' Week Fair. During its moment in the sun, it attracted a galaxy of impressive personalities to entertain its members, often as part of a charity-raising endeavour, with speakers such as Edward Heath, Frankie Howerd, Jeffrey Archer (he gets everywhere, doesn't he?), Michael Winner and Nicholas Parsons gracing its functions. A few years later, it was to be shut down unceremoniously by the university authorities for embezzlement – the funds were apparently lavished on weekend breaks in Paris for the officers, rather than promoting the aims and objectives in its articles. But, in 1985, it was still a society in good standing, and, as I put the finishing touches to my piece, I was particularly proud of a couple of paragraphs I'd drafted about whether the Union Society might be a stepping stone towards the greasy pole of politics (if you'll pardon the slightly strained metaphors):

> Taking life less seriously than others does annoy the 'others', which is even more reason to take it less seriously. Politics is a dirty game, so if you're thinking of getting involved, think twice. But make sure your second thought is different to the first, otherwise you're wasting time, and time-wasters are the last people who should be getting involved.
>
> Fame and fortune may be fun but it's not as much fun as ripping into politicians. I have learnt a little about practical politics whilst in Cambridge, and though my opponents will argue that I'm just pointing the finger away from my own apparent selfishness when I say that mostly they care for no-one but themselves, I will be able to go home at the end of the day, cuddle up in bed with a cup of hot chocolate, secure in the knowledge that it's rude to point. Also I'm well aware that when I become senile and consider a political career, they'll all be waving this article about, even though it will be thirty years later and I might have had the bad fortune to change my mind.

I folded up my handwritten article (no such thing as laptops in those days), tucked it into an envelope that I'd need to hand-deliver to Jesus College (no such thing as emails either), and wondered whether I could be bothered finally to turn my mind back to that wretched essay. René was staying with me for the weekend, and had waited patiently whilst I penned the article. With a look of daggers, she warned me not to dare start any more writing. 'Looking at you hunched over your desk isn't my idea of a good night out,' she said, and if it'd been six years later would probably have added, 'Try it, and it's "hasta la vista, baby!"'

I knew where the conversation was headed. A sumptuous dinner at Angeline's, René's favourite Cambridge restaurant, nestled above the student art's cinema in the corner of one of the city's many pedestrianised passageways. Apart from the pleasure of René's company, and the exquisite cuisine, a strong attraction of the restaurant was the opportunity to brush up on my rusty French – every item on the menu was described in evocative terms – but in the 'language of romance'.

As we walked along Sidney Street, René took my arm and whispered, 'When you're in this city, you almost forget about the outside world. It's like you're spending three years in a bubble.'

'A bubble with lots of intrigue. Think about Clive Blackwood.' Even halfway through my presidential term, Blackwood – author of the put-down 'I like ye style, but I na' like ye' – still nurtured a special place in my Rogues Gallery.

'But it's all quite harmless here,' said René. 'I'm sure that when you eventually get a job…'

'A job!' I exclaimed in mock horror.

'Yes, a job. I'm sure that when you eventually get a job, you'll come across people far worse than Clive Blackwood!'

'What are you saying? I'll shrivel up and die, since I won't be able to cope with the real world?'

'Not at all. You know I have faith in you. You can do whatever you put your mind to.'

'You're only saying that because I'm gallant and handsome and…'

'Stop with the ego. You'll do some things well, and some things not so well. That's life.'

'Not so well?'

'If something is … too much for you.'

'Wait … "too much for me". I'm not sure I know what you mean!'

'It's things like, I don't know…'

'Like what?'

'Like … like … suspending horizontally from that lamp post over there.'

I perked up. 'Is that a challenge?'

'No, silly.'

'It certainly sounded like one.'

I needed no further encouragement. Thirty seconds later, René was holding my jacket, and I was sizing up a lamppost a few feet from the entrance to Sidney Sussex College's Chapel Court. I knew enough about physics to appreciate that selecting the correct height to place my hands was going to be crucial in defying gravity. I figured placing my bottom hand at about waist level would enable me to channel as much strength as possible into maintaining the grip, without needing to bend my legs when I swung my body off the ground. Next, I needed to determine the optimal spacing between my hands; too close or too far apart and my ability to balance would be jeopardised; I guessed around eighteen inches apart; that felt a comfortable (and metric!) distance. Next I needed to ensure the surface of the post would be conducive to a solid grip. They may speak of greasy poles in politics, but they can be a severe impediment to any fledgling career as an amateur lamp post acrobat.

The object seemed reliable. I'd selected my positions. In my mind's eye, I'd picture a successful outcome. There wasn't any other option but to go for it.

As I lifted my feet from the pavement, I realised that my upper arm wasn't actually doing that much. I'd wrapped it around the post for a bit of stability, but in truth it was the bottom arm that was doing all the work. I felt the arm dig deeper into my shoulder socket as all my weight was channelled through the one arm, then the hand, and finally the fingers, which were digging into the steel of the post like a falcon with its claws around a field mouse.

For a moment, I struggled to keep my balance, and one of my feet brushed back against the floor. My legs had drifted apart. Dammit. I wouldn't be able to maintain my stability unless they were tight together as if bound by invisible masking tape. My second attempt was more successful. As I pushed harder into the post, I felt my torso elevating. But still the position was awkward, unnatural, I wouldn't be able to sustain it for more than a few seconds.

It was time to take a risk. I twisted my pelvis so that my legs were pointing not to the horizontal but upwards – not by a severe angle; I didn't have the contortionist's ability to assume an L-shape, but enough that I could hold my body in place without agonising discomfort. My lower hand was firm now, I could feel the rust of the post against my palm, and that provided valuable friction against any temptation to slide. So, here I was, a student at an internationally renowned university, President of the Cambridge Union, a life of drama and adversity no doubt lying ahead. Hanging horizontally from a lamppost as passers-by stopped to gawk.

'Is this illuminating?' I asked, my teeth clenched with concentration.

René loved a pun as much as I do. 'I always said you're a shady character,' she chuckled. 'Whatever next?'

'Well, whatever's next, I hope it hurries up.'

'Why's that?'

'Because, René ... the suspense ... is killing me.'

DRAMATIS PERSONAE

Rahman Ali	Brother of Muhammad Ali
Jeffrey Archer	Novelist
Nick Balcombe	Loss adjuster
Gareth Blacker	LDA Director of Development
Clive Blackwood	Cambridge hack
Tony Blair	Prime Minister
John Cherrie	Forman's General Manager
Peter Chiswick	Forman's driver
Sebastian Coe	LOCOG Chairman
Shimon Cohen	PR consultant
Paul Deighton	LOCOG Chief Executive
Richard Fieldsend	Estate agent
Michael Finlay	Owner of a building contracting firm
Annabel Forman	Daughter
Marcel Forman	Father
Matthew Forman	Son
Oliver Forman	Son
René Forman	Wife
Jeremy Fraser	Lobbyist
Seamus Gannon	Owner of a concrete crushing firm
Lloyd Hardwick	Forman's Operations Director

Debbie Hartley	BBC showrunner
Damian Hockney	UKIP member of the GLA
Phil Hudson	Architect
Boris Johnson	London Mayor
Tessa Jowell	Culture Secretary
Dan Lafayeedney	Director of Cleveland Development
Rita Law	Forman's tea lady, sage and mentor
Mike Lee	London 2012 Director of Communications
Manny Lewis	LDA Chief Executive
Ken Livingstone	London Mayor
Darren Matson	Forman's salmon carver
Stuart Meachin	Forman's General Manager
David Russell	PR consultant
Emma Peters	Tower Hamlets Head of Planning
Ian Rose	Director, M&A Associates
Arthur Somerset	Events and hospitality genius
Mark Stephens	Media lawyer
Tony Winterbottom	Gareth Blacker's boss
Nick Young	Adman
Anita Zabludowicz	Art patron